The Minimal English Test 研究
(最小英語テスト)

牧 秀樹 [著]

音声CD付

開拓社

まえがき

本書は，現在，中学・高校・大学で英語教育に携わっている方，また，今後，小学校で英語教育に関わる方に，英語能力の簡易的測定方法をお知らせし，同時に，その測定法に使われるテスト自体が，繰り返し実施することで，英語能力の向上にもつながるという事実をお伝えするものである．このテストは，実施時間が3分から5分程度であるため，最小英語テスト（The Minimal English Test＝MET）と呼んでいる．あまりにも簡易的過ぎるため，最初は，このようなテストがTOEICや英検などで測定されるような英語能力を測定できるとは思えないかもしれないが，読み進めていくうちに，その疑いが次第に晴れていくだろう．

本書の構成は，以下の通りである．まず，第1章で，METの起源を示す．METは，英語能力測定テストであるが，その起源は，日本語教育において提案された簡易型日本語能力測定テストであるSPOTにある．SPOTの要領を工夫し，成美堂から出版されたKawana and WalkerによるThis is Media.comという大学1年生向けの教科書から，METの最初の版が作成され，METの得点とセンター試験英語の得点との相関がある程度高いことが発見された．第2章では，METの英語能力測定機能について示す．具体的には，METの得点と，いくつかの主要な英語テスト（センター試験英語，TOEIC，Paul Nation's Vocabulary Size Test，英検など）の得点との相関に関する調査を示す．

第3章では，METの作成上の簡易性について論じ，METは，作成上の規則を調整すれば，どのようなバージョンのMETも作成できることを示す．さらに，新たな版のMETが，主要な英語テストの得点をどの程度予測するかも示している．第4章では，METの英語能力向上機能について示す．METは，その作成上の簡易性により，いくつもの版を短時間に作成することができる．これを利用し，英語学習者に，異なる版のMETをいくつも実施し，一番最初に実施したMETを再度実施すると，解答を見せていないにもかかわらず，その得点が統計的有意に向上する．

第 5 章では，MET をアジア諸国（韓国，中国，内モンゴル）で実施した結果を示す．第 6 章では，MET の中学生版，The junior Minimal English Test (jMET) を紹介する．第 7 章では，MET／jMET の第二言語習得研究機能について論ずる．具体的には，英語における *That*-Trace 現象の英語学習者による判断についての研究，中学生による Wh 疑問文習得に関する研究，そして，大学生による関係節・Wh 疑問文習得に関する研究に，MET が重要な形で寄与することを示す．

　第 8 章では，新たな版の MET を，センター試験英語の聴解テスト部分を利用することで作成し，そのセンター試験版 MET の得点が，TOEIC や中国における高校の中間テストの得点をどの程度予測するか示す．第 9 章では，さらに，中国で出版され，中国の中学，高校，大学で使用されている教科書を利用して，新たな版の MET を作成し，その中国版 MET の得点が，中国の中学，高校，大学で実施されるテストの得点とどのような相関を持つかを示す．最後に，第 10 章では，実際にこれまで使用されてきた MET（成美堂から出版された *This is Media.com* に基づいて作成された版とセンター試験聴解問題に基づいて作成された版）の問題と解答を提示する．付録として，これらの実際の MET の音声が，CD として添付されている．第二言語習得研究や，まだ私が思いつかない研究に，効果的に利用されることを願っている．

　なお，MET の実際のテストはそれぞれの番号で 1 行に収まる形式となっているが，本書で収録するにあたっては，可読性を考慮して 2 行にわたるものはそのままとした．

謝　辞

　本書は，2002年4月に私が岐阜大学に赴任してから，本日まで，私が英語教育に携わる中で，多くの方々の善意・協力・示唆・慈悲を戴きながら，新たな簡易型英語能力測定テストを開発し，その性質を調査した結果をまとめたものである．関係してくださった全ての方に，心から，感謝の意を表したい．
　まず，MET の開発に，Kawana and Walker (2002) のテキストの一部の使用を許可してくださった著者の川名典人氏・Stuart Walker 氏，Kawana and Walker (2002) の付随音声教材の使用を許可してくださった佐野英一郎氏・松本健治氏・宍戸貢氏（成美堂），石黒 (2000) の付随音声教材の使用を許可してくださった谷垣誠也氏（美誠社），jMET の開発に，New Horizon English Courses 1, 2, 3 の教科書付随音声教材の使用を許可してくださった五十嵐政則氏（東京書籍），新たな jMET の開発に，New Crown English Series 1, 2, 3 の教科書付随音声教材の使用を許可してくださった富岡次男氏（三省堂書店），中国人英語学習者向けの MET の開発に，中国における中学・高校・大学教科書の使用を許可してくださった王守仁氏・何鋒氏（江蘇訳林出版社（中学・高校教科書））と李蔭華氏（上海外語教育出版社（大学教科書）），英語検定2級一次試験問題の利用を許可してくださった日本英語検定協会，センター試験聴解問題の利用を許可してくださった大学入試センター，そして，経済的支援に関して，岐阜大学技術交流研究会（岐阜大学産官学融合本部）に，心より，感謝する．
　そして，本書の基となる論文を共同で作成してくださった方々（天野万喜男氏，Hee-Won Lee 氏，Myung-Hwan Lee 氏，飯島拓也氏，池田順子氏，石川茜氏，市原賢優氏，伊藤英氏，伊藤たかね氏，伊藤徳一郎氏，今牧浩隆氏，上田由紀子氏，内堀朝子氏，梅澤敏郎氏，及川裕偉氏，王燦氏，大友麻子氏，大野幸恵氏，岡田明菜氏，奥聡氏，越智正男氏，笠井千勢氏，葛西宏信氏，樫村真由氏，加藤恵氏，岸貴彦氏，Dae-Jin Kim 氏，Jeong-Seok Kim 氏，木村由美氏，久保比呂美氏，久保田信孝氏，倉地裕子氏，黒下明日香氏，高永新氏，餾燏崴氏，呉姝静氏，後藤健一氏，Sarenqimuge 氏，澤崎宏一氏，篠田

弥那氏，柴田洋子氏，杉山美月氏，鈴木健吾氏，Michael Sevier 氏，Keun-Won Sohn 氏，田頭美穂氏，高橋和誉氏，田川憲二郎氏，田口茂樹氏，伊達雅彦氏，Jessica Dunton 氏，張月環氏，張壽文氏，鶴田涼子氏，徳川翔吾氏，永末康介氏，新沼史和氏，西田晴美氏，任文祺氏，白春花氏，橋本永貢子氏，橋本洋平氏，長谷部めぐみ氏，浜崎通世氏，濱谷浩正氏，范凌云氏，廣田則夫氏，Alexandra von Fragstein 氏，古川真哉氏，牧野友紀氏，松井久恵氏，宮本陽一氏，森島玉峰氏，森田祐佳氏，宗像孝氏，大和隆介氏，由本陽子氏，吉村純里氏，和佐田裕昭氏），データ収集・管理をしてくださった方々（井上俊英氏，内田勝氏，呉文亮氏，石海英氏，杉山容子氏，長尾裕子氏，中川一雄氏，中村典生氏，黄堅氏，黄章龙氏，马雯氏，森井那奈美氏，楊瑛玲氏，John Russell 氏，李大舵氏，李艶芝氏，劉怡氏，王希宾氏，張獅翔氏），そして，本書を執筆する上で，有益な助言をくださった方々（江坂栄子氏，小林桂一郎氏，沢陽彩美氏，白木茜氏，高橋幸雄氏，南波あゆみ氏，長谷川信子氏，嶺岸玲子氏，神田外語大学 FLP-BH ワークショップ参加者諸氏，国内外の英語教育関連学会において，コメントを下さった方々）に，お礼を申し上げる．

最後に，本書の出版を，困難な時世の中，引き受けてくださった開拓社の川田賢氏に，万謝する．

本刊行物は，JSPS 科研費 JP18HP5064 の助成を受けたものである．

目　次

まえがき ………………………………………………………………… iii
謝　辞 …………………………………………………………………… v

第1章　MET：起源（成美堂版） ……………………………… 1
1.1　The Minimal English Test（MET）の誕生 ………………… 1
1.2　MET 成美堂版 ……………………………………………… 6

第2章　MET：能力測定機能 …………………………………… 13
2.1　大学入試センター試験英語 ………………………………… 13
　　2.1.1　2002年-2009年 ……………………………………… 13
　　2.1.2　2009年-2016年 ……………………………………… 16
2.2　TOEIC ………………………………………………………… 22
2.3　Paul Nation's Vocabulary Size Test ………………………… 24
2.4　高校生の英語能力 …………………………………………… 28
　　2.4.1　進研模試英語 2005 ………………………………… 28
　　2.4.2　The Global Test of English Communication for Students
　　　　　（GTEC）2005 ………………………………………… 29
2.5　実用英語技能検定 …………………………………………… 30

第3章　MET：作成の簡易性 …………………………………… 33
3.1　5文字以下版 ………………………………………………… 33
3.2　8単語・10単語目ごと版 …………………………………… 38
3.3　4文字以下数単語目ごと版 ………………………………… 44

vii

3.4　美誠社版 ……………………………………………… 52
3.5　その他 ………………………………………………… 55

第 4 章　MET：能力向上機能 …………………………………… 57

4.1　Maki and Niinuma (2005) ……………………………… 57
4.2　Maki et al. (2011b) ……………………………………… 62

第 5 章　アジアにおける MET …………………………………… 73

5.1　韓国 ……………………………………………………… 73
5.2　中国 ……………………………………………………… 74
5.3　内モンゴル ……………………………………………… 77

第 6 章　中学生版 MET：jMET ………………………………… 79

6.1　東京書籍 New Horizon 版 ……………………………… 80
6.2　三省堂 New Crown 版 …………………………………… 90

第 7 章　MET：第二言語習得研究機能 ………………………… 97

7.1　*That*-Trace 現象 ………………………………………… 98
7.2　日本人中学生による Wh 疑問文習得 ………………… 101
7.3　日本人大学生による関係節・Wh 疑問文習得 ……… 107

第 8 章　センター試験版 MET ………………………………… 115

8.1　日本：MET CT 2015 と MET CT 2016 ………………… 123
8.2　中国：MET CT 2014-MET CT 2017 …………………… 125
　8.2.1　MET CT 2014 と MET CT 2015 …………………… 125
　8.2.2　MET CT 2016 と MET CT 2017 …………………… 126

第 9 章　中国版 MET ·································· 129

9.1　中学生 ·································· 140
9.2　高校生 ·································· 142
9.3　大学生 ·································· 143

第 10 章　MET：実際の問題と解答 ·································· 147

10.1　成美堂版（4 文字以下版） ·································· 148
10.2　成美堂版（6 単語目ごと版） ·································· 175
10.3　センター試験版 ·································· 201

参考文献 ·································· 235

索　引 ·································· 243

付録 CD（成美堂版 MET & センター試験版 MET）

第 1 章

MET：起源（成美堂版）

1.1 The Minimal English Test (MET) の誕生

　第二言語習得調査のために，どの第二言語を調査する研究者も，基本データとして，被験者のその第二言語の能力を測定しておきたいと願っているであろう．そのために，第二言語としての英語の習得調査であれば，(1) に示すような，何らかの英語能力測定試験が必要となる．

(1)　英語能力測定試験
　　a.　実用英語技能検定（英検）
　　b.　大学入試センター試験英語
　　c.　TOEIC
　　d.　TOEFL
　　e.　Paul Nation's Vocabulary Size Test

しかし，上記の試験は，最も短くても，30 分以上かかり，長ければ，2 時間かかる．そうなると，本調査の前に，被験者は，疲労を感じ，本調査の結果に影響を与えかねない．さらに，研究者も，その英語能力測定試験の採点のために，疲労を感じる．このような背景をもとに，本調査の前に，疲労を感じないような，しかも，信頼性がある英語能力測定試験が求められている．しかし，2003 年までは，そのような英語能力測定試験は，存在しなかった．

　このような背景の中で，牧ほか (2003) は，日本語教育において，小林・

フォード (1992), 小林ほか (1994, 1995, 1996), フォード丹羽ほか (1994, 1995) によって開発された The Simple Performance-Oriented Test (SPOT) (簡易型日本語運用能力測定試験) に注目した．私が SPOT について知ったのは，1997年3月にジョージア工科大学で開催された第12回 Southeast Association of Teachers of Japanese 学会でであった．そこで初めて，SPOT 開発者の小林典子筑波大学教授による SPOT に関する講演を拝聴した．

SPOT は，テープを聞きながら，空いている括弧の中に，ひらがなを1つ入れるだけの試験である．具体的には，(2) の形式をしている．

(2) そこ (　) 何をしているんですか？

(フォード丹羽ほか (1995) より改定し，引用)

(　) には，「で」が入る．SPOT は，(3) に示す5つの規則にしたがって作成されている．

(3) a. 音声テープを使用する．
　　 b. 各問題は，一文単位の独立した文である．
　　 c. 空所には，ひらがな一文字だけが対応する．
　　 d. 空所は，各文につき一箇所である．
　　 e. 空所は，機械的に設けられず，文法項目と関与している．

SPOT は，1996年までに4バージョン開発され，問題数は，最大で65問，最小で30問である．実施時間は，数分である．

小林グループは，一連の調査の中で，筑波大学留学生センターが留学生に実施するプレースメントテスト (以下，PT) の得点と，SPOT の得点の間に強い相関があることを発見した．PT は，聴解，文法，読解，語彙，漢字の読み書きを含み，実施時間は，150分である．両得点の相関は，(4) に示される．

(4) a. SPOT-Ver.1 (61問) 得点と PT 総合得点との相関係数　$r = .82$

(小林ほか (1992))

　　 b. SPOT-Ver.4 (30問) 得点と PT 総合得点との相関係数　$r = .86$

(フォード丹羽ほか (1995))

相関係数の解釈に関して，柳井 (1998) に従い，(5) の対応を仮定すると，SPOT 得点と PT 総合得点の間には，強い相関があることが分かる．

(5) 相関係数とその性質

相関係数	性質
$.0 \leq r < 1.2\vert$	ほとんど相関がない
$\vert.2\vert \leq r < \vert.4\vert$	やや相関がある
$\vert.4\vert \leq r < \vert.7\vert$	相関がある
$\vert.7\vert \leq r < \vert.9\vert$	強い相関がある
$\vert.9\vert \leq r \leq \vert1.0\vert$	極めて強い相関がある

したがって，SPOT は，PT 総合得点をほぼ予測できるようになり，150 分必要とする PT に代わるプレースメントテストとして機能するようになった．

私は，SPOT という形式のテストが，他の材料を用いても，その機能が再現できるかどうか調査した．その当時勤務していた米国 West Virginia 州にある Salem-Teikyo University の日本研究学部の日本語を学ぶ英語母語話者の学生を対象に実験を行った．SPOT 形式のテストに，時間が最小であるという意味から，The Minimal Japanese Test (MJT)（最小日本語テスト）と名付け，当時，米国の大学における日本語教育でよく使用されていた Tohsaku (1994) による『ようこそ！』という教科書の文法項目を利用して，MJT を作成した．音声は，自分の声を録音したものを使用した．MJT は，(6) に示されるように，46 問からなり，実施時間は，数分である．

(6) The Minimal Japanese Test (MJT)

テープを聞きながら，空いている括弧の中に，ひらがなを 1 つ入れて下さい．
(Please fill a Hiragana into each blank spot, while listening to the tape.)
1 （　）の人は，町田さんです．
2 これは，だれ（　）セーターですか？
3 図書館は，（　）そこです．
4 （　）こで昼ごはんを食べますか？
5 その大学は，あまり有名（　）ゃありません．
6 うちに，犬が（　）ます．
7 銀行は，どこに（　）りますか？
8 ブラウンさんのみ（　）に川村さんがいます．
9 テーブルの上にバナナが五（　）んあります．
10 どんなスポーツが（　）きですか？

11 シュミットさんは，日本語を話さ（　）い．
12 今日の午後，山田さんに会（　）ます．
13 昨日，日本語のクラスがありまし（　）か？
14 ここからあそこ（　）で二時間かかります．
15 わたしが，ワインを買いま（　）ょうか？
16 机の上にペン（　）ノートがあります．
17 大野先生は，とてもきび（　）かったです．
18 今年の冬は，去年の冬（　）り雨がたくさん降りました．
19 強い風が，一日中吹（　）た．
20 なぜ顔が赤い（　）ですか？
21 川村さんは，東京大学の学生（　），専攻は，工学です．
22 ここに名前を書い（　）下さい．
23 明日は，雪が降るかもし（　）ません．
24 この三つつの中から（　）れか選んで下さい．
25 歌がじょうず（　）人は，だれですか？
26 漢字を書く（　）は，おもしろいです．
27 クラッシック音楽（　）ロックもあまり好きじゃありません．
28 山口さんは，昨日来（　）れなかった．
29 川村さんは，毎日ジョギングをし（　）います．
30 昨日食べ（　）ピザはおいしかったですか？
31 掃除をしたので，部屋がきれいに（　）った．
32 十年前にカナダへ行った（　）とがあります．
33 妹は，あまりお金をほし（　）らない．
34 その日は，レストランで食事をしたと（　）もいます．
35 この部屋は，ちょっと暑す（　）ますね．
36 日本人は，これをたこ（　）言います．
37 チンさんの誕生日にすしを作る（　）もりです．
38 一度すしを食べて（　）ました．
39 コーヒーを飲みな（　）ら，ブラウンさんと話した．
40 買い物をする（　）き，クレジットカードを使います．
41 もっと地味な（　）はありませんか？
42 お金があった（　），いいコンピューターを買いたい．
43 服を着替え（　），アパートに帰りました．
44 あの魚屋は，とても安い（　）うです．
45 その車を買うか（　）うかまだわからない．
46 買い物もした（　），映画も見たし，もう帰りましょうか？

Maki et al. (1999) は，被験者 40 名に，日本語能力試験 3 級の過去問題を実施し，その得点と，MJT の得点の相関を測定した．日本語能力試験の主催者である国際交流基金と日本国際教育支援協会によると，日本語能力試験 3 級は，日本語を 300 時間学習した後に到達できるレベルであるとされており，語彙，漢字（300 字の知識まで），聴解，読解，文法の諸問題からなっている．実施時間は，130 分である．両得点の相関は，(7) に示される．本書では，一貫して，有意水準を，5%（=.05）と設定している．実験によって得られた p 値 = 有意確率（帰無仮説（= 否定されることを目的として立てられる仮説）が正しいという条件の下で，実際の実験によって得られた値以上に極端な統計量が観測される確率）が，有意水準より小さければ，帰無仮説が否定されるので，以下の相関分析においては，帰無仮説は，「2 変量（日本語能力試験 3 級の得点と MJT の得点）の間に相関はない」となり，得られた p 値が，有意水準 =.05 を下回れば，その帰無仮説は，否定され，相関は，有意であると判定される．

(7) 日本語能力試験 3 級の得点と MJT の得点の相関
$n = 40$
$r = .87$
$p < .001$

両得点の相関の様子は，以下の図 1 のように視覚化すると，より明確に理解できる．(図 1 では，分かりやすくするために，両得点を％で表している．)

図 1　日本語能力試験 3 級得点と MJT 得点との相関

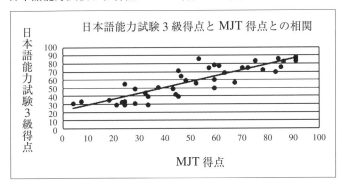

(7) によれば，$p < .001$ であるため，日本語能力試験 3 級の得点と MJT の得点の相関は，有意であり，また，両得点の相関係数は，.87 であるため，両者には，有意に強い相関があると言える．したがって，MJT は，日本語能力試験 3 級の得点をほぼ予測できることが分かった．これは，まさに，SPOT が PT の得点をほぼ予測できるのと同じ状況であり，したがって，SPOT 形式のテストが他の材料を用いても，その機能が再現できることが明らかになった．

この結果，MJT は，第二言語としての日本語教育における諸調査に利用できることになった．牧ほか (2003) は，この MJT を英語能力測定試験に応用し，The Minimal English Test (MET) を作成し，MET が誕生することになった．

1.2 MET 成美堂版

牧ほか (2003) は，大学 1 年生の英語能力を 5 分で測定する目的で，Kawana and Walker (2002) による成美堂が出版したテキストの 1 章と 2 章の英文と，付随する CD を基に，The Minimal English Test (MET) を作成した．MET の主な特徴は，(8) に示すように，5 点である．

(8)　MET の特徴
　　a.　A4 用紙 1 枚に書かれた英文の中の空所に，CD から流れてくる英語を聞きながら，単語を埋めるだけである．
　　b.　空所にある単語は，すべて 4 文字以下である．
　　c.　空所は，各行につき二箇所である．
　　d.　英文は，2 つの話からできているため，18 行目と 19 行目に 3 秒のインターバルがある．
　　e.　所要時間は，約 5 分である．

MET の中の空所は，72 で，括弧内の語が長すぎると，音声を聞いている間に書ききれないことを考慮に入れ，単語の長さは，最大で 4 文字とした．(9) にオリジナルの MET 成美堂版を示す．(10) には，その解答を示す．

(9) MET 成美堂版 4 文字以下版

CD を聞きながら，空いている（　）の中に，4 文字以下（最大で 4 文字）の英単語を入れて下さい．

01. The majority of people have at least one pet at (　)¹ time in their (　)².
02. Sometimes the relationship between a pet (　)³ or cat and its owner is (　)⁴ close
03. that (　)⁵ begin to resemble (　)⁶ other in their appearance and behavior.
04. On the other (　)⁷, owners of unusual pets (　)⁸ as tigers or snakes
05. sometimes (　)⁹ to protect themselves (　)¹⁰ their own pets.
06. Thirty years (　)¹¹ the idea of an inanimate (　)¹² first arose.
07. This was the pet (　)¹³, which became a craze (　)¹⁴ the United States and
08. spread (　)¹⁵ other countries as (　)¹⁶.
09. People (　)¹⁷ large sums of money for ordinary rocks and assigned (　)¹⁸ names.
10. They tied a leash around the rock and pulled (　)¹⁹ down the street just (　)²⁰ a dog.
11. The rock owners (　)²¹ talked (　)²² their pet rocks.
12. Now (　)²³ we have entered the computer age, (　)²⁴ have virtual pets.
13. The Japanese Tamagotchi— (　)²⁵ imaginary chicken (　)²⁶—
14. (　)²⁷ the precursor of (　)²⁸ virtual pets.
15. Now there (　)²⁹ an ever-increasing number of such virtual (　)³⁰
16. which mostly young people are adopting (　)³¹ their (　)³².
17. And (　)³³ your virtual pet (　)³⁴,
18. you (　)³⁵ reserve a permanent resting place (　)³⁶ the Internet in a virtual pet cemetery.
19. Sports are big business. Whereas Babe Ruth, the (　)³⁷ famous athlete of (　)³⁸ day,
20. was well-known (　)³⁹ earning as (　)⁴⁰ as the President of the United States, the average
21. salary (　)⁴¹ today's professional baseball players is (　)⁴² times that of the President.
22. (　)⁴³ a handful of sports superstars earn 100 times (　)⁴⁴ through their contracts
23. (　)⁴⁵ manufacturers of clothing, (　)⁴⁶, and sports equipment.
24. But every generation produces (　)⁴⁷ or two legendary athletes (　)⁴⁸ rewrite

25. the record books, and whose ability and achievements (   )⁴⁹ remembered (   )⁵⁰ generations.
26. (   )⁵¹ the current generation Tiger Woods and Michael Jordan are two (   )⁵² legendary
27. figures, (   )⁵³ of whom (   )⁵⁴ achieved almost mythical status.
28. The (   )⁵⁵ that a large number of professional athletes (   )⁵⁶ huge incomes
29. has (   )⁵⁷ to increased competition throughout (   )⁵⁸ sports world.
30. Parents (   )⁵⁹ their children to sports training camps (   )⁶⁰ an early age.
31. Such (   )⁶¹ typically practice three to (   )⁶² hours a day,
32. (   )⁶³ weekend (   )⁶⁴ during their school vacations
33. in order (   )⁶⁵ better their chances of eventually obtaining (   )⁶⁶ well-paid position
34. on a professional (   )⁶⁷ when they grow (   )⁶⁸.
35. As for the (   )⁶⁹ young aspirants who do (   )⁷⁰ succeed,
36. one wonders if they (   )⁷¹ regret having (   )⁷² their childhood.

(10) MET 成美堂版 4 文字以下版 (解答)

CD を聞きながら，空いている (   ) の中に，4 文字以下 (最大で 4 文字) の英単語を入れて下さい．

01. The majority of people have at least one pet at (some)¹ time in their (life)².
02. Sometimes the relationship between a pet (dog)³ or cat and its owner is (so)⁴ close
03. that (they)⁵ begin to resemble (each)⁶ other in their appearance and behavior.
04. On the other (hand)⁷, owners of unusual pets (such)⁸ as tigers or snakes
05. sometimes (have)⁹ to protect themselves (from)¹⁰ their own pets.
06. Thirty years (ago)¹¹ the idea of an inanimate (pet)¹² first arose.
07. This was the pet (rock)¹³, which became a craze (in)¹⁴ the United States and
08. spread (to)¹⁵ other countries as (well)¹⁶.
09. People (paid)¹⁷ large sums of money for ordinary rocks and assigned (them)¹⁸ names.
10. They tied a leash around the rock and pulled (it)¹⁹ down the street just (like)²⁰ a dog.
11. The rock owners (even)²¹ talked (to)²² their pet rocks.

12. Now (that)²³ we have entered the computer age, (we)²⁴ have virtual pets.
13. The Japanese Tamagotchi—(the)²⁵ imaginary chicken (egg)²⁶—
14. (was)²⁷ the precursor of (many)²⁸ virtual pets.
15. Now there (are)²⁹ an ever-increasing number of such virtual (pets)³⁰
16. which mostly young people are adopting (as)³¹ their (own)³².
17. And (if)³³ your virtual pet (dies)³⁴,
18. you (can)³⁵ reserve a permanent resting place (on)³⁶ the Internet in a virtual pet cemetery.
19. Sports are big business. Whereas Babe Ruth, the (most)³⁷ famous athlete of (his)³⁸ day,
20. was well-known (for)³⁹ earning as (much)⁴⁰ as the President of the United States, the average
21. salary (of)⁴¹ today's professional baseball players is (ten)⁴² times that of the President.
22. (And)⁴³ a handful of sports superstars earn 100 times (more)⁴⁴ through their contracts
23. (with)⁴⁵ manufacturers of clothing, (food)⁴⁶, and sports equipment.
24. But every generation produces (one)⁴⁷ or two legendary athletes (who)⁴⁸ rewrite
25. the record books, and whose ability and achievements (are)⁴⁹ remembered (for)⁵⁰ generations.
26. (In)⁵¹ the current generation Tiger Woods and Michael Jordan are two (such)⁵² legendary
27. figures, (both)⁵³ of whom (have)⁵⁴ achieved almost mythical status.
28. The (fact)⁵⁵ that a large number of professional athletes (earn)⁵⁶ huge incomes
29. has (led)⁵⁷ to increased competition throughout (the)⁵⁸ sports world.
30. Parents (send)⁵⁹ their children to sports training camps (at)⁶⁰ an early age.
31. Such (kids)⁶¹ typically practice three to (four)⁶² hours a day,
32. (all)⁶³ weekend (and)⁶⁴ during their school vacations
33. in order (to)⁶⁵ better their chances of eventually obtaining (a)⁶⁶ well-paid position
34. on a professional (team)⁶⁷ when they grow (up)⁶⁸.
35. As for the (many)⁶⁹ young aspirants who do (not)⁷⁰ succeed,
36. one wonders if they (will)⁷¹ regret having (lost)⁷² their childhood.

METを作成後，実際に，SPOTやMJTのように，他の長時間かかる試験の得点とMETの得点との間に，統計的有意な相関があるかどうか調査した．他の長時間の英語試験として，2002年1月に実施された2001年度センター試験英語を利用した．以下では，実際に実施された年をもとに，このテストをCT 2002と呼ぶ．大学入試センターの報告によると，CT 2002の結果は，(11)に要約される．

(11)　CT 2002概要
　　　受験者数　549,224
　　　満点　　　200
　　　設問数　　50
　　　平均点　　109.68
　　　標準偏差　33.24
　　　制限時間　80分
　　　実施日　　2002年1月19日

CT 2002は，発音，文法，文章構成，読解について問い，聴解問題はない．
　METは，2003年1月に実施された．データは，岐阜大学の4つの学部から，合計で，154収集された．METの得点とCT 2002の得点に対して，単回帰分析（相関分析）が行われた．その結果は，(12)に示される．

(12)　CT 2002得点とMET得点の相関
　　　$n = 154$
　　　$r = .68$
　　　$p < .001$

この分析結果は，図2で，視覚的により明確に示される．

図2 CT 2002 得点と MET 得点の相関

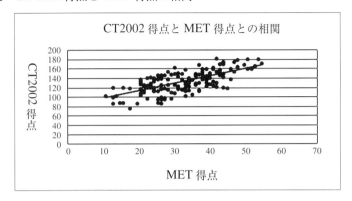

(12) によれば，$p < .001$ であるため，CT 2002 の得点と MET の得点の相関は，有意であり，また，両得点の相関係数は，.68 であるため，両者には，有意に相関があると言える．ただし，図1は，$r = .87$（強い相関）であったのに対し，図2は，$r = .68$（相関）であるため，図2の得点分布は，図1の得点分布と比べ，近似曲線を軸に，膨らみがある程度大きくなっている．

この初期調査の結果，私達が開発した MET の得点と CT 2002 の得点の間には，統計的有意な相関があることが判明した．つまり，MET の得点が，短時間で，センター試験英語の得点をある程度予測できるようになったのである．

第 2 章

MET：能力測定機能

　前章で見たように，MET の得点は，2002 年 1 月実施の大学入試センター試験英語（CT 2002）の得点と比較的強い相関があり（$r=.68$），したがって，MET 得点は，ある程度，大学入試センター試験英語の得点を予測できる見通しがついた．本章では，まず，2009 年までの MET 得点とセンター試験英語の得点の相関を示し，MET 得点は，ある程度，大学入試センター試験英語で測定される英語能力を予測できることを示す．その後，MET が，TOEIC，Paul Nation's Vocabulary Size Test，高校生向け英語テスト（進研模試英語・GTEC），実用英語検定試験で測定される英語能力を予測できることを示す．

2.1　大学入試センター試験英語

2.1.1　2002 年-2009 年

　前章で示されたように，牧ほか（2003）は，大学 1 年生の英語能力を 5 分で測定する目的で，Kawana and Walker（2002）による成美堂が出版したテキストの内部の英文と，付随する CD を基に，The Minimal English Test（MET）を作成した．MET の主な特徴は，(1) に示すように，5 点である．

(1)　MET の特徴
　　　a.　A4 用紙 1 枚に書かれた英文の中の空所に，CD から流れてくる英語を聞きながら，単語を埋めるだけである．

b. 空所にある単語は，すべて4文字以下である．
   c. 空所は，各行につき二箇所である．
   d. 英文は，2つの話からできているため，18行目と19行目に3秒のインターバルがある．
   e. 所要時間は，約5分である．

(2) に，2002年から2009年までのセンター試験の詳細を示し，(3) に，牧グループの調査における MET の得点と 2002 年から 2009 年までのセンター試験英語の得点との相関を示す．2006 年より，センター試験英語に，聴解問題が課されるようになった．(3) のデータに関しては，牧ほか (2003)，Maki et al. (2004, 2005a, 2006a, 2007a, 2008a, 2009a, 2010a) を参照．MET 調査の詳細に関しては，Goto et al. (2010)，Maki (2010)，牧 (2015) を参照．

(2) 2002 年から 2009 年までのセンター試験の詳細

	受験者数（読解）	満点（読解）	設問数（読解）	平均点（読解）	標準偏差（読解）	制限時間（読解）
CT 2002	549,224	200	50	109.68	33.24	80分
CT 2003	551,891	200	50	126.82	40.78	80分
CT 2004	535,944	200	50	130.11	37.27	80分
CT 2005	520,048	200	50	116.18	37.98	80分
CT 2006	499,630	200	50	127.52	39.37	80分
CT 2007	500,995	200	53	131.09	40.35	80分
CT 2008	497,101	200	51	125.26	39.28	80分
CT 2009	500,297	200	50	115.02	37.54	80分

	受験者数（聴解）	満点（聴解）	設問数（聴解）	平均点（聴解）	標準偏差（聴解）	制限時間（聴解）
CT 2002						
CT 2003						
CT 2004						
CT 2005						
CT 2006	492,555	50	25	36.25	8.27	約30分
CT 2007	493,213	50	25	32.48	9.14	約30分
CT 2008	490,853	50	25	29.45	8.72	約30分
CT 2009	494,342	50	25	24.03	9.65	約30分

第 2 章　MET：能力測定機能

	実施日
CT 2002	2002 年 1 月 19 日
CT 2003	2003 年 1 月 18 日
CT 2004	2004 年 1 月 17 日
CT 2005	2005 年 1 月 15 日
CT 2006	2006 年 1 月 21 日
CT 2007	2007 年 1 月 20 日
CT 2008	2008 年 1 月 19 日
CT 2009	2009 年 1 月 17 日

(3) MET の得点とセンター試験英語（2002 年から 2009 年まで）の得点との相関

	被験者数	相関係数（r）	回帰直線
CT 2002	154	.68（読解）	y = 1.53x + 82.13
CT 2003	629	.72（読解）	y = 2.39x + 67.62
CT 2004	657	.72（読解）	y = 2.18x + 75.95
CT 2005	600	.61（読解）	y = 2.09x + 66.06
CT 2006	610	.59（読解）	y = 1.49x + 101.55
		.55（聴解）	y = .33x + 29.34
		.62（読解と聴解）	y = 1.82x + 130.89
CT 2007	895	.62（読解）	y = 1.41x + 109.21
		.61（聴解）	y = .40x + 23.97
		.66（読解と聴解）	y = 1.80x + 133.18
CT 2008	563	.60（読解）	y = 1.73x + 88.22
		.67（聴解）	y = .52x + 16.2
		.65（読解と聴解）	y = 2.25x + 104.43
CT 2009	877	.533（読解）	y = 1.34x + 93.19
		.589（聴解）	y = .49x + 12.49
		.592（読解と聴解）	y = 1.83x + 105.68

(3) において，相関係数に関する p 値は，すべて $p < .001$ である．(3) からは，以下のことが分かる．

(4) a. MET 得点とセンター試験英語総合得点との相関係数は，8 年間の調査において，$.59 \leq r \leq .72$ である．

  b. MET 得点とセンター試験英語総合得点との相関係数は，8 年間の調査の内 CT 2008 を除いて，MET 得点とセンター試験英語読解だけの得点との相関係数と MET 得点とセンター試験英語聴解だけの得点との相関係数よりも，高い．

 このことから，MET 得点とセンター試験英語総合得点との相関は，比較的強い相関があり，また，MET は，単なる聴解力測定試験ではなく，読解力も含めた，総合的能力を測定する試験であると言える．この一連の調査を基に，Goto et al. (2010) は，MET の信頼係数を算出し，MET は，信頼度が保証された試験であることを示している．これにより，MET は，第二言語習得調査における，英語能力測定試験として機能すると考えてもよいことになったと言える．

2.1.2 2009 年-2016 年

 しかしながら，MET 調査を進めていく中で，他の研究者から，次の質問が上がった．「MET の中で選ばれている語は，なぜ，4 文字以下であるのか？しかも，4 文字以下の語の中でも，選ばれている語とそうでない語があるのはなぜか？」最初の問いに関しては，「それ以上の文字数を持つ語では，聞きながら書く際に，時間が不足すると考えたからである．」と答えることができるとしても，では，「5 文字以上の語を用いて，調査をしたことがあるのか？」という新たな問いには，満足がいく回答が与えられない．さらに，2 つ目の問いに関しては，「同じ語を避けるため．」，あるいは，「選ばれた語が接近しすぎないため．」と答えることもできるが，「同じ語を使用した場合と，そうでない場合を比較したか？」，あるいは，「選ばれた二語が接近しすぎている距離とは，どの程度の距離であるか？」という新たな問いには，回答が与えらない．

 そこで，これらの問いをなるべく回避するために，Maki et al. (2010b) は，2009 年に，新たな MET を作成した．その作成には，Cloze Test の手法を用い，ターゲットとなる語を，ランダムに選んだ．その際，手始めに，6 単語目ごと版を作成した．2011 年にそれを最小限修正した．最初の版は，MET 6 単語目ごと版 A (MET E6A)，次の版を，MET 6 単語目ごと版 B (MET E6B) と呼ぶ．本書では，以後，MET 6 単語目ごと版 B を単に MET E6 と呼び，MET 4 文字以下版を，MET E6 と明確に区別する必要がある時には，MET 4

と呼び，そうでない時には，MET と呼ぶことにする．MET E6A と MET E6B（＝MET E6）は，それぞれ，(5) と (6) に示される．

(5) MET 成美堂版 6 単語目ごと版（MET E6A）

CD を聞きながら，空いている（　）の中に英単語を書き入れて下さい．
01. The (　)¹ of people have at least (　)² pet at some time
02. in (　)³ life. Sometimes the relationship between (　)⁴ pet dog or cat
03. and (　)⁵ owner is so close that (　)⁶ begin to resemble
04. each other (　)⁷ their appearance and behavior. On (　)⁸ other hand,
05. owners of unusual (　)⁹ such as tigers or snakes (　)¹⁰ have to protect
06. themselves from (　)¹¹ own pets. Thirty years ago (　)¹² idea of
07. an inanimate pet (　)¹³ arose. This was the pet (　)¹⁴, which became a craze
08. in (　)¹⁵ United States and spread to (　)¹⁶ countries as well.
09. People paid (　)¹⁷ sums of money for ordinary (　)¹⁸ and assigned them names.
10. They (　)¹⁹ a leash around the rock (　)²⁰ pulled it down
11. the street (　)²¹ like a dog. The rock (　)²² even talked to
12. their pet (　)²³. Now that we have entered (　)²⁴ computer age,
13. we have virtual (　)²⁵. The Japanese Tamagotchi—
14. the imaginary chicken (　)²⁶—was the precursor of many (　)²⁷ pets.
15. Now there are an (　)²⁸-increasing number of such virtual (　)²⁹
16. which mostly young people are (　)³⁰ as their own.
17. And if (　)³¹ virtual pet dies, you can (　)³² a permanent resting
18. place on (　)³³ Internet in a virtual pet (　)³⁴.
19. Sports (　)³⁵ big business. Whereas Babe Ruth, the most (　)³⁶
20. athlete of his day, was (　)³⁷-known for earning as much (　)³⁸ the President
21. of the United (　)³⁹, the average salary of today's (　)⁴⁰ baseball players
22. is ten times (　)⁴¹ of the President. And a (　)⁴² of sports superstars
23. earn 100 times (　)⁴³ through their contracts with manufacturers (　)⁴⁴
24. clothing, food, and sports equipment. (　)⁴⁵ every generation produces
25. one or (　)⁴⁶ legendary athletes who rewrite the (　)⁴⁷ books,
26. and whose ability and (　)⁴⁸ are remembered for generations.
27. In (　)⁴⁹ current generation Tiger Woods and Michael Jordan are two (　)⁵⁰

28. legendary figures, both of whom ( )⁵¹ achieved almost mythical status.
29. The ( )⁵² that a large number of ( )⁵³ athletes earn huge incomes
30. has ( )⁵⁴ to increased competition throughout the ( )⁵⁵ world.
31. Parents send their children ( )⁵⁶ sports training camps at an ( )⁵⁷ age.
32. Such kids typically practice ( )⁵⁸ to four hours a day, ( )⁵⁹ weekend
33. and during their school ( )⁶⁰ in order to better their ( )⁶¹ of eventually
34. obtaining a well-( )⁶² position on a professional team ( )⁶³ they grow up.
35. As for ( )⁶⁴ many young aspirants who do ( )⁶⁵ succeed,
36. one wonders if they ( )⁶⁶ regret having lost their childhood.

(6) MET 成美堂版 6 単語目ごと版 (MET E6B = MET E6)

CD を聞きながら，空いている ( ) の中に英単語を書き入れて下さい．

01. The majority of people have ( )¹ least one pet at some ( )² in their life.
02. Sometimes the ( )³ between a pet dog or ( )⁴ and its owner
03. is so ( )⁵ that they begin to resemble ( )⁶ other in their appearance
04. and ( )⁷. On the other hand, owners ( )⁸ unusual pets
05. such as tigers ( )⁹ snakes sometimes have to protect ( )¹⁰ from their own pets.
06. Thirty ( )¹¹ ago the idea of an ( )¹² pet first arose.
07. This was ( )¹³ pet rock, which became a ( )¹⁴ in the United States
08. and ( )¹⁵ to other countries as well. ( )¹⁶ paid large sums of money
09. ( )¹⁷ ordinary rocks and assigned them ( )¹⁸.
10. They tied a leash around ( )¹⁹ rock and pulled it down ( )²⁰ street just like a dog.
11. ( )²¹ rock owners even talked to ( )²² pet rocks.
12. Now that we ( )²³ entered the computer age, we ( )²⁴ virtual pets.
13. The Japanese *Tamagotchi*—the ( )²⁵ chicken egg—
14. was the precursor ( )²⁶ many virtual pets.
15. Now there ( )²⁷ an ever-increasing number of such ( )²⁸ pets
16. which mostly young people ( )²⁹ adopting as their own.
17. And ( )³⁰ your virtual pet dies, you ( )³¹ reserve a permanent resting place
18. ( )³² the Internet in a virtual ( )³³ cemetery.

第2章　MET：能力測定機能　　19

19. Sports are big business. (　)³⁴ Babe Ruth, the most famous athlete of (　)³⁵ day,
20. was well-known for earning (　)³⁶ much as the President of (　)³⁷ United States,
21. the average salary (　)³⁸ today's professional baseball players
22. is (　)³⁹ times that of the President. (　)⁴⁰ a handful of sports superstars
23. (　)⁴¹ one hundred times more through (　)⁴² contracts with manufacturers
24. of clothing, (　)⁴³, and sports equipment. But every (　)⁴⁴ produces
25. one or two legendary (　)⁴⁵ who rewrite the record books,
26. (　)⁴⁶ whose ability and achievements are (　)⁴⁷ for generations.
27. In the current (　)⁴⁸ Tiger Woods and Michael Jordan are two such legendary (　)⁴⁹,
28. both of whom have achieved (　)⁵⁰ mythical status.
29. The fact that (　)⁵¹ large number of professional athletes (　)⁵² huge incomes
30. has led to (　)⁵³ competition throughout the sports world.
31. (　)⁵⁴ send their children to sports (　)⁵⁵ camps at an early age.
32. (　)⁵⁶ kids typically practice three to (　)⁵⁷ hours a day,
33. all weekend (　)⁵⁸ during their school vacations in (　)⁵⁹ to better their chances
34. of (　)⁶⁰ obtaining a well-paid position on (　)⁶¹ professional team
35. when they grow (　)⁶². As for the many young (　)⁶³ who do not succeed,
36. one (　)⁶⁴ if they will regret having (　)⁶⁵ their childhood.

MET E6 を作る規則は，(7) の2点のみである．

(7) MET E6 作成規則
　　a. 6単語目ごとに，空所が設けられる．
　　b. 空所を設ける際，固有名詞，ハイフンで繋がれた長い語，数字，日本語，年，括弧の中にある発音されない語は，除外される．

この結果，MET E6 の問題数は，MET 4 の 72 問から，65 問へと減少した．（厳密には，MET E6A は，66 問，MET E6B は，65 問である．）

　以下に，MET 修正版（MET E6A と MET E6B = MET E6）の得点とセン

ター試験英語の得点との相関を示す．まず，(8) に，2009 年から 2016 年までのセンター試験の詳細を示し，(9) に，MET の得点とセンター試験英語 (2009 年から 2016 年まで) の得点との相関を示す．(9) のデータに関しては，Maki et al. (2010a, 2011a, 2012a, 2013a, 2014a, 2015a, 2016a, 2017a) を参照．CT 2009 に関しては，MET 4 の得点との相関を見るために，877 のデータを得，また，MET E6A の得点との相関を見るために，それとは別に，さらに 520 のデータを得ている．

(8) 2009 年から 2016 年までのセンター試験の詳細

	受験者数 (読解)	満点 (読解)	設問数 (読解)	平均点 (読解)	標準偏差 (読解)	制限時間 (読解)
CT 2009	500,297	200	50	115.02	37.54	80 分
CT 2010	512,451	200	51	118.14	39.96	80 分
CT 2011	519,538	200	51	122.78	41.24	80 分
CT 2012	519,867	200	54	124.15	42.05	80 分
CT 2013	535,835	200	55	119.15	41.20	80 分
CT 2014	525,217	200	55	118.87	41.06	80 分
CT 2015	523,354	200	55	116.17	40.96	80 分
CT 2016	529,688	200	55	112.43	42.15	80 分

	受験者数 (聴解)	満点 (聴解)	設問数 (聴解)	平均点 (聴解)	標準偏差 (聴解)	制限時間 (聴解)
CT 2009	494,342	50	25	24.03	9.65	約 30 分
CT 2010	506,898	50	25	29.39	9.24	約 30 分
CT 2011	513,817	50	25	25.17	9.55	約 30 分
CT 2012	514,748	50	25	24.55	8.03	約 30 分
CT 2013	529,440	50	25	31.45	8.61	約 30 分
CT 2014	519,172	50	25	33.16	9.40	約 30 分
CT 2015	516,429	50	25	35.39	9.77	約 30 分
CT 2016	522,950	50	25	30.81	9.35	約 30 分

第 2 章　MET：能力測定機能　　　　　　　　　　21

	実施日
CT 2009	2009 年 1 月 17 日
CT 2010	2010 年 1 月 16 日
CT 2011	2011 年 1 月 15 日
CT 2012	2012 年 1 月 14 日
CT 2013	2013 年 1 月 19 日
CT 2014	2014 年 1 月 18 日
CT 2015	2015 年 1 月 17 日
CT 2016	2016 年 1 月 16 日

(9) MET E6 の得点とセンター試験英語（2009 年から 2016 年まで）の得点との相関

	MET	被験者数	相関係数 (r)	回帰直線
CT 2009	MET E6A	520	.51（読解）	$y = 1.59x + 100.55$
			.54（聴解）	$y = .53x + 16.56$
			.56（読解と聴解）	$y = 2.12x + 117.11$
CT 2010	MET E6A	1188	.48（読解）	$y = 1.45x + 109.12$
			.52（聴解）	$y = .45x + 23.14$
			.53（読解と聴解）	$y = 1.90x + 132.26$
CT 2011	MET E6B (MET E6)	217	.54（読解）	$y = 1.60x + 117.46$
			.56（聴解）	$y = .51x + 19.75$
			.60（読解と聴解）	$y = 2.13x + 136.36$
CT 2012	MET E6B (MET E6)	127	.52（読解）	$y = 1.89x + 112.07$
			.58（聴解）	$y = .56x + 15.02$
			.57（読解と聴解）	$y = 2.45x + 127.09$
CT 2013	MET E6B (MET E6)	142	.57（読解）	$y = 1.87x + 110.37$
			.48（聴解）	$y = .46x + 26.16$
			.60（読解と聴解）	$y = 2.33x + 136.53$
CT 2014	MET E6B (MET E6)	573	.58（読解）	$y = 2.00x + 97.39$
			.51（聴解）	$y = .45x + 27.15$
			.61（読解と聴解）	$y = 2.45x + 124.54$
CT 2015	MET E6B (MET E6)	444	.50（読解）	$y = 1.82x + 96.80$
			.50（聴解）	$y = .44x + 29.70$
			.54（読解と聴解）	$y = 2.26x + 126.50$
CT 2016	MET E6B (MET E6)	125	.55（読解）	$y = 1.58x + 109.75$
			.57（聴解）	$y = .46x + 25.54$
			.60（読解と聴解）	$y = 2.04x + 135.29$

(9) において，相関係数に関する p 値は，すべて $p < .001$ である．(9) からは，以下のことが分かる．

(10) a. MET E6（A）得点とセンター試験英語総合得点との相関係数は，8年間の調査において，$.53 \leq r \leq .61$ である．
b. MET E6（A）得点とセンター試験英語総合得点との相関係数は，8年間の調査の内，CT 2012 を除いて，MET E6（A）得点とセンター試験英語読解だけの得点との相関係数と MET E6（A）得点とセンター試験英語聴解だけの得点との相関係数よりも，高い．

このことから，MET E6（A）得点とセンター試験英語総合得点との間には，相関があり，また，MET E6（A）は，MET 4 と同様に，単なる聴解力測定試験ではなく，読解力も含めた，総合的能力を測定する試験であると言える．ただし，MET 4 に関する相関係数は，2002 年から 2009 年までの 8 年間の調査において，$.59 \leq r \leq .72$ であったのに対し，MET E6（A）に関する相関係数は，2009 年から 2016 年までの 8 年間の調査において，$.53 \leq r \leq .61$ となっており，若干，低下している．この事実は，MET 作成に関して，一定の示唆を与えてくれるかもしれない．つまり，MET 4 の方式のほうが，Cloze Test タイプの MET E6（A）の方式よりも，センター試験英語によって測定される英語能力をよりよく予測するということである．

2.2　TOEIC

Maki et al.（2010c）は，MET の得点と The Test of English for International Communication（TOEIC）の得点との間に，相関があるか調査した．TOEIC は，Educational Testing Service（ETS）によって提供されるテストで，ETS によれば，その試験内容は，(11) に示されるように，聴解問題と読解問題を含んでいる．

(11)　TOEIC の試験内容

	聴解問題	読解問題	総合
問題数	100 問	100 問	200 問
最高点	495 点	495 点	990 点
制限時間	45 分	75 分	120 分

TOEICは，大学入試センター試験とは異なり，希望者のみが受験する．したがって，同一のテストを多数の被験者が受験していないため，大量のデータを一度に集めることができない．そこで，被験者には，2004年から2009年までに受験したTOEICの最高総合得点を報告してもらい，その受験時期から時間的に隔たりがない時期に，METを実施した．2004年から2009年までに得られた被験者は，57名である．その調査結果は，(12)に示される．

(12) METの得点とTOEICの得点との相関
$n = 57$
$r = .74$
$p < .001$

この結果，METの得点とTOEICの得点との間に，強い相関（$.7 < r$）があることが明らかになった．したがって，METは，TOEICによって測定される英語能力をある程度予測できることが分かった．

ただし，この調査には，不完全な部分があることに注意しなければならない．被験者には，TOEICの最高獲得合計点を報告してもらっているが，毎回，TOEICの問題の難易度や平均点が同一であるわけではない．そのため，この調査結果をより確固たるものにするためには，同じTOEICの公式試験を大量に被験者に受験してもらい，その時期と時間的に隔たりがない時期に，METを実施することが必要となる．

そこで，Maki et al. (2017b) は，上記の問題を一部回避するために，2015年5月に，The Test of English for International Communication Institutional Testing Program (TOEIC ITP) を受験した被験者16名にMET E6を実施し，MET E6の得点とTOEIC ITPの得点との相関を調査した．TOEIC ITPは，非公式なものであるが，その問題は，公式TOEICの問題と同じ構成である．この調査において重要な点は，これら16名は，全員同じTOEIC ITPの問題を解いているということである．その調査結果は，(13)に示される．

(13) MET E6の得点とTOEIC ITPの得点との相関
$n = 16$
$r = .73$
$p < .001$

この結果，MET E6 の得点と TOEIC ITP の得点との間に，強い相関（$.7 < r$）があることが明らかになった．これは，Maki（2010c）の結果を支持するもので，MET は，TOEIC によって測定される英語能力をある程度予測できるという仮説をより強固なものにした．

2.3　Paul Nation's Vocabulary Size Test

　Kasai et al.（2005）は，MET の得点と Paul Nation's Vocabulary Size Test（PNT）の得点との間に，相関があるかどうか調査した．PNT は，Nation（1990）によって開発され，第二言語習得研究分野においては，最も確立された英語能力測定テストの1つである．被験者の英語能力測定において，広く採用されてきているが，被験者に応じて，10分から30分と，ある程度の時間を消費する．以下に，PNT の特徴を見る．

　PNT は，語彙テストであり，5つのレベルの異なるグループに分かれた，合計 90 の語彙問題から構成されている．最も低いレベルであるレベル A は，大学生になじみのある，最も頻繁に使用される 1,000 の語彙から選択されている．その次のレベルのレベル B は 2,000，その上のレベル C は 3,000，その上のレベル D は 5,000，そして，最も上のレベル E は 10,000 の語彙から選択されている．(14) に PNT の具体例を示す．テスト内容は，語彙が与えられ，その語彙と，その語彙の定義をマッチさせるものである．

(14) Paul Nation's Vocabulary Size Test の例

Paul Nation's Vocabulary Size Test

How to Administer the Test

Find the most suitable vocabulary from 1 to 6 that matches the words/phrases on the right. Use the separate answer sheet when you fill in the answers.

Examples
Level F

[1]	1. business	☐ part of a house
	2. clock	
	3. horse	☐ animal with four legs
	4. pencil	
	5. shoe	☐ something used for writing
	6. wall	

The actual test is divided into 5 levels from A to E. As you proceed, the level will be higher. Turn the page and begin the test.

Level A

[1]	1. original	☐ complete	[2]	1. apply	☐ choose by voting
	2. private			2. elect	
	3. royal	☐ first		3. jump	☐ become like water
	4. slow			4. manufacture	
	5. sorry	☐ not public		5. melt	☐ make
	6. total			6. threaten	
[3]	1. blame	☐ keep away from sight	[4]	1. accident	☐ having a high opinion of yourself
	2. hide			2. choice	
	3. hit	☐ have a bad effect on something		3. debt	☐ something you must pay
	4. invite			4. fortune	
	5. pour	☐ ask		5. pride	☐ loud, deep sound
	6. spoil			6. roar	

[5]	1. basket	☐ money paid regularly for doing a job	[6]	1. birth	☐ being born
	2. crop			2. dust	
	3. flesh	☐ heat		3. operation	☐ game
	4. salary			4. row	
	5. temperature	☐ meat		5. sport	☐ wining
	6. thread			6. victory	

…

Level E

[5]	1. dregs	☐ worst and most useless parts of anything	[6]	1. auspices	☐ being away from other people
	2. flurry			2. casualty	
	3. hostage	☐ natural liquid present in the mouth		3. froth	☐ someone killed or injured
	4. jumble			4. haunch	
	5. saliva	☐ confused mixture		5. revelry	☐ noisy and happy celebration
	6. truce			6. seclusion	

(15) に，回答用紙を示す．

(15)　Paul Nation's Vocabulary Size Test の回答用紙

	Level A	Level B	Level C	Level D	Level E
Paul Nation's Vocabulary Size Test					
Name: _____ Date: Month____Day____Year_____					
[1]					
[2]					
[3]					
[4]					
[5]					
[6]					
Points	A: /18	B: /18	C: /18	D: /18	E: /18
Total	/90	%			

　Kasai et al.（2005）は，159 人の大学生被験者に，PNT と MET を実施し，その得点の間の相関を調査した．その結果は，（16）に示される．

(16) METの得点とPNTの得点との相関
$n = 159$
$r = .81$
$p < .001$

この結果，METの得点とPNTの得点との間に，強い相関（$.7 < r$）があることが明らかになった．したがって，METは，PNTによって測定される英語能力をある程度予測できることが分かった．

2.4 高校生の英語能力

次に，Maki et al. (2007b, 2008b) は，METが，高校1年までの英語教育を修了した直後の高校2年生の英語能力を測定できるかどうか調査した．

2.4.1 進研模試英語 2005

Maki et al. (2007b) は，ある1つの日本の高校において，2005年7月に，ベネッセによる進研模試英語を受験した2年生に，その直後にMETを実施した．これらの学生の進研模試英語2005の結果は，(17) に示される．

(17) 当該高校における進研模試英語2005の結果
受験者数　135
満点　　　100
平均点　　37.2
標準偏差　14.1
制限時間　90分
実施日　　2005年7月9日

進研模試英語2005は，聴解，文法，読解，作文を含み，マルティプル・チョイスのテストではない．

Maki et al. (2007b) は，METの得点と進研模試英語2005の得点との相関を調査した．その調査結果は，(18) に示される．

(18) MET の得点と進研模試英語 2005 の得点との相関
$n = 135$
$r = .63$
$p < .001$

この結果，MET の得点と進研模試英語 2005 の得点との間に，相関（$.4 < r$）があることが明らかになった．したがって，MET は，進研模試英語 2005 によって測定される英語能力をある程度予測できることが分かった．

2.4.2 The Global Test of English Communication for Students (GTEC) 2005

さらに，Maki et al. (2008b) は，ある 1 つの日本の高校において，2005 年 7 月に，ベネッセによる The Global Test of English Communication for Students (GTEC) を受験した 2 年生に，その直後に MET を実施した．GTEC 2005 は，聴解，読解，作文から構成される．これらの学生の GTEC 2005 の結果は，(19) に示される．

(19) 当該高校における GTEC 2005 の結果

	聴解	読解	作文	合計
被験者数	134			
満点	320	320	160	800
平均点	158.4	168.4	93.7	420.5
標準偏差	33.2	28.1	16.2	63.8
テスト時間	25 分	45 分	20 分	90 分

Maki et al. (2008b) は，MET の得点と GTEC 2005 の得点に対して，単回帰分析（相関分析）を行った．その調査結果は，(20) に示される．

(20) MET の得点と GTEC 2005 の読解・聴解・総合得点との相関

	読解	聴解	総合
被験者数	134		
相関係数	$.63 < r$	$.61 < r$	$.7 < r$
p 値	$p < .001$		

この結果，MET の得点と GTEC 2005 の総合得点との間に，強い相関（.7 <

r) があることが明らかになった．また，MET 得点と GTEC 2005 総合得点との相関係数（$.7 < r$）は，MET 得点と GTEC 2005 読解だけの得点との相関係数（$.63 < r$）と MET 得点と GTEC 2005 聴解だけの得点との相関係数（$.61 < r$）よりも，高い．このことから，MET は，単なる聴解力測定試験ではなく，読解力も含めた，総合的能力を測定する試験であると言える．したがって，MET は，GTEC 2005 総合得点によって測定される英語能力をある程度予測できることが明らかになった．

2.5 実用英語技能検定

Maki and Hasebe (2013) は，MET E6 の得点と英語検定 2 級一次試験問題（読解と聴解）の得点との間に，どの程度の相関があるか調査した．日本英語検定協会（英検）によれば，英検の級と受験推奨目安の関係は，(21) に示される．

(21) 英検の級と受験推奨目安

級	推奨目安
5	中学初級程度
4	中学中級程度
3	中学卒業程度
準2	高校中級程度
2	高校卒業程度
準1	大学中級程度
1	大学上級程度

Maki and Hasebe (2013) は，大学 1 年生被験者 22 名に対して，英語検定 2 級一次試験問題（2010-1）の読解と聴解テストを実施し，それと同時に，MET E6 も実施した．その調査結果を (22) に示す．

(22) MET E6 の得点と英語検定 2 級 (2010-1) の得点との相関

	読解	聴解	総合
被験者数	22		
相関係数	$.47 < r$	$.57 < r$	$.59 < r$
p 値	$p < .05$	$p < .001$	$p < .001$

この結果，MET の得点と英語検定 2 級（2010-1）の総合得点との間に，相関（$.59 < r$）があることが明らかになった．また，MET 得点と英語検定 2 級（2010-1）総合得点との相関係数（$.59 < r$）は，MET 得点と英語検定 2 級（2010-1）読解だけの得点との相関係数（$.47 < r$）と MET 得点と英語検定 2 級（2010-1）聴解だけの得点との相関係数（$.57 < r$）よりも，高い．このことから，改めて，MET は，単なる聴解力測定試験ではなく，読解力も含めた，総合的能力を測定する試験であると言える．したがって，MET は，英語検定 2 級（2010-1）総合得点によって測定される英語能力をある程度予測できることが明らかになった．

第 3 章

MET：作成の簡易性

　MET は，その性質上，一定の規則を守りさえすれば，同じ材料を用いながら，いくつでも，新たな版を作成することができる．そして，新たに作成された版とこれまで作成された版から得られるデータを基に，どの版が，TOEIC や英検などの総合的テストの得点に対して，より予測力が高いか調査することができる．本章では，オリジナル MET の MET 4 文字以下版 (MET 4) と MET 6 単語目ごと版 (MET E6) 以外に，これまで開発された版を提示し，その得点と他のテストとの得点との相関を見る．具体的には，MET 5 文字以下版 (MET 5)，MET 8・10 単語目ごと版，MET 4 文字以下版で，かつ，3・4・5 単語目ごと版，他の材料（石黒 (2000) *All-Round Level B*）を用いた MET 美誠社版 (MET ARB)，そして，最後に，後の章で詳細に扱われる版について示す．

3.1　5 文字以下版

　Maki et al. (2009b) は，「MET の中で選ばれている語は，なぜ，4 文字以下であるのか？」という他の研究者からの問いに部分的に答えるために，その問いを，「MET 4 文字以下版と，MET X 文字以下版とでは，センター試験英語の得点の予測力に，差があるのか？」と鋳直し，まず，最初の試みとして，MET の中で選ばれる語を，5 文字以下とし，新たな版の MET，MET 5 を作成した．MET 5 の作成規則 (2) は，MET 4 の作成規則 (1) に最小限変更を

加えただけのものである．

(1) MET 4 作成規則
　a. 空所にある単語は，すべて 4 文字以下である．
　b. 空所は，各行につき二箇所である．

(2) MET 5 作成規則
　a. 空所にある単語は，すべて 5 文字以下である．
　b. 空所は，各行につき二箇所である．

(2) の規則にしたがって，(3) に示すように，MET 5 が作成された．

(3) MET 成美堂版 5 文字以下版 (MET 5)

CD を聞きながら，空いている（　）の中に，5 文字以下（最大で 5 文字）の英単語を入れて下さい．

01. The majority of people have at (　)¹ one pet at some time in their (　)².
02. Sometimes the relationship between a pet (　)³ or cat and its (　)⁴ is so close
03. that they (　)⁵ to resemble each other (　)⁶ their appearance and behavior.
04. On the (　)⁷ hand, owners of unusual pets (　)⁸ as tigers or snakes
05. sometimes (　)⁹ to protect themselves from their (　)¹⁰ pets.
06. Thirty years ago the (　)¹¹ of an inanimate pet first (　)¹².
07. This was the pet (　)¹³, which became a craze (　)¹⁴ the United States and
08. spread (　)¹⁵ other countries as (　)¹⁶.
09. People paid large sums of (　)¹⁷ for ordinary rocks and assigned them (　)¹⁸.
10. They (　)¹⁹ a leash around the rock and pulled it (　)²⁰ the street
11. just like a (　)²¹. The rock owners (　)²² talked to their pet rocks.
12. Now (　)²³ we have entered the computer (　)²⁴,
13. we have virtual (　)²⁵. The Japanese Tamagotchi— (　)²⁶ imaginary chicken egg—
14. (　)²⁷ the precursor of (　)²⁸ virtual pets.
15. Now there (　)²⁹ an ever-increasing number (　)³⁰ such virtual pets
16. which mostly (　)³¹ people are adopting (　)³² their own.

17. And if (   )³³ virtual pet dies, you (   )³⁴ reserve a permanent resting place
18. (   )³⁵ the Internet in (   )³⁶ virtual pet cemetery.
19. Sports are (   )³⁷ business. Whereas Babe Ruth, the (   )³⁸ famous athlete
20. of his (   )³⁹, was well-known for earning as (   )⁴⁰ as the President of the United States,
21. the average salary (   )⁴¹ today's professional baseball players is ten times (   )⁴²
22. of the President. And a handful of sports superstars (   )⁴³ 100 (   )⁴⁴ more
23. through their contracts (   )⁴⁵ manufacturers of clothing, (   )⁴⁶, and sports equipment.
24. But (   )⁴⁷ generation produces (   )⁴⁸ or two legendary athletes
25. who rewrite the record (   )⁴⁹, and whose ability and achievements (   )⁵⁰ remembered
26. for generations. (   )⁵¹ the current generation Tiger Woods (   )⁵² Michael Jordan
27. are (   )⁵³ such legendary figures, both of (   )⁵⁴ have achieved almost mythical status.
28. The fact that a (   )⁵⁵ number of professional athletes earn (   )⁵⁶ incomes
29. has (   )⁵⁷ to increased competition throughout the sports (   )⁵⁸.
30. Parents (   )⁵⁹ their children to sports training (   )⁶⁰ at an early age.
31. Such (   )⁶¹ typically practice (   )⁶² to four hours a day,
32. (   )⁶³ weekend and during (   )⁶⁴ school vacations
33. in (   )⁶⁵ to better their chances of eventually obtaining a well-(   )⁶⁶ position
34. on a professional (   )⁶⁷ when they (   )⁶⁸ up.
35. As for the (   )⁶⁹ young aspirants who do (   )⁷⁰ succeed,
36. one wonders (   )⁷¹ they will regret having (   )⁷² their childhood.

Maki et al. (2009b) は，CT 2008 の得点と MET 5 の得点に対して，単回帰分析（相関分析）を行った．まず，Maki et al. (2009a) から，(4) に CT 2008 の詳細を，(5) に MET 4 得点と CT 2008 得点との相関を再掲する．

(4) 2008年のセンター試験の詳細

	受験者数 (読解)	満点 (読解)	設問数 (読解)	平均点 (読解)	標準偏差 (読解)	制限時間 (読解)
CT 2008	497,101	200	51	125.26	39.28	80分

	受験者数 (聴解)	満点 (聴解)	設問数 (聴解)	平均点 (聴解)	標準偏差 (聴解)	制限時間 (聴解)
CT 2008	490,853	50	25	29.45	8.72	約30分

	実施日
CT 2008	2008年1月19日

(5) MET 4の得点と2008年センター試験英語の得点との相関

	MET	被験者数	相関係数 (r)	回帰直線
CT 2008	MET 4	563	.60 (読解)	y = 1.73x + 88.22
			.67 (聴解)	y = .52x + 16.2
			.65 (読解と聴解)	y = 2.25x + 104.43

続いて，Maki et al. (2009b) による MET 5 の得点と CT 2008 の得点に対する，単回帰分析（相関分析）の結果を (6) に示す．

(6) MET 5の得点と2008年センター試験英語の得点との相関

	MET	被験者数	相関係数 (r)	回帰直線
CT 2008	MET 5	367	.63 (読解)	y = 1.73x + 88.22
			.57 (聴解)	y = .52x + 16.2
			.66 (読解と聴解)	y = 2.25x + 104.43

Maki et al. (2009b) は，VassarStats: Web Site for Statistical Computation による Fisher r-to-z 変換を使用し，各相関係数間に，統計的有意な差があるかどうか調査した．Fisher r-to-z 変換においては，p 値（片側）が，.05 未満の場合に，統計的有意な差があると言う．以下，読解得点，聴解得点，総合得点に関する MET 5 得点と MET 4 得点の相関係数間の差の有意性を，(7)-(9) に示す．

(7) CT 2008 読解得点に関する MET 5 得点と MET 4 得点の相関係数間の差の有意性

	MET 5	MET 4
相関係数 r	.63	.60
被験者数 n	367	563
z 値		.72
p 値（片側）		.24

(8) CT 2008 聴解得点に関する MET 5 得点と MET 4 得点の相関係数間の差の有意性

	MET 5	MET 4
相関係数 r	.57	.67
被験者数 n	367	563
z 値		-2.42
p 値（片側）		.01

(9) CT 2008 総合得点に関する MET 5 得点と MET 4 得点の相関係数間の差の有意性

	MET 5	MET 4
相関係数 r	.66	.65
被験者数 n	367	563
z 値		.26
p 値（片側）		.40

この結果，CT 2008 聴解得点に関する MET 5 得点と MET 4 得点の相関係数間には，有意な差があったが，CT 2008 読解得点と CT 2008 総合得点に関する MET 5 得点と MET 4 得点の相関係数間には，有意な差がないことが分かった．このことは，MET 4 のほうが MET 5 より，CT 2008 の聴解得点をよりよく予測するが，CT 2008 の読解得点と総合得点に関しては，どちらも，その予測力には，有意な差がないことを意味している．

そうなると，「MET 4 文字以下版と，MET 5 文字以下版とでは，センター試験英語の得点の予測力に，差があるのか？」という当初の問いに対して，総合得点に関する限り，その 2 版の MET の予測力に，統計的有意な差はないという回答が与えられる．この調査によって，MET の作成基準は，ある程度

自由があってもよいということが分かった．

3.2　8単語・10単語目ごと版

Maki et al. (2012a) は，MET 6 単語目ごと版 (MET E6) を作成し，その得点と CT 2011 の得点との相関を調査した．($n = 217$, r（読解と聴解）= .60, $p < .001$) Maki et al. (2012b, 2013b, 2014b) は，さらに，8 単語目ごと版 (MET E8) と 10 単語目ごと版 (MET E10) を作成し，MET E6, MET E8, MET E10 のセンター試験英語の得点の予測力に差があるかどうか調査した．(10) の規則にしたがって，(12) に示すように，MET E8 が作成され，(11) の規則にしたがって，(13) に示すように，MET 10 が作成された．

(10)　MET E8 作成規則
   a.　8 単語目ごとに，空所が設けられる．
   b.　空所を設ける際，固有名詞，ハイフンで繋がれた長い語，数字，日本語，年，括弧の中にある発音されない語は，除外される．

(11)　MET E10 作成規則
   a.　10 単語目ごとに，空所が設けられる．
   b.　空所を設ける際，固有名詞，ハイフンで繋がれた長い語，数字，日本語，年，括弧の中にある発音されない語は，除外される．

(12)　MET 8 単語目ごと版 (MET E8)

CD を聞きながら，空いている（　）の中に，英単語を入れて下さい．
01.　The majority of people have at least (　)^1 pet at some time in their life.
02.　(　)^2 the relationship between a pet dog or (　)^3 and its owner
03.　is so close that (　)^4 begin to resemble each other in their (　)^5
04.　and behavior. On the other hand, owners (　)^6 unusual pets
05.　such as tigers or snakes (　)^7 have to protect themselves from their own (　)^8.
06.　Thirty years ago the idea of an (　)^9 pet first arose.
07.　This was the pet (　)^{10}, which became a craze in the United (　)^{11}
08.　and spread to other countries as well. (　)^{12} paid large sums of money
09.　for ordinary (　)^{13} and assigned them names.

10. They tied a (　　)¹⁴ around the rock and pulled it down (　　)¹⁵ street just like a dog.
11. The rock (　　)¹⁶ even talked to their pet rocks.
12. Now (　　)¹⁷ we have entered the computer age, we (　　)¹⁸ virtual pets.
13. The Japanese *Tamagotchi*—the imaginary chicken (　　)¹⁹—
14. was the precursor of many virtual pets.
15. (　　)²⁰ there are an ever-increasing number of such (　　)²¹ pets
16. which mostly young people are adopting (　　)²² their own.
17. And if your virtual pet (　　)²³, you can reserve a permanent resting place
18. (　　)²⁴ the Internet in a virtual pet cemetery.
19. Sports are big business. Whereas Babe Ruth, the most famous (　　)²⁵ of his day,
20. was well-known for earning (　　)²⁶ much as the President of the United (　　)²⁷,
21. the average salary of today's professional baseball (　　)²⁸
22. is ten times that of the President. (　　)²⁹ a handful of sports superstars
23. earn one (　　)³⁰ times more through their contracts with manufacturers
24. (　　)³¹ clothing, food, and sports equipment. But every (　　)³² produces
25. one or two legendary athletes who (　　)³³ the record books,
26. and whose ability and (　　)³⁴ are remembered for generations.
27. In the current (　　)³⁵ Tiger Woods and Michael Jordan are two such legendary figures,
28. both (　　)³⁶ whom have achieved almost mythical status.
29. The (　　)³⁷ that a large number of professional athletes (　　)³⁸ huge incomes
30. has led to increased competition (　　)³⁹ the sports world.
31. Parents send their children (　　)⁴⁰ sports training camps at an early age.
32. (　　)⁴¹ kids typically practice three to four hours (　　)⁴² day,
33. all weekend and during their school (　　)⁴³ in order to better their chances
34. of (　　)⁴⁴ obtaining a well-paid position on a professional (　　)⁴⁵
35. when they grow up. As for the (　　)⁴⁶ young aspirants who do not succeed,
36. one (　　)⁴⁷ if they will regret having lost their (　　)⁴⁸.

(13) MET 10 単語目ごと版 (MET E10)

CD を聞きながら，空いている（　）の中に，英単語を入れて下さい．

01. The majority of people have at least one pet (　)¹ some time in their life.
02. Sometimes the relationship between (　)² pet dog or cat and its owner
03. is so (　)³ that they begin to resemble each other in their (　)⁴
04. and behavior. On the other hand, owners of unusual (　)⁵
05. such as tigers or snakes sometimes have to protect (　)⁶ from their own pets.
06. Thirty years ago the idea (　)⁷ an inanimate pet first arose.
07. This was the pet (　)⁸, which became a craze in the United States
08. and (　)⁹ to other countries as well. People paid large sums (　)¹⁰ money
09. for ordinary rocks and assigned them names.
10. They (　)¹¹ a leash around the rock and pulled it down (　)¹² street just like a dog.
11. The rock owners even (　)¹³ to their pet rocks.
12. Now that we have entered (　)¹⁴ computer age, we have virtual pets.
13. The Japanese *Tamagotchi*—the (　)¹⁵ chicken egg—
14. was the precursor of many virtual pets.
15. (　)¹⁶ there are an ever-increasing number of such virtual pets
16. (　)¹⁷ mostly young people are adopting as their own.
17. And (　)¹⁸ your virtual pet dies, you can reserve a permanent (　)¹⁹ place
18. on the Internet in a virtual pet cemetery.
19. Sports are big business. Whereas Babe Ruth, the most famous athlete of (　)²⁰ day,
20. was well-known for earning as much as the (　)²¹ of the United States,
21. the average salary of today's (　)²² baseball players
22. is ten times that of the President. (　)²³ a handful of sports superstars
23. earn one hundred times (　)²⁴ through their contracts with manufacturers
24. of clothing, food, and (　)²⁵ equipment. But every generation produces
25. one or two legendary (　)²⁶ who rewrite the record books,
26. and whose ability and (　)²⁷ are remembered for generations.
27. In the current generation Tiger Woods and Michael Jordan (　)²⁸ two such legendary figures,
28. both of whom have achieved (　)²⁹ mythical status.

29. The fact that a large number of ( )³⁰ athletes earn huge incomes
30. has led to increased competition ( )³¹ the sports world.
31. Parents send their children to sports ( )³² camps at an early age.
32. Such kids typically practice ( )³³ to four hours a day,
33. all weekend and during ( )³⁴ school vacations in order to better their chances
34. of ( )³⁵ obtaining a well-paid position on a professional team
35. when ( )³⁶ grow up. As for the many young aspirants who ( )³⁷ not succeed,
36. one wonders if they will regret having ( )³⁸ their childhood.

Maki et al. (2013b) は，CT 2012 を受験した学生をランダムに3つのグループに分け，それぞれ，MET E6, MET E8, MET E10 を実施した．それぞれのグループの人数と CT 2012 の平均点を (14) に示す．

(14) 3グループの CT 2012 の平均点

MET 種類	人数	CT 2012 平均点
MET E6	127	161.66/200（読解） 29.78/50（聴解） 191.44/250（読解と聴解）
MET E8	125	161.10/200（読解） 29.48/50（聴解） 190.58/250（読解と聴解）
MET E10	118	161.37/200（読解） 30.01/50（聴解） 191.38/250（読解と聴解）

MET E6, MET E8, MET E10 の得点と CT 2012 の得点の相関は，(15) に示される．

(15) MET E6, MET E8, MET E10 の得点と CT 2012 の得点の相関

年	MET 種類	人数	相関係数（r）	回帰直線
2012	MET E6	127	.52（読解）	y = 1.89x + 112.07
			.58（聴解）	y = .56x + 15.02
			.57（読解と聴解）	y = 2.45x + 127.09
	MET E8	125	.54（読解）	y = 2.26x + 109.89
			.53（聴解）	y = .53x + 17.46
			.58（読解と聴解）	y = 2.79x + 127.36
	MET E10	118	.53（読解）	y = 2.39x + 117.49
			.53（聴解）	y = .60x + 19.03
			.57（読解と聴解）	y = 2.99x + 136.52

　読解，聴解，読解と聴解の得点と 3 種類の MET の得点の相関は，読解（.52 ≤ r ≤ .54），聴解（.53 ≤ r ≤ .58），読解と聴解（.57 ≤ r ≤ .58）であり，3 種類の MET の間で，ほぼ差がなかった．

　Maki et al. (2013b) は，VassarStats: Web Site for Statistical Computation による Fisher r-to-z 変換を使用し，各相関係数間に，統計的有意な差があるかどうか調査した．その結果，読解得点，聴解得点，総合得点に関する 3 種類の MET の得点の相関係数間の差の有意性は，認められなかった．この結果，MET E6, MET E8, MET E10 の得点の CT 2012 の読解得点，聴解得点，総合得点についての予測力には，有意な差がないことが分かった．

　続けて，Maki et al. (2014b) は，CT 2013 を受験した学生をランダムに 3 つのグループに分け，それぞれ，MET E6, MET E8, MET E10 を実施した．それぞれのグループの人数と CT 2013 の平均点を（16）に示す．

第3章 MET：作成の簡易性　　43

(16) 3グループのCT 2013の平均点

MET 種類	人数	CT 2013 平均点
MET E6	142	157.73/200（読解）
		37.70/50（聴解）
		195.44/250（読解と聴解）
MET E8	155	162.31/200（読解）
		38.74/50（聴解）
		201.05/250（読解と聴解）
MET E10	153	160.65/200（読解）
		38.10/50（聴解）
		198.72/250（読解と聴解）

MET E6, MET E8, MET E10 の得点と CT 2013 の得点の相関は，(17) に示される．

(17) MET E6, MET E8, MET E10 の得点と CT 2013 の得点の相関

年	MET 種類	人数	相関係数 (r)	回帰直線
2013	MET E6	142	.57（読解）	$y = 1.87x + 110.37$
			.48（聴解）	$y = .46x + 26.16$
			.60（読解と聴解）	$y = 2.33x + 136.53$
	MET E8	155	.43（読解）	$y = 1.83x + 120.41$
			.24（聴解）	$y = .49x + 27.54$
			.44（読解と聴解）	$y = 2.32x + 147.95$
	MET E10	153	.53（読解）	$y = 2.23x + 119.58$
			.62（聴解）	$y = .75x + 24.18$
			.62（読解と聴解）	$y = 2.99x + 136.52$

読解，聴解，読解と聴解の得点と3種類のMETの得点の相関は，読解（$.43 \leq r \leq .57$），聴解（$.24 \leq r \leq .62$），読解と聴解（$.44 \leq r \leq .62$）であり，3種類のMETの間で，ばらつきが見られた．

Maki et al. (2014b) は，VassarStats: Web Site for Statistical Computation による Fisher r-to-z 変換を使用し，各相関係数間に，統計的有意な差があるかどうか調査した．その結果，読解得点に関する3種類のMETの得点の相関係数間の差の有意性は，認められなかったが，聴解得点と総合得点に関する3種類のMETの得点の相関係数間には，総合得点に関するMET E6（$r = .60$）

とMET E10（$r=.62$）の相関係数以外は，有意な差があった．このことから，CT 2013の各得点に関して，3種類のMETの予測能力は，総合得点に関するMET E6とMET E10以外は，一定ではないことが分かった．

したがって，Maki et al.（2012b, 2013b, 2014b）の調査は，MET E6, MET E8, MET E10のセンター試験英語の読解，聴解，読解と聴解の各得点への予測能力を正確に明らかにするためには，長期的調査が必要であることを示している．

3.3　4文字以下数単語目ごと版

Maki et al.（2010a）は，初めて6単語目ごと版を作成したが，この版においては，ターゲットとなる語の文字数には，制限がなく，*relationship*などの12文字からなる語もターゲットとなっている．これでは，ランダム性は保障されても，一単語を書く速度に負担がかかり，正しく被験者の英語能力を測定しているとは言いにくい．そこで，Maki et al.（2015b）は，さらに新たなMETの版を作成した．その版においては，一単語を書く速度の負担を減らすために，すべてのターゲットとなる語を4文字以下のものに限定し，その上で，ランダム性を維持するために，3単語おき，4単語おきに空欄を設けている．

Maki et al.（2015b）は，MET 4文字以下3単語目ごと版（MET 4E3）とMET 4文字以下4単語目ごと版（MET 4E4）を作成し，MET 4E3, MET 4E4, MET E6の得点とCT 2014の得点との相関を調査した．さらに，Maki et al.（2016b）は，MET 4文字以下5単語目ごと版（MET 4E5）を作成し，MET 4E3, MET 4E4, MET 4E5, MET E6の得点とCT 2015の得点との相関を調査した．そして，Maki et al.（2015b, 2016b）は，それぞれの版のMETのセンター試験英語の得点の予測力に差があるかどうか調査した．MET 4文字以下X単語目ごと版は，(18)の規則にしたがって作成された．

(18)　MET 4文字以下X単語目ごと版作成規則（X = 3, 4, 5）
　　　a.　ターゲット語は，4文字以下である．
　　　b.　X単語目ごとに，空所が設けられる．
　　　c.　空所を設ける際，固有名詞，ハイフンで繋がれた長い語，数字，

第 3 章　MET：作成の簡易性

日本語，年，括弧の中にある発音されない語は，除外される．

MET 4E3，MET 4E4，MET 4E5 は，(19)-(21) に示される．

(19)　MET 4 文字以下 3 単語目ごと版 (MET 4E3)

CD を聞きながら，空いている (　) の中に，英単語を入れて下さい．

01. The majority of people (　)¹ at least one (　)² at some (　)³ in their life.
02. Sometimes (　)⁴ relationship between a pet (　)⁵ or cat (　)⁶ its owner
03. is (　)⁷ close that they begin (　)⁸ resemble each other in their appearance
04. (　)⁹ behavior. On the other (　)¹⁰, owners of unusual pets
05. (　)¹¹ as tigers or snakes sometimes (　)¹² to protect themselves
06. from their (　)¹³ pets. Thirty years ago (　)¹⁴ idea of (　)¹⁵ inanimate pet first arose.
07. This (　)¹⁶ the pet (　)¹⁷, which became a craze in (　)¹⁸ United States
08. and spread to other countries (　)¹⁹ well. People paid large (　)²⁰ of money
09. for ordinary rocks (　)²¹ assigned them names. They (　)²² a leash around the (　)²³
10. and pulled it (　)²⁴ the street just (　)²⁵ a dog.
11. (　)²⁶ rock owners even talked (　)²⁷ their pet rocks.
12. Now (　)²⁸ we have entered (　)²⁹ computer age, we (　)³⁰ virtual pets.
13. The Japanese *Tamagotchi*—(　)³¹ imaginary chicken egg—
14. was (　)³² precursor of many virtual (　)³³.
15. Now there are (　)³⁴ ever-increasing number of such virtual (　)³⁵
16. which mostly young people are adopting as their (　)³⁶.
17. And if your virtual (　)³⁷ dies, you (　)³⁸ reserve a permanent resting place
18. on (　)³⁹ Internet in a virtual (　)⁴⁰ cemetery.
19. Sports are big business. Whereas Babe Ruth, (　)⁴¹ most famous athlete of (　)⁴² day,
20. was well-known (　)⁴³ earning as much (　)⁴⁴ the President

21. of ( )⁴⁵ United States, the average salary of today's professional baseball players
22. ( )⁴⁶ ten times that ( )⁴⁷ the President. And ( )⁴⁸ handful of sports superstars
23. earn ( )⁴⁹ hundred times more through their contracts with manufacturers
24. ( )⁵⁰ clothing, food, and sports equipment. ( )⁵¹ every generation produces
25. one or ( )⁵² legendary athletes who rewrite the record books,
26. ( )⁵³ whose ability and achievements are remembered ( )⁵⁴ generations.
27. In the current generation Tiger Woods ( )⁵⁵ Michael Jordan are two ( )⁵⁶ legendary figures,
28. both of ( )⁵⁷ have achieved almost mythical status.
29. The ( )⁵⁸ that a large number ( )⁵⁹ professional athletes earn huge incomes
30. ( )⁶⁰ led to increased competition throughout ( )⁶¹ sports world.
31. Parents send their children to sports training camps ( )⁶² an early age.
32. ( )⁶³ kids typically practice three to ( )⁶⁴ hours a day,
33. ( )⁶⁵ weekend and during their school vacations in order ( )⁶⁶ better their chances
34. of eventually obtaining a well-paid position ( )⁶⁷ a professional team
35. ( )⁶⁸ they grow ( )⁶⁹. As for ( )⁷⁰ many young aspirants
36. who ( )⁷¹ not succeed, one wonders ( )⁷² they will regret having ( )⁷³ their childhood.

(20) MET 4 文字以下 4 単語目ごと版 (MET 4E4)

CD を聞きながら，空いている ( ) の中に，英単語を入れて下さい．

01. The majority of people have ( )¹ least one pet at ( )² time in their life.
02. Sometimes ( )³ relationship between a pet dog ( )⁴ cat and its owner
03. ( )⁵ so close that they begin ( )⁶ resemble each other in their appearance
04. and behavior. ( )⁷ the other hand, owners of unusual ( )⁸
05. such as tigers or snakes sometimes ( )⁹ to protect themselves from their own ( )¹⁰.
06. Thirty years ago the idea ( )¹¹ an inanimate pet first arose.
07. This ( )¹² the pet rock, which became ( )¹³ craze in the United States

第 3 章　MET：作成の簡易性　　47

08. and spread (　)¹⁴ other countries as well. People paid large (　)¹⁵ of money
09. for ordinary rocks and assigned (　)¹⁶ names. They tied a leash around (　)¹⁷ rock
10. and pulled it (　)¹⁸ the street just like (　)¹⁹ dog.
11. The rock owners (　)²⁰ talked to their pet rocks.
12. Now (　)²¹ we have entered the computer (　)²², we have virtual pets.
13. (　)²³ Japanese *Tamagotchi*—the imaginary chicken egg—
14. was (　)²⁴ precursor of many virtual pets.
15. (　)²⁵ there are an ever-increasing number of (　)²⁶ virtual pets
16. which mostly young people are adopting as their (　)²⁷.
17. And if your virtual (　)²⁸ dies, you can reserve (　)²⁹ permanent resting place
18. on the Internet in (　)³⁰ virtual pet cemetery.
19. Sports are big business. Whereas Babe Ruth, (　)³¹ most famous athlete of his (　)³²,
20. was well-known for earning as (　)³³ as the President of (　)³⁴ United States,
21. the average salary of today's professional baseball players
22. is (　)³⁵ times that of the President. (　)³⁶ a handful of sports superstars
23. earn (　)³⁷ hundred times more through their contracts with manufacturers
24. of clothing, (　)³⁸, and sports equipment. But every generation produces
25. one (　)³⁹ two legendary athletes who rewrite the record books,
26. (　)⁴⁰ whose ability and achievements are remembered for generations.
27. (　)⁴¹ the current generation Tiger Woods and Michael Jordan are (　)⁴²
28. such legendary figures, both of (　)⁴³ have achieved almost mythical status.
29. The fact (　)⁴⁴ a large number of professional athletes earn (　)⁴⁵ incomes
30. has led to increased competition throughout (　)⁴⁶ sports world.
31. Parents send their children to sports training camps at (　)⁴⁷ early age.
32. Such kids typically practice three (　)⁴⁸ four hours a day,
33. (　)⁴⁹ weekend and during their school vacations in order to better their chances
34. (　)⁵⁰ eventually obtaining a well-paid position on a professional (　)⁵¹
35. when they grow (　)⁵². As for the (　)⁵³ young aspirants who do not succeed,
36. (　)⁵⁴ wonders if they will regret having (　)⁵⁵ their childhood.

(21) MET 4 文字以下 5 単語目ごと版 (MET 4E5)

CD を聞きながら，空いている（　）の中に，英単語を入れて下さい．

01. The majority of people have at least (　)¹ pet at some time (　)² their life.
02. Sometimes the relationship between a pet (　)³ or cat and its owner
03. (　)⁴ so close that they begin to resemble (　)⁵ other in their appearance
04. and behavior. On the other (　)⁶, owners of unusual pets
05. such as tigers (　)⁷ snakes sometimes have to protect themselves
06. from their own (　)⁸. Thirty years ago the idea of (　)⁹ inanimate pet first arose.
07. This was the (　)¹⁰ rock, which became a craze in the United States
08. (　)¹¹ spread to other countries as well. People paid large (　)¹² of money
09. for ordinary rocks and assigned them names. (　)¹³ tied a leash around the rock
10. (　)¹⁴ pulled it down the street just (　)¹⁵ a dog.
11. The rock owners (　)¹⁶ talked to their pet rocks.
12. Now that (　)¹⁷ have entered the computer age, we (　)¹⁸ virtual pets.
13. The Japanese *Tamagotchi*—the imaginary chicken egg—
14. (　)¹⁹ the precursor of many virtual pets.
15. (　)²⁰ there are an ever-increasing number of such virtual (　)²¹
16. which mostly young people are adopting as their own.
17. And (　)²² your virtual pet dies, you can reserve (　)²³ permanent resting place
18. on the Internet in a virtual (　)²⁴ cemetery.
19. Sports are big business. Whereas Babe Ruth, the most famous athlete (　)²⁵ his day,
20. was well-known for earning (　)²⁶ much as the President
21. of (　)²⁷ United States, the average salary of today's professional baseball players
22. is ten times (　)²⁸ of the President. And a handful (　)²⁹ sports superstars
23. earn one hundred times more through their contracts with manufacturers
24. (　)³⁰ clothing, food, and sports equipment. But every generation produces

第3章　MET：作成の簡易性

25. one（　　）³¹ two legendary athletes who rewrite the record books,
26. and whose ability（　　）³² achievements are remembered for generations.
27. In the current generation Tiger Woods（　　）³³ Michael Jordan are two such legendary figures,
28. both（　　）³⁴ whom have achieved almost mythical status.
29. The fact（　　）³⁵ a large number of professional athletes earn huge incomes
30. （　　）³⁶ led to increased competition throughout the sports world.
31. Parents send their children（　　）³⁷ sports training camps at an early age.
32. Such（　　）³⁸ typically practice three to four hours a day,
33. （　　）³⁹ weekend and during their school vacations in order to better their chances
34. of eventually obtaining（　　）⁴⁰ well-paid position on a professional team
35. when（　　）⁴¹ grow up. As for（　　）⁴² many young aspirants
36. who do not succeed, （　　）⁴³ wonders if they will regret having lost their childhood.

Maki et al. (2015b) は，CT 2014 を受験した学生をランダムに 3 つのグループに分け，それぞれ，MET 4E3, MET 4E4, MET E6 を実施した．それぞれのグループの人数と CT 2014 の平均点を (22) に示す．

(22)　3 グループの CT 2014 の平均点

MET 種類	人数	CT 2014 平均点
MET 4E3	549	146.67/200（読解） 38.42/50（聴解） 185.08/250（読解と聴解）
MET 4E4	573	144.88/200（読解） 37.46/50（聴解） 182.34/250（読解と聴解）
MET E6	573	146.87/200（読解） 38.35/50（聴解） 185.22/250（読解と聴解）

MET 4E3, MET 4E4, MET E6 の得点と CT 2014 の得点の相関は，(23) に示される．

(23) MET 4E3, MET 4E4, MET E6 の得点と CT 2014 の得点の相関

年	MET 種類	人数	相関係数 (r)	回帰直線
2014	MET 4E3	549	.56（読解）	$y = 1.54x + 92.72$
			.51（聴解）	$y = .35x + 26.14$
			.59（読解と聴解）	$y = 1.90x + 118.85$
	MET 4E4	573	.55（読解）	$y = 1.79x + 93.00$
			.57（聴解）	$y = .50x + 22.85$
			.59（読解と聴解）	$y = 2.29x + 115.85$
	MET E6	573	.58（読解）	$y = 2.00x + 97.39$
			.51（聴解）	$y = .45x + 27.15$
			.61（読解と聴解）	$y = 2.45x + 124.54$

読解, 聴解, 読解と聴解の得点と 3 種類の MET の得点の相関は, 読解 (.55 $\leq r \leq$ .58), 聴解 (.51 $\leq r \leq$ .57), 読解と聴解 (.59 $\leq r \leq$ .61) であり, 3 種類の MET の間で, ほぼ差がなかった.

Maki et al. (2015b) は, VassarStats: Web Site for Statistical Computation による Fisher r-to-z 変換を使用し, 各相関係数間に, 統計的有意な差があるかどうか調査した. その結果, 読解得点, 聴解得点, 総合得点に関する 3 種類の MET の得点の相関係数間の差の有意性は, 認められなかった. この結果, MET 4E3, MET 4E4, MET E6 の得点の CT 2014 の読解得点, 聴解得点, 総合得点についての予測力には, 有意な差がないことが分かった.

続けて, Maki et al. (2016b) は, CT 2015 を受験した学生をランダムに 3 つのグループに分け, それぞれ, MET 4E3, MET 4E4, MET 4E5, MET E6 を実施した. それぞれのグループの人数と CT 2015 の平均点を (24) に示す.

(24) 4グループの CT 2015 の平均点

MET 種類	人数	CT 2015 平均点
MET 4E3	399	138.86/200（読解）
		40.00/50（聴解）
		178.86/250（読解と聴解）
MET 4E4	419	139.85/200（読解）
		40.48/50（聴解）
		180.34/250（読解と聴解）
MET 4E5	418	139.38/200（読解）
		40.27/50（聴解）
		179.65/250（読解と聴解）
MET E6	444	139.41/200（読解）
		39.99/50（聴解）
		179.39/250（読解と聴解）

MET 4E3, MET 4E4, MET 4E5, MET E6 の得点と CT 2015 の得点の相関は，(25) に示される．

(25) MET 4E3, MET 4E4, MET 4E5, MET E6 の得点と CT 2015 の得点の相関

年	MET 種類	人数	相関係数 (r)	回帰直線
2015	MET 4E3	399	.55（読解）	y = 1.60x + 82.45
			.55（聴解）	y = .40x + 25.89
			.60（読解と聴解）	y = 2.00x + 108.34
	MET 4E4	419	.53（読解）	y = 1.70x + 91.19
			.47（聴解）	y = .39x + 29.45
			.56（読解と聴解）	y = 2.09x + 120.64
	MET 4E5	418	.56（読解）	y = 1.82x + 71.91
			.55（聴解）	y = .57x + 24.11
			.59（読解と聴解）	y = 2.97x + 96.02
	MET E6	444	.50（読解）	y = 2.40x + 96.80
			.50（聴解）	y = .44x + 29.70
			.54（読解と聴解）	y = 2.26x + 126.50

読解，聴解，読解と聴解の得点と 4 種類の MET の得点の相関は，読解（.50 $\leq r \leq$ .56），聴解（.47 $\leq r \leq$ .55），読解と聴解（.54 $\leq r \leq$ .60）であり，4 種

類の MET の間で，ほぼ差がなかった．

Maki et al. (2016b) は，VassarStats: Web Site for Statistical Computation による Fisher r-to-z 変換を使用し，各相関係数間に，統計的有意な差があるかどうか調査した．その結果，読解得点，聴解得点，総合得点に関する 4 種類の MET の得点の相関係数間の差の有意性は，認められなかった．この結果，MET 4E3, MET 4E4, MET 4E5, MET E6 の得点の CT 2015 の読解得点，聴解得点，総合得点についての予測力には，有意な差がないことが分かった．

Maki et al. (2015b, 2016b) の調査により，MET 4E3, MET 4E4, MET 4E5, MET E6 の得点のセンター試験英語の読解，聴解，読解と聴解の各得点への予測能力は，ほぼ等しいことが明らかになった．そうなると，驚くことに，MET におけるターゲットとなる語の文字数は，センター試験英語の得点への予測に対して，決定的要因とならないことになる．同時に，MET におけるターゲット語間の距離も，センター試験英語の得点への予測に対して，決定的要因とならないことになる．

3.4 美誠社版

Maki et al. (2012c) は，成美堂から出版された Kawana and Walker (2002) 以外の材料からでも，同様の英語能力測定効果がある MET を作成できるかどうか調査するために，美誠社から出版された石黒 (2000) の大学一年生向け教科書 *All-Round Level B* の 1 章と 2 章を用いて，MET の新たな版 MET ARB 版（ARB = All-Round Level B）を作成した．MET ARB の作成規則は，MET 4 の作成規則 (1) と同様で，(26) に示される．

(26) MET ARB 作成規則
    a. 空所にある単語は，すべて 4 文字以下である．
    b. 空所は，各行につき二箇所である．

MET ARB は，(27) に，その解答は，(28) に示される．

第 3 章 MET：作成の簡易性

(27) MET 美誠社版 (MET ARB)

CD を聞きながら，空いている（　）の中に，4 文字以下（最大で4文字）の英単語を入れて下さい．

01. Adonis was the (　)¹ handsome man (　)² Greek mythology.
02. He was (　)³ from a tree, not (　)⁴ a woman. The older
03. he (　)⁵, the more handsome he became. He had (　)⁶ skin,
04. long blond (　)⁷, clear blue eyes, and a well-proportioned (　)⁸.
05. Aphrodite, the goddess (　)⁹ beauty, fell in love (　)¹⁰ him. "What a
06. handsome (　)¹¹ he is!" she cried. Her (　)¹² for him was very passionate.
07. She (　)¹³ so much attracted to him not (　)¹⁴ because he was so
08. handsome, (　)¹⁵ because Eros, her son, pierced (　)¹⁶ breast
09. with his arrow (　)¹⁷ mistake. The legend (　)¹⁸ that Eros
10. had a golden arrow and (　)¹⁹ this arrow pierced (　)²⁰ heart,
11. you would (　)²¹ captured by love. Eros accidentally (　)²² his own
12. mother with (　)²³ golden arrow. This is (　)²⁴ Aphrodite
13. fell (　)²⁵ love with Adonis. However, her love was (　)²⁶ fulfilled,
14. because Adonis was still (　)²⁷ young to accept it. (　)²⁸ interest
15. was only (　)²⁹ hunting. Aphrodite (　)³⁰ very
16. (　)³¹ worried about (　)³² danger Adonis might encounter
17. during hunting. (　)³³ was always thinking, "(　)³⁴ he should
18. (　)³⁵ wounded in a flight (　)³⁶ a fierce animal..."
19. "Don't be too brave. (　)³⁷ you are in danger, please (　)³⁸ my name.
20. I will be with you in (　)³⁹ time," Aphrodite (　)⁴⁰ to say to Adonis.
21. One (　)⁴¹, he chased a boar (　)⁴² the bushes and shot at it.
22. Unfortunately, the arrow missed (　)⁴³ heart and only injured (　)⁴⁴ boar's body.
23. Nothing is (　)⁴⁵ horrible and dangerous than an injured (　)⁴⁶ beast.
24. It caught (　)⁴⁷ and attacked him. The sharp tusks (　)⁴⁸ the boar pierced
25. Adonis's body (　)⁴⁹ and then twice. Aphrodite, (　)⁵⁰ was on a trip
26. in a (　)⁵¹ carriage in the sky, was struck by a sensation (　)⁵² her
27. beloved was (　)⁵³ danger. She looked (　)⁵⁴ to earth and discovered
28. the boy's (　)⁵⁵ covered with blood. (　)⁵⁶ with her magical powers,
29. it (　)⁵⁷ impossible to revive the (　)⁵⁸ boy.
30. Aphrodite decided (　)⁵⁹ she would (　)⁶⁰ Adonis into a flower

31. which would bloom every (   )⁶¹ so that she could still (   )⁶² him.
32. The (   )⁶³ that absorbed Adonis's blood brought (   )⁶⁴ a beautiful
33. crimson flower, (   )⁶⁵ the life of the flower was (   )⁶⁶ short as
34. Adonis's (   )⁶⁷. This flower is (   )⁶⁸ known as an anemone.
35. Aphrodite (   )⁶⁹ her beloved forever and could not (   )⁷⁰ crying.
36. The tears (   )⁷¹ Aphrodite (   )⁷² for this beloved boy turned into roses.

(28)　MET 美誠社版 (MET ARB)（解答）

CD を聞きながら，空いている（　　）の中に，4 文字以下（最大で 4 文字）の英単語を入れて下さい．

01. Adonis was the (most)¹ handsome man (in)² Greek mythology.
02. He was (born)³ from a tree, not (from)⁴ a woman. The older
03. he (grew)⁵, the more handsome he became. He had (rosy)⁶ skin,
04. long blond (hair)⁷, clear blue eyes, and a well-proportioned (body)⁸.
05. Aphrodite, the goddess (of)⁹ beauty, fell in love (with)¹⁰ him. "What a
06. handsome (boy)¹¹ he is!" she cried. Her (love)¹² for him was very passionate.
07. She (was)¹³ so much attracted to him not (only)¹⁴ because he was so
08. handsome, (but)¹⁵ because Eros, her son, pierced (her)¹⁶ breast
09. with his arrow (by)¹⁷ mistake. The legend (said)¹⁸ that Eros
10. had a golden arrow and (if)¹⁹ this arrow pierced (your)²⁰ heart,
11. you would (be)²¹ captured by love. Eros accidentally (shot)²² his own
12. mother with (the)²³ golden arrow. This is (why)²⁴ Aphrodite
13. fell (in)²⁵ love with Adonis. However, her love was (not)²⁶ fulfilled,
14. because Adonis was still (too)²⁷ young to accept it. (His)²⁸ interest
15. was only (in)²⁹ hunting. Aphrodite (was)³⁰ very
16. (much)³¹ worried about (the)³² danger Adonis might encounter
17. during hunting. (She)³³ was always thinking, "(if)³⁴ he should
18. (be)³⁵ wounded in a flight (with)³⁶ a fierce animal..."
19. "Don't be too brave. (When)³⁷ you are in danger, please (call)³⁸ my name.
20. I will be with you in (no)³⁹ time," Aphrodite (used)⁴⁰ to say to Adonis.
21. One (day)⁴¹, he chased a boar (into)⁴² the bushes and shot at it.
22. Unfortunately, the arrow missed (its)⁴³ heart and only injured (the)⁴⁴ boar's body.
23. Nothing is (more)⁴⁵ horrible and dangerous than an injured (wild)⁴⁶ beast.
24. It caught (him)⁴⁷ and attacked him. The sharp tusks (of)⁴⁸ the boar pierced

> 25. Adonis's body (once)[49] and then twice. Aphrodite, (who)[50] was on a trip
> 26. in a (swan)[51] carriage in the sky, was struck by a sensation (that)[52] her
> 27. beloved was (in)[53] danger. She looked (down)[54] to earth and discovered
> 28. the boy's (body)[55] covered with blood. (Even)[56] with her magical powers,
> 29. it (was)[57] impossible to revive the (dead)[58] boy.
> 30. Aphrodite decided (that)[59] she would (turn)[60] Adonis into a flower
> 31. which would bloom every (year)[61] so that she could still (see)[62] him.
> 32. The (land)[63] that absorbed Adonis's blood brought (out)[64] a beautiful
> 33. crimson flower, (but)[65] the life of the flower was (as)[66] short as
> 34. Adonis's (life)[67]. This flower is (now)[68] known as an anemone.
> 35. Aphrodite (lost)[69] her beloved forever and could not (stop)[70] crying.
> 36. The tears (that)[71] Aphrodite (shed)[72] for this beloved boy turned into roses.

Maki et al. (2012c) は，46名の被験者にMET ARBとMET 4を期間を空けずに実施し，その得点間に相関があるかどうか調査した．両得点に対する，単回帰分析（相関分析）の結果を (29) に示す．

(29) MET ARBの得点とMET 4の得点との相関

被験者数	相関係数 (r)	回帰直線	p 値
46	.67	y = .60x + 5.68	$p < .05$

この結果，MET ARB得点とMET 4得点との間に，比較的強い相関があることが分かった ($n = 46, r = .67, p < .05$)．したがって，MET ARBは，MET 4と同様の機能を果たす能力があることが分かり，同時に，METは，Kawana and Walker (2002) 以外のテキストを用いても，作成することが可能であることが分かった．

3.5 その他

牧グループは，上記以外にも，さまざまな版のMETを作成し，その機能を調査している．6章以降で詳述されるように，Hasebe et al. (2010) とMaki et al. (2010d) は，中学生版MET, junior Minimal English Test (jMET) を作成した．また，Morii (2018), Xu (2018), Wu (2018) は，日本の大学入

試センター試験英語聴解部分を基に，センター試験版 MET を作成し，Ma（in progress）は，中国で使用されている教科書を基に，中国版 MET を作成した．これらの版の MET の機能は，後の章で，詳述される．

第4章

MET：能力向上機能

4.1 Maki and Niinuma (2005)

　Maki and Niinuma (2005) は，MET が，単に英語能力を測定する機能を持つだけでなく，繰り返し実施することで，英語能力を向上させる機能があることを明らかにした．Maki (2003) は，Kawana and Walker (2002) を利用して，MET 4文字以下版を Version 1 (MET 4-1) から Version 10 (MET 4-10) まで作成した．MET 4全10バージョンは，10章に提示される．以下に，MET 4-1, MET 4-2, MET 4-10 を提示する．

　(1)　MET 4-1

CD を聞きながら，空いている（　）の中に，4文字以下（最大で4文字）の英単語を入れて下さい．

01. The majority of people have at least one pet at (　　)^1 time in their (　　)^2.
02. Sometimes the relationship between a pet (　　)^3 or cat and its owner is (　　)^4 close
03. that (　　)^5 begin to resemble (　　)^6 other in their appearance and behavior.
04. On the other (　　)^7, owners of unusual pets (　　)^8 as tigers or snakes
05. sometimes (　　)^9 to protect themselves (　　)^{10} their own pets.
06. Thirty years (　　)^{11} the idea of an inanimate (　　)^{12} first arose.
07. This was the pet (　　)^{13}, which became a craze (　　)^{14} the United States and
08. spread (　　)^{15} other countries as (　　)^{16}.

09. People (   )^{17} large sums of money for ordinary rocks and assigned (   )^{18} names.
10. They tied a leash around the rock and pulled (   )^{19} down the street just (   )^{20} a dog.
11. The rock owners (   )^{21} talked (   )^{22} their pet rocks.
12. Now (   )^{23} we have entered the computer age, (   )^{24} have virtual pets.
13. The Japanese Tamagotchi— (   )^{25} imaginary chicken (   )^{26}—
14. (   )^{27} the precursor of (   )^{28} virtual pets.
15. Now there (   )^{29} an ever-increasing number of such virtual (   )^{30}
16. which mostly young people are adopting (   )^{31} their (   )^{32}.
17. And (   )^{33} your virtual pet (   )^{34},
18. you (   )^{35} reserve a permanent resting place (   )^{36} the Internet in a virtual pet cemetery.
19. Sports are big business. Whereas Babe Ruth, the (   )^{37} famous athlete of (   )^{38} day,
20. was well-known (   )^{39} earning as (   )^{40} as the President of the United States, the average
21. salary (   )^{41} today's professional baseball players is (   )^{42} times that of the President.
22. (   )^{43} a handful of sports superstars earn 100 times (   )^{44} through their contracts
23. (   )^{45} manufacturers of clothing, (   )^{46}, and sports equipment.
24. But every generation produces (   )^{47} or two legendary athletes (   )^{48} rewrite
25. the record books, and whose ability and achievements (   )^{49} remembered (   )^{50} generations.
26. (   )^{51} the current generation Tiger Woods and Michael Jordan are two (   )^{52} legendary
27. figures, (   )^{53} of whom (   )^{54} achieved almost mythical status.
28. The (   )^{55} that a large number of professional athletes (   )^{56} huge incomes
29. has (   )^{57} to increased competition throughout (   )^{58} sports world.
30. Parents (   )^{59} their children to sports training camps (   )^{60} an early age.
31. Such (   )^{61} typically practice three to (   )^{62} hours a day,
32. (   )^{63} weekend (   )^{64} during their school vacations
33. in order (   )^{65} better their chances of eventually obtaining (   )^{66} well-paid position

第4章　MET：能力向上機能　　　　　　　　　　59

34. on a professional (　　)⁶⁷ when they grow (　　)⁶⁸.
35. As for the (　　)⁶⁹ young aspirants who do (　　)⁷⁰ succeed,
36. one wonders if they (　　)⁷¹ regret having (　　)⁷² their childhood.

(2)　MET 4-2

CDを聞きながら，空いている(　　)の中に，4文字以下（最大で4文字）の英単語を入れて下さい．

01. Many people (　　)¹ experienced the (　　)² of standing on a
02. moving (　　)³ and watching a group (　　)⁴ dolphins swim alongside.
03. Dolphins are (　　)⁵ only playful animals (　　)⁶ they are also highly
04. intelligent. They (　　)⁷ mammals that can be found in (　　)⁸ of
05. the world's oceans (　　)⁹ well as (　　)¹⁰ fresh water.
06. Dolphins (　　)¹¹ swim at speeds of (　　)¹² to
07. 56 k.p.h., and (　　)¹³ can dive (　　)¹⁴ depths of 200 meters
08. and (　　)¹⁵ under water (　　)¹⁶ 5-8 minutes without resurfacing
09. for (　　)¹⁷. They are well-known for (　　)¹⁸ unique
10. clicking sound they (　　)¹⁹ like sonar to locate (　　)²⁰ as
11. well (　　)²¹ obstacles. Every dolphin (　　)²² has
12. its (　　)²³ individual whistling sound (　　)²⁴ for communication.
13. (　　)²⁵ dolphins sleep, they sleep in (　　)²⁶ semi-alert
14. state (　　)²⁷ resting one side of their brain (　　)²⁸ a time.
15. They (　　)²⁹ help sick or injured dolphins as (　　)³⁰ as
16. they can, and they (　　)³¹ as a team (　　)³² there is danger.
17. It (　　)³³ because of these (　　)³⁴ other human-like
18. qualities (　　)³⁵ people have a special feeling (　　)³⁶ dolphins.
19. Everybody seems to (　　)³⁷ or be interested (　　)³⁸ the ostrich.
20. This (　　)³⁹ be because it is unique (　　)⁴⁰ appearance and
21. character. The ostrich is a (　　)⁴¹, but it cannot (　　)⁴².
22. It (　　)⁴³ the tallest and heaviest bird in (　　)⁴⁴ world,
23. and (　　)⁴⁵ it is the fastest two-legged creature (　　)⁴⁶ Earth,
24. (　　)⁴⁷ the ability to reach a speed (　　)⁴⁸ 70 k.p.h.
25. Ostriches (　　)⁴⁹ been successfully domesticated and are (　　)⁵⁰
26. farmed throughout the world (　　)⁵¹ meat, feathers (　　)⁵² leather.
27. Ostrich (　　)⁵³, although red, (　　)⁵⁴ fewer calories and less
28. cholesterol (　　)⁵⁵ chicken (　　)⁵⁶ turkey meat.
29. There (　　)⁵⁷ several myths about ostriches. Perhaps the (　　)⁵⁸

30. enduring myth about ( )⁵⁹ ostrich is ( )⁶⁰ it hides
31. its ( )⁶¹ in the sand ( )⁶² in danger.
32. Although ( )⁶³ can read ( )⁶⁴ myth in stories
33. written ( )⁶⁵ ancient Romans 2000 years ( )⁶⁶, it is not at
34. all ( )⁶⁷. But people continue to believe this ( )⁶⁸ and
35. think ( )⁶⁹ the ostrich is ( )⁷⁰ stupid animal. Maybe people
36. think this ( )⁷¹ because ostriches' eyes are larger ( )⁷² their brains.

(3) MET 4-10

CDを聞きながら，空いている（　）の中に，4文字以下（最大で4文字）の英単語を入れて下さい．

01. The human mouth ( )¹ three major functions. ( )² of them—eating
02. and breathing— ( )³ shared by members ( )⁴ the animal kingdom.
03. ( )⁵ third function—speaking—is ( )⁶ of the principal features which
04. distinguishes human beings ( )⁷ the rest ( )⁸ living creatures.
05. Although primitive ( )⁹ must have ( )¹⁰ a spoken language,
06. social scientists ( )¹¹ no evidence of language as ( )¹² until the
07. appearance ( )¹³ written records ( )¹⁴ ancient Mesopotamia and Egypt
08. 5-6000 years ( )¹⁵. Present-day linguists can identify ( )¹⁶ 1500
09. spoken languages, ( )¹⁷ Mandarin Chinese being spoken by more ( )¹⁸ three-quarters
10. of ( )¹⁹ billion people. After Mandarin Chinese, English is the ( )²⁰ widely spoken first
11. language, and ( )²¹ become the language of choice ( )²² international communication.
12. English has ( )²³ always been the international language. ( )²⁴ hundred years ago
13. French ( )²⁵ the dominant language. ( )²⁶ ancient times, Aramaic, Greek and Latin
14. ( )²⁷ international languages ( )²⁸ different points in time. Efforts have
15. ( )²⁹ made throughout history ( )³⁰ adopt a common universal language for
16. ( )³¹ peoples of the world. The most successful such effort to ( )³² was Esperanto

第 4 章　MET：能力向上機能　　　　　　　　　　　　　　　　61

17. which was spoken（　　）[33] about 750,000 people at one（　　）[34] in the mid-20th century.
18. However, such universal languages always（　　）[35] because of the absence（　　）[36] a cultural foundation.
19. Hinduism, the primary religion（　　）[37] India, has produced a wealth of（　　）[38],
20. customs and rituals since（　　）[39] origins in prehistory.（　　）[40] of its more colorful
21. aspects（　　）[41] the large number（　　）[42] wandering beggars called *sadhus*.
22. Traditionally a *sadhu* renounces（　　）[43] comforts of ordinary（　　）[44] and leads
23. a life（　　）[45] a begging nomad. He travels（　　）[46] one holy
24. place to another on（　　）[47], often barefoot with hardly（　　）[48] clothes,
25. carrying a begging（　　）[49] and perhaps a walking stick. In（　　）[50] way,
26. he hopes（　　）[51] escape from the evils（　　）[52] a materialistic life.
27. Indian people believe（　　）[53] giving food, shelter（　　）[54]
28. money（　　）[55] *sadhus* improves their chances of escaping（　　）[56] reincarnation.
29. Reincarnation（　　）[57] the belief that one's（　　）[58] is repeatedly
30. reborn in a different（　　）[59]. For Hindus, never-ending rebirth（　　）[60]
31. equivalent（　　）[61] the Christian idea of（　　）[62]. Hindus believe that by
32. performing（　　）[63] good actions (such（　　）[64] giving
33. to *sadhus*),（　　）[65] can enter（　　）[66] Hindu heaven.
34. Some *sadhus*（　　）[67] truly holy people with（　　）[68] minds and hearts.
35. Others（　　）[69] that they can（　　）[70] through their whole life without working simply
36. （　　）[71] pretending to be a holy（　　）[72] and living off the kindness of others.

　Maki and Niinuma（2005）は，2004 年 4 月から 2004 年 7 月の間に，大学 1 年生英語学習者に，週に一度のペースで，MET 4-1，MET 4-2，MET 4-10 の順に，10 バージョンの MET 4 文字以下版を実施し，その後，第 11 週目に，MET 4-1 を再度実施した．MET 用紙は，毎回，すべて回収され，学生は，試験後，一切，MET の内容を確認できなかった．合計 64 名の学生が，この実験に参加した．

　Maki and Niinuma（2005）は，*t*-Test を用いて，第 1 回目の MET 4-1 の得点の平均点と，10 週後に行われた第 2 回目の MET 4-1 の得点の平均点と

の間に,有意な差があるかどうか調査した.その結果は,(4)に示される.

(4) 第1回目の MET 4-1 の得点の平均点と第2回目の MET 4-1 の得点の平均点に対する t-Test の結果

	第1回目 MET 4-1	第2回目 MET 4-1
平均点	19.66	26.09
被験者数	64	64
t Stat	-10.06	
$p(T < t)$ two-tail	.001	
t Critical two-tail	2.00	

(4) において,|t-Stat|= 10.06 > |t Critical two-tail|= 2.00 であり,また,p < .05 であるので,2 得点の間には,統計的有意な差があることになる.具体的には,第2回目の得点の平均点は,第1回目の得点の平均点に対し,6.43点,また,%では,8.93%上昇している.

したがって,この調査結果は,MET が,単に英語能力を測定する機能を持つだけでなく,繰り返し実施することで,英語能力を向上させる機能があることを意味している.前章で見たように,MET は,その作成方法が極めて簡易的であるため,同じ音源を利用しながら,何バージョンもの MET を作成することができる.したがって,英語教育者が,あらかじめ,何バージョンも MET を用意しておけば,英語学習者が,何度も挑戦することで,少しずつ英語能力を向上させることができる.

4.2 Maki et al. (2011b)

Maki et al. (2011b) は,Maki and Niinuma (2005) の調査を継続して行い,どのタイプの MET を用いても,MET が,単に英語能力を測定する機能を持つだけでなく,繰り返し実施することで,英語能力を向上させる機能があることを明らかにしている.この調査のために,Maki et al. (2011b) は,MET 4文字以下版,MET 5文字以下版,そして,MET 6単語目ごと版 (MET E6A) の3種類の MET を使用した.

Maki et al. (2011b) は,2005年10月から2011年2月まで,この調査を行った.(5) は,各年の MET の種類と被験者の数を示している.

(5) 年毎の MET の種類と被験者数

年	MET の種類	満点	被験者数
2005	MET 4	72	31
2006	MET 4	72	32
2007	MET 4	72	27
2008	MET 5	72	33
2009	MET E6A	66	31
2010	MET E6A	66	24

以下に，各種類の MET の最初のバージョン (MET 4-1, MET 5-1, MET E6A-1) を提示する．

(6) MET 4-1

CD を聞きながら，空いている（　）の中に，4文字以下（最大で4文字）の英単語を入れて下さい．

01. The majority of people have at least one pet at (　)[1] time in their (　)[2].
02. Sometimes the relationship between a pet (　)[3] or cat and its owner is (　)[4] close
03. that (　)[5] begin to resemble (　)[6] other in their appearance and behavior.
04. On the other (　)[7], owners of unusual pets (　)[8] as tigers or snakes
05. sometimes (　)[9] to protect themselves (　)[10] their own pets.
06. Thirty years (　)[11] the idea of an inanimate (　)[12] first arose.
07. This was the pet (　)[13], which became a craze (　)[14] the United States and
08. spread (　)[15] other countries as (　)[16].
09. People (　)[17] large sums of money for ordinary rocks and assigned (　)[18] names.
10. They tied a leash around the rock and pulled (　)[19] down the street just (　)[20] a dog.
11. The rock owners (　)[21] talked (　)[22] their pet rocks.
12. Now (　)[23] we have entered the computer age, (　)[24] have virtual pets.
13. The Japanese Tamagotchi—(　)[25] imaginary chicken (　)[26]—
14. (　)[27] the precursor of (　)[28] virtual pets.
15. Now there (　)[29] an ever-increasing number of such virtual (　)[30]
16. which mostly young people are adopting (　)[31] their (　)[32].

17. And (   )³³ your virtual pet (   )³⁴,
18. you (   )³⁵ reserve a permanent resting place (   )³⁶ the Internet in a virtual pet cemetery.
19. Sports are big business. Whereas Babe Ruth, the (   )³⁷ famous athlete of (   )³⁸ day,
20. was well-known (   )³⁹ earning as (   )⁴⁰ as the President of the United States, the average
21. salary (   )⁴¹ today's professional baseball players is (   )⁴² times that of the President.
22. (   )⁴³ a handful of sports superstars earn 100 times (   )⁴⁴ through their contracts
23. (   )⁴⁵ manufacturers of clothing, (   )⁴⁶, and sports equipment.
24. But every generation produces (   )⁴⁷ or two legendary athletes (   )⁴⁸ rewrite
25. the record books, and whose ability and achievements (   )⁴⁹ remembered (   )⁵⁰ generations.
26. (   )⁵¹ the current generation Tiger Woods and Michael Jordan are two (   )⁵² legendary
27. figures, (   )⁵³ of whom (   )⁵⁴ achieved almost mythical status.
28. The (   )⁵⁵ that a large number of professional athletes (   )⁵⁶ huge incomes
29. has (   )⁵⁷ to increased competition throughout (   )⁵⁸ sports world.
30. Parents (   )⁵⁹ their children to sports training camps (   )⁶⁰ an early age.
31. Such (   )⁶¹ typically practice three to (   )⁶² hours a day,
32. (   )⁶³ weekend (   )⁶⁴ during their school vacations
33. in order (   )⁶⁵ better their chances of eventually obtaining (   )⁶⁶ well-paid position
34. on a professional (   )⁶⁷ when they grow (   )⁶⁸.
35. As for the (   )⁶⁹ young aspirants who do (   )⁷⁰ succeed,
36. one wonders if they (   )⁷¹ regret having (   )⁷² their childhood.

(7) MET 5-1

CD を聞きながら，空いている（　）の中に，5文字以下（最大で5文字）の英単語を入れて下さい．

01. The majority of people have at (　)¹ one pet at some time in their (　)².
02. Sometimes the relationship between a pet (　)³ or cat and its (　)⁴ is so close
03. that they (　)⁵ to resemble each other (　)⁶ their appearance and behavior.
04. On the (　)⁷ hand, owners of unusual pets (　)⁸ as tigers or snakes
05. sometimes (　)⁹ to protect themselves from their (　)¹⁰ pets.
06. Thirty years ago the (　)¹¹ of an inanimate pet first (　)¹².
07. This was the pet (　)¹³, which became a craze (　)¹⁴ the United States and
08. spread (　)¹⁵ other countries as (　)¹⁶.
09. People paid large sums of (　)¹⁷ for ordinary rocks and assigned them (　)¹⁸.
10. They (　)¹⁹ a leash around the rock and pulled it (　)²⁰ the street
11. just like a (　)²¹. The rock owners (　)²² talked to their pet rocks.
12. Now (　)²³ we have entered the computer (　)²⁴,
13. we have virtual (　)²⁵. The Japanese Tamagotchi—(　)²⁶ imaginary chicken egg—
14. (　)²⁷ the precursor of (　)²⁸ virtual pets.
15. Now there (　)²⁹ an ever-increasing number (　)³⁰ such virtual pets
16. which mostly (　)³¹ people are adopting (　)³² their own.
17. And if (　)³³ virtual pet dies, you (　)³⁴ reserve a permanent resting place
18. (　)³⁵ the Internet in (　)³⁶ virtual pet cemetery.
19. Sports are (　)³⁷ business. Whereas Babe Ruth, the (　)³⁸ famous athlete
20. of his (　)³⁹, was well-known for earning as (　)⁴⁰ as the President of the United States,
21. the average salary (　)⁴¹ today's professional baseball players is ten times (　)⁴².
22. of the President. And a handful of sports superstars (　)⁴³ 100 (　)⁴⁴ more
23. through their contracts (　)⁴⁵ manufacturers of clothing, (　)⁴⁶, and sports equipment.

24. But (　　)⁴⁷ generation produces (　　)⁴⁸ or two legendary athletes
25. who rewrite the record (　　)⁴⁹, and whose ability and achievements (　　)⁵⁰ remembered
26. for generations. (　　)⁵¹ the current generation Tiger Woods (　　)⁵² Michael Jordan
27. are (　　)⁵³ such legendary figures, both of (　　)⁵⁴ have achieved almost mythical status.
28. The fact that a (　　)⁵⁵ number of professional athletes earn (　　)⁵⁶ incomes
29. has (　　)⁵⁷ to increased competition throughout the sports (　　)⁵⁸.
30. Parents (　　)⁵⁹ their children to sports training (　　)⁶⁰ at an early age.
31. Such (　　)⁶¹ typically practice (　　)⁶² to four hours a day,
32. (　　)⁶³ weekend and during (　　)⁶⁴ school vacations
33. in (　　)⁶⁵ to better their chances of eventually obtaining a well-(　　)⁶⁶ position
34. on a professional (　　)⁶⁷ when they (　　)⁶⁸ up.
35. As for the (　　)⁶⁹ young aspirants who do (　　)⁷⁰ succeed,
36. one wonders (　　)⁷¹ they will regret having (　　)⁷² their childhood.

(8) MET E6-1 (MET E6A-1)

CDを聞きながら，空いている (　　) の中に英単語を入れて下さい．

01. The (　　)¹ of people have at least (　　)² pet at some time
02. in (　　)³ life. Sometimes the relationship between (　　)⁴ pet dog or cat
03. and (　　)⁵ owner is so close that (　　)⁶ begin to resemble
04. each other (　　)⁷ their appearance and behavior. On (　　)⁸ other hand,
05. owners of unusual (　　)⁹ such as tigers or snakes (　　)¹⁰ have to protect
06. themselves from (　　)¹¹ own pets. Thirty years ago (　　)¹² idea of
07. an inanimate pet (　　)¹³ arose. This was the pet (　　)¹⁴, which became a craze
08. in (　　)¹⁵ United States and spread to (　　)¹⁶ countries as well.
09. People paid (　　)¹⁷ sums of money for ordinary (　　)¹⁸ and assigned them names.
10. They (　　)¹⁹ a leash around the rock (　　)²⁰ pulled it down
11. the street (　　)²¹ like a dog. The rock (　　)²² even talked to
12. their pet (　　)²³. Now that we have entered (　　)²⁴ computer age,
13. we have virtual (　　)²⁵. The Japanese Tamagotchi—

第4章 MET：能力向上機能

14. the imaginary chicken (　　)²⁶—was the precursor of many (　　)²⁷ pets.
15. Now there are an (　　)²⁸-increasing number of such virtual (　　)²⁹
16. which mostly young people are (　　)³⁰ as their own.
17. And if (　　)³¹ virtual pet dies, you can (　　)³² a permanent resting
18. place on (　　)³³ Internet in a virtual pet (　　)³⁴.
19. Sports (　　)³⁵ big business. Whereas Babe Ruth, the most (　　)³⁶
20. athlete of his day, was (　　)³⁷-known for earning as much (　　)³⁸ the President
21. of the United (　　)³⁹, the average salary of today's (　　)⁴⁰ baseball players
22. is ten times (　　)⁴¹ of the President. And a (　　)⁴² of sports superstars
23. earn 100 times (　　)⁴³ through their contracts with manufacturers (　　)⁴⁴
24. clothing, food, and sports equipment. (　　)⁴⁵ every generation produces
25. one or (　　)⁴⁶ legendary athletes who rewrite the (　　)⁴⁷ books,
26. and whose ability and (　　)⁴⁸ are remembered for generations.
27. In (　　)⁴⁹ current generation Tiger Woods and Michael Jordan are two (　　)⁵⁰
28. legendary figures, both of whom (　　)⁵¹ achieved almost mythical status.
29. The (　　)⁵² that a large number of (　　)⁵³ athletes earn huge incomes
30. has (　　)⁵⁴ to increased competition throughout the (　　)⁵⁵ world.
31. Parents send their children (　　)⁵⁶ sports training camps at an (　　)⁵⁷ age.
32. Such kids typically practice (　　)⁵⁸ to four hours a day, (　　)⁵⁹ weekend
33. and during their school (　　)⁶⁰ in order to better their (　　)⁶¹ of eventually
34. obtaining a well-(　　)⁶² position on a professional team (　　)⁶³ they grow up.
35. As for (　　)⁶⁴ many young aspirants who do (　　)⁶⁵ succeed,
36. one wonders if they (　　)⁶⁶ regret having lost their childhood.

Maki et al. (2011b) は，大学1年生英語学習者に，週に一度のペースで，各種類の MET 8 バージョンを実施し，その後，第9週目に，第1週目に実施した MET を再度実施した．MET 用紙は，毎回，すべて回収され，学生は，試験後，一切，MET の内容を確認できなかった．

Maki et al. (2011b) は，t-Test を用いて，第1回目の MET の得点の平均点と，8週後に行われた第2回目の MET の得点の平均点との間に，有意な差があるかどうか調査した．その結果は，以下に示される．まず，2005年における結果は，(9) に示される．

(9) 第1回目の MET 4-1 の得点の平均点と第2回目の MET 4-1 の得点の平均点に対する t-Test の結果

	第1回目 MET 4-1	第2回目 MET 4-1
実施年	2005 年	2005 年
平均点	34.66	43.58
被験者数	31	31
t Stat	-9.82	
$p(T \leq t)$ two-tail	.001	
t Critical two-tail	2.04	

(9) において, $|t\text{-Stat}|=9.82 > |t \text{ Critical two-tail}|=2.04$ であり, また, $p < .05$ であるので, 2 得点の間には, 統計的有意な差があることになる. 具体的には, 第2回目の得点の平均点は, 第1回目の得点の平均点に対し, 8.92 点, また, %では, 12.39%上昇している.

第二に, 2006 年における結果は, (10) に示される.

(10) 第1回目の MET 4-1 の得点の平均点と第2回目の MET 4-1 の得点の平均点に対する t-Test の結果

	第1回目 MET 4-1	第2回目 MET 4-1
実施年	2006 年	2006 年
平均点	37.34	47.44
被験者数	32	32
t Stat	-10.82	
$p(T \leq t)$ two-tail	.001	
t Critical two-tail	2.04	

(10) において, $|t\text{-Stat}|=10.82 > |t \text{ Critical two-tail}|=2.04$ であり, また, $p < .05$ であるので, 2 得点の間には, 統計的有意な差があることになる. 具体的には, 第2回目の得点の平均点は, 第1回目の得点の平均点に対し, 10.10 点, また, %では, 14.03%上昇している.

第三に, 2007 年における結果は, (11) に示される.

(11) 第 1 回目の MET 4-1 の得点の平均点と第 2 回目の MET 4-1 の得点の平均点に対する t-Test の結果

	第 1 回目 MET 4-1	第 2 回目 MET 4-1
実施年	2007 年	2007 年
平均点	33.44	42.44
被験者数	27	27
t Stat	-11.55	
$p(T \leq t)$ two-tail	.001	
t Critical two-tail	2.06	

(11) において,|t-Stat|= 11.55 > |t Critical two-tail|= 2.06 であり,また,$p < .05$ であるので,2 得点の間には,統計的有意な差があることになる.具体的には,第 2 回目の得点の平均点は,第 1 回目の得点の平均点に対し,9.00 点,また,%では,12.50%上昇している.

第四に,2008 年における結果は,(12) に示される.

(12) 第 1 回目の MET 5-1 の得点の平均点と第 2 回目の MET 5-1 の得点の平均点に対する t-Test の結果

	第 1 回目 MET 5-1	第 2 回目 MET 5-1
実施年	2008 年	2008 年
平均点	31.52	43.64
被験者数	33	33
t Stat	-11.08	
$p(T \leq t)$ two-tail	.001	
t Critical two-tail	2.04	

(12) において,|t-Stat|= 11.08 > |t Critical two-tail|= 2.04 であり,また,$p < .05$ であるので,2 得点の間には,統計的有意な差があることになる.具体的には,第 2 回目の得点の平均点は,第 1 回目の得点の平均点に対し,12.12 点,また,%では,16.83%上昇している.

第五に,2009 年における結果は,(13) に示される.

(13) 第 1 回目の MET E6A-1 の得点の平均点と第 2 回目の MET E6A-1 の得点の平均点に対する t-Test の結果

	第 1 回目 MET 6A-1	第 2 回目 MET 6A-1
実施年	2009 年	2009 年
平均点	26.00	33.71
被験者数	31	31
t Stat	－8.54	
$p(T<t)$ two-tail	.001	
t Critical two-tail	2.04	

(13) において, |t-Stat| = 8.54 > |t Critical two-tail| = 2.04 であり, また, p < .05 であるので, 2 得点の間には, 統計的有意な差があることになる. 具体的には, 第 2 回目の得点の平均点は, 第 1 回目の得点の平均点に対し, 7.71 点, また, ％では, 11.68％上昇している.

第六に, 2010 年における結果は, (14) に示される.

(14) 第 1 回目の MET E6A-1 の得点の平均点と第 2 回目の MET E6A-1 の得点の平均点に対する t-Test の結果

	第 1 回目 MET 6A-1	第 2 回目 MET 6A-1
実施年	2010 年	2010 年
平均点	23.25	34.71
被験者数	24	24
t Stat	－8.87	
$p(T<t)$ two-tail	.001	
t Critical two-tail	2.07	

(14) において, |t-Stat| = 8.87 > |t Critical two-tail| = 2.07 であり, また, p < .05 であるので, 2 得点の間には, 統計的有意な差があることになる. 具体的には, 第 2 回目の得点の平均点は, 第 1 回目の得点の平均点に対し, 11.46 点, また, ％では, 17.36％上昇している.

これらの結果より, Maki and Niinuma (2005) が最初に指摘した「MET が, 単に英語能力を測定する機能を持つだけでなく, 繰り返し実施することで, 英語能力を向上させる機能があること」が, さらに確証されたことになる.

このことは，英語学習において，英語の格言"Practice makes perfect!"どおり，「習うより慣れろ．」「継続は力なり．」ということが，有効な学習手段であることを示している．

第 5 章

アジアにおける MET

牧グループは，MET が，ある程度日本人英語学習者の英語能力を測定することを明らかにした後，同様のことがアジア諸国の英語学習者にも当てはまるかどうか明らかにするために，韓国，中国，内モンゴルにおいて，大学生にMET を実施し，他の英語能力測定試験の得点との間の相関を調査した．

5.1 韓国

日本と同様，韓国にも，大学入試センター試験に相当する試験がある．それは，The College Scholastic Achievement Test と呼ばれている．Maki et al. (2006b) は，The College Scholastic Achievement Test (English Part) 2005 (CSAT 2005) を使用し，MET の得点と CSAT 2005 の得点との間に，どの程度の相関があるか調査した．まず，CSAT 2005 の概要を (1) に示す．

(1) CAST 2005 概要
    受験者数　570,431
    満点　　　100
    設問数　　50(聴解 17)
    平均点　　58
    標準偏差　20
    制限時間　70 分（聴解 20 分）
    実施日　　2004 年 11 月 17 日

Maki et al.（2006b）は，2005 年 4 月に，韓国にある 2 大学にて，155 名の大学 1 年生英語学習者に MET 4 文字以下版（MET 4）を実施した．その調査結果は，(2) に示される．

(2) MET の得点と CSAT 2005 の得点との相関
 $n = 155$
 $r = .61$
 $p < .05$

MET の得点と CSAT 2005 の得点の相関係数は，$r = .61$ であった．この結果，両得点間に，相関があることが明らかになった．

5.2 中国

次に，Bai（2007）は，中国人英語学習者を対象に，中国において調査を行い，MET の得点と Paul Nation's Vocabulary Size Test（PNT）の得点との間に，どの程度の相関があるか調査した．PNT は，Nation（1990）によって開発され，第二言語習得研究分野においては，最も確立された英語能力測定テストの 1 つである．PNT は，語彙テストであり，5 つのレベルの異なるグループに分かれた，合計 90 の語彙問題から構成されている．最も低いレベルであるレベル A は，大学生になじみのある，最も頻繁に使用される 1,000 の語彙から選択されている．その次のレベルのレベル B は 2,000，その上のレベル C は 3,000，その上のレベル D は 5,000，そして，最も上のレベル E は 10,000 の語彙から選択されている．(3) に PNT の具体例を示す．テスト内容は，語彙が与えられ，その語彙と，その語彙の定義をマッチさせるものである．

(3) Paul Nation's Vocabulary Size Test の例

Paul Nation's Vocabulary Size Test

How to Administer the Test

Find the most suitable vocabulary from 1 to 6 that matches the words/phrases on the right. Use the separate answer sheet when you fill in the answers.

Examples

Level F

[1]	1. business	☐ part of a house
	2. clock	
	3. horse	☐ animal with four legs
	4. pencil	
	5. shoe	☐ something used for writing
	6. wall	

The actual test is divided into 5 levels from A to E. As you proceed, the level will be higher. Turn the page and begin the test.

Level A

[1]	1. original	☐ complete	[2]	1. apply	☐ choose by voting
	2. private			2. elect	
	3. royal	☐ first		3. jump	☐ become like water
	4. slow			4. manufacture	
	5. sorry	☐ not public		5. melt	☐ make
	6. total			6. threaten	
[3]	1. blame	☐ keep away from sight	[4]	1. accident	☐ having a high opinion of yourself
	2. hide			2. choice	
	3. hit	☐ have a bad effect on something		3. debt	☐ something you must pay
	4. invite			4. fortune	
	5. pour	☐ ask		5. pride	☐ loud, deep sound
	6. spoil			6. roar	

[5]	1. basket	☐ money paid regularly for doing a job	[6]	1. birth	☐ being born
	2. crop			2. dust	
	3. flesh	☐ heat		3. operation	☐ game
	4. salary			4. row	
	5. temperature	☐ meat		5. sport	☐ wining
	6. thread			6. victory	

…

Level E

[5]	1. dregs	☐ worst and most useless parts of anything	[6]	1. auspices	☐ being away from other people
	2. flurry			2. casualty	
	3. hostage	☐ natural liquid present in the mouth		3. froth	☐ someone killed or injured
	4. jumble			4. haunch	
	5. saliva	☐ confused mixture		5. revelry	☐ noisy and happy celebration
	6. truce			6. seclusion	

　Bai (2007) は，2006年9月から12月までの間に，中国の3大学で，549名の英語学習者に，MET 4文字以下版 (MET 4) と PNT を実施した．その調査結果は，(4) に示される．

(4) MET の得点と PNT の得点との相関
　　 $n = 549$
　　 $r = .70$
　　 $p < .05$

MET の得点と PNT の得点の相関係数は，$r = .70$ であった．この結果，両得点間に，強い相関があることが明らかになった．

5.3 内モンゴル

最後に，Wu (2011) は，中国国内の内モンゴル自治区に住むモンゴル語母語話者の英語学習者を対象に，調査を行った．この調査に参加した内モンゴル自治区に住むモンゴル語母語話者は，第二言語として，中国語を学び，第三言語として，英語を学んでいる．中国語に関しては，日常生活に支障なく使用している．Wu (2011) は，日本で実施された 2009 年センター試験英語（読解と聴解）を中国語に翻訳して使用し，MET の得点と 2009 年センター試験英語の総合得点との間に，どの程度の相関があるか調査した．

Wu (2011) は，2009 年 12 月から 2010 年 2 月までの間に，内モンゴル内にある 3 大学で，326 名の英語学習者に，MET 6 単語目ごと版（MET E6）と 2009 年センター試験英語を実施した．その 3 大学のうち，2 大学では，被験者（223 名）の専攻は，英語であり，残りの 1 大学では，被験者（103 名）の専攻は，英語ではなかった．

まず，全英語学習者（326 名）に対する調査結果は，(5) に示される．

(5) MET E6 の得点と 2009 年センター試験英語の総合得点との相関
 $n = 326$
 $r = .19$
 $p < .001$

MET E6 の得点と 2009 年センター試験英語の総合得点との相関係数は，$r = .19$ であった．この結果，これまでの調査結果とは異なり，両得点間に，相関がないことが明らかになった．

しかしながら，専攻が英語ではない被験者（103 名）の 2009 年センター試験英語の総合得点があまりにも低いことから，この被験者を取り除き，専攻が英語である被験者（223 名）に関して，両テストの得点の相関を調査した．その結果は，(6) に示される．

(6) MET E6 の得点と 2009 年センター試験英語の総合得点との相関
 $n = 223$（専攻が英語である被験者のみ）
 $r = .60$
 $p < .05$

MET E6 の得点と 2009 年センター試験英語の総合得点の相関係数は，$r = .60$ であった．この結果，専攻が英語である被験者のみに限定した場合，両得点間に，相関があることが明らかになった．

　この調査結果だけからは，決定的なことは言えないが，MET E6 の英語能力測定に関する予測能力は，被験者の学問的背景によってある程度影響を受けるかもしれない．とりわけ，センター試験のような長時間かかるテストを，英語を専門としない被験者に実施すれば，英語能力以外の要因が，獲得する得点に関与してくるかもしれない．今後は，MET の精密化のために，そのような要因が存在するかどうか，調査する必要があるだろう．

第 6 章

中学生版 MET：jMET

　牧グループは，Kawana and Walker (2002) を基にして開発した MET を使用し，主に日本人を中心としたアジア人大学生の英語能力の測定を行ってきた．Hasebe et al. (2008) は，これまで，中学生の英語能力を測定する MET がないことから，MET 調査上初めて，中学生版 MET = junior Minimal English Test (jMET) の開発に着手した．Hasebe et al. (2008) は，Nakagawa and Yamawaki (2004)『グリとグラ』の Peter Howlett and Richard McNamara による英訳版とそれに付随する CD を使用し，最初の jMET を作成し，中学 2 年生 505 名に，jMET Guri and Gura Version = jMET (GG) を実施した．jMET (GG) は，72 点満点であった．その中学 2 年生は，全員，業者による英語の実力テストを受けていた．その英語実力テストは，100 点満点で，読解・文法・聴解問題から構成されていた．試験時間は，35 分であった．得られた結果に対して，単回帰分析を行った．その結果は，被験者 505 名全体に対しては，jMET (GG) の得点と実力テストの得点との間には，ほぼ，相関が見られなかった ($n = 505$, $r = .28$, $p < .05$) が，実力試験の得点が 36 点以上（平均 = 66.7 点）の被験者 288 名に限定すると，相関が見られた ($n = 288$, $r = .48$, $p < .05$)．

　その後，牧グループは，jMET の材料を検討し，jMET 東京書籍 New Horizon 版と jMET 三省堂 New Crown 版を作成した．前者は，6.1 節で，後者は，6.2 節で詳述される．

6.1 東京書籍 New Horizon 版

Maki et al. (2010d) は，日本の中学校で最も頻繁に使用されている教科書の1つ，笠島ほか (2006c) の *New Horizon English Course 3* に基づいて，新たな中学生版 junior Minimal English Test (jMET) を作成し，jMET NH3 と名付けた．jMET NH3 は，(1) に示される．

(1) The junior Minimal English Test NH3 (The jMET NH3)

CD を聞きながら，空いている（　）の中に英単語を書き入れて下さい．

01. When you want to (　)^1 in Japanese restaurants, you usually (　)^2,
02. "Sumimasen," in a loud voice. But (　)^3 America, we just make eye (　)^4
03. or raise our hand. So (　)^5 still have a hard time (　)^6
04. Japanese restaurants. I always say, "Sumi ... uh, uh, sumimasen," (　)^7 quietly.
05. It's not easy for (　)^8 to get food. So I (　)^9 very hungry.
06. My Japanese friend (　)^{10} a different problem. One day (　)^{11} family
07. took him to an (　)^{12} American restaurant. He ate a (　)^{13} and
08. became thirsty. He wanted (　)^{14} water, so he shouted, "I'm (　)^{15}!
09. I'm sorry!" Everyone in the (　)^{16} stopped eating and looked at (　)^{17}.
10. This is one of the (　)^{18} telephones. It was made in 1876.
11. (　)^{19} is another telephone made in 1877. (　)^{20} is a picture taken
12. about 70 (　)^{21} ago. The people answering the (　)^{22} here are operators.
13. I'm fifteen. (　)^{23} mother says junior high school (　)^{24} shouldn't have
14. cell phones. What (　)^{25} you think? (Mike Davis)
15. I agree with (　)^{26} mother. You can use your (　)^{27} phone or a public
16. phone. (　)^{28} don't understand why you need (　)^{29} cell phone. (T. J.)
17. But it's not (　)^{30} to find public phones in (　)^{31} emergency. (Kaori)
18. That may be true. (　)^{32} people using cell phones sometimes (　)^{33} careful.
19. Some accidents are caused (　)^{34} people using cell phones. (R. B.)
20. Cell (　)^{35} are very useful. But people (　)^{36} understand
21. when and where to (　)^{37} them. (Bird)

第6章 中学生版 MET：jMET

22. In my opinion, people (   )^38 use cell phones in trains (   )^39 restaurants,
23. and never in school!（Hungry Lion）
24. (   )^40 is a book I bought (   )^41 the United States.
25. These are (   )^42 of the people you can (   )^43 in it.
26. Choose one and (   )^44 a report about her or (   )^45.
27. Carson was a scientist who (   )^46 about the danger of farm (   )^47.
28. Few people worried about it (   )^48 the 1950's, but she did.
29. In 1962 (   )^49 finished her book Silent Spring. "(   )^50 Spring" means
30. "a spring without (   )^51." The book became a best-seller.
31. (   )^52 was a book that changed (   )^53 view of nature.
32. Carson was (   )^54 on farm. She loved nature (   )^55 her life.
33. She especially loved (   )^56 sea. When she was a (   )^57, she liked to write.
34. Later (   )^58 wanted to be a writer (   )^59 a scientist. She became both.
35. (   )^60 had cancer while she was (   )^61 Silent Spring.
36. But she worked (   )^62 hard and finished it. Some (   )^63 books that
37. she wrote are (   )^64 Sea Around Us and The (   )^65 of Wonder.

jMET NH3 は，7つのダイアローグで構成され，合計 65 問からなり，jMET NH3 作成規則は，(2) の2点のみである．

 (2) jMET NH3 作成規則
  a. 6 単語目ごとに，空所が設けられる．
  b. 空所を設ける際，固有名詞，ハイフンで繋がれた長い語，数字，日本語，年，括弧の中にある発音されない語は，除外される．

Maki et al. (2010d) は，jMET NH3 の得点と他の長時間かかる英語試験の得点との間に相関があるかどうか見るために，*New Horizon English Course 3* を使用している中学 3 年生 171 名に，jMET NH3 を実施した．171 名の被験者は，すべて，その中学において，2 学期期末テスト英語試験を受けていた．その期末テスト英語試験は，50 問からなり，45 の読解問題と 5 つの聴解問題からなっていた．読解問題の満点は，90 点，聴解問題の満点は，10 点であり，合計 100 点の試験であった．その期末テストの範囲は，jMET NH3 の範囲と同様であった．

分析結果は，以下の通りである．jMET NH3 の得点と期末試験英語の総合得点との間には，強い相関（$n=171, r=.87, p<.001$）があった．相関係数 $r=.87$ は，牧グループの MET 調査史上，最も高い相関係数で，$.9\leq r$ であれば，極めて強い相関を示すことから，jMET NH3 の中学 3 年生の英語総合能力（読解と聴解）の予測力は，極めて強いことが分かった．この結果は，図 1 によって，より明確に示される．

図1　jMET NH3 の得点と期末試験英語総合得点との相関

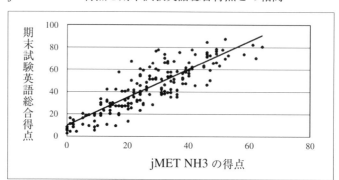

また，jMET NH3 の得点と期末試験英語の読解得点との間には，強い相関（$n=171, r=.87, p<.001$）があり，jMET NH3 の得点と期末試験英語の聴解得点との間には，相関（$n=171, r=.56, p<.001$）があった．

この結果から，jMET NH3 は，中学生 3 年生の英語能力（読解と聴解の総合英語能力）を，かなりの程度予測できることが明らかになった．

さらに，Yoshimura et al. (2011) は，jMET NH3 の得点と，*New Horizon English Course 3* と独立に作成された業者による実力テストの得点との間に，相関があるかどうか調査した．そのために，この調査では，*New Horizon English Course 3* を基に作成された 2 学期期末テストと，業者による実力テストを使用した．期末テストは，100 点満点で，読解 52 点満点，聴解 30 点満点，書き 18 点満点であった．実力テストも，期末テスト同様に，100 点満点で，読解 52 点満点，聴解 30 点満点，書き 18 点満点であった．両テストとも，制限時間は，45 分であった．この調査には，71 名の中学 3 年生が参加した．

分析結果は，以下の通りである．jMET NH3 の得点と期末試験英語の総合得点との間には，強い相関（$n=71, r=.783, p<.05$）があった．同様に，

jMET NH3 の得点と実力テスト英語の総合得点との間にも，強い相関（$n = 71$, $r = .777$, $p < .05$）があった．

Yoshimura et al. (2011) は，VassarStats: Web Site for Statistical Computation による Fisher r-to-z 変換を使用し，両相関係数間に，統計的有意な差があるかどうか調査した．Fisher r-to-z 変換においては，p 値（片側）が，.05 未満の場合に，統計的有意な差があると言う．分析の結果，(3) に示すように，総合得点に関する両相関係数間に統計的有意な差は，なかった．

(3) jMET NH3 得点と期末テスト得点の相関係数と jMET NH3 得点と実力テスト得点の相関係数間の差の有意性

	期末テスト	実力テスト
相関係数 r	.783	.777
被験者数 n	71	71
z 値		.09
p 値（片側）		.46

この結果から，jMET NH3 は，その内容を内含するテスト（期末テスト）であっても，その内容を内含しないテスト（実力テスト）であっても，その総合点を，おおむね予測することができることが分かった．

次に，Hasebe et al. (2010) は，jMET NH3 が，中学 3 年生向けに作成されたことから，中学 2 年生向けに，新たに，笠島ほか (2006b) の *New Horizon English Course 2* に基づいて，junior Minimal English Test NH 2 (jMET NH2) を作成した．jMET NH2 は，(4) に示される．

(4) The junior Minimal English Test NH2 (The jMET NH2)

CD を聞きながら，空いている（　）の中に英単語を書き入れて下さい．

01. My name is Cool. I'm fourteen (　)[1] I live in Korea. I (　)[2] comics.
02. In Korea they're very (　)[3]. Are they popular in your (　)[4], too?
03. Write me soon. Hi, Cool! (　)[5] Lucky. I'm in the fifth grade (　)[6] Thailand.
04. We also like to (　)[7] comics. We have a manga club (　)[8] school.
05. Do you know the (　)[9] manga? I'm Sea. I'm seventeen and I (　)[10] in China.
06. I know the (　)[11] manga. It comes from the Japanese (　)[12]

07. In 2000 Hong Kong hosted the (　)^{13} Asian Manga Summit.
08. Many people got (　)^{14} to talk about manga culture. I (　)^{15} manga.
09. It can tell us about (　)^{16} cultures. I hope to hear (　)^{17} you soon.

10. Communication is important. (　)^{18} have to speak English.
11. But (　)^{19} don't have to speak perfect (　)^{20}.
12. You're a member of the (　)^{21}. You have to help with (　)^{22} housework.

13. Everyone in my host (　)^{23} is nice to me.
14. But (　)^{24} host mother always gives me (　)^{25} much food.
15. Do I have (　)^{26} eat everything? It's too much (　)^{27} me.
16. You must tell your (　)^{28} mother. Say, "I'm sorry. It's (　)^{29} good,
17. but I can't eat (　)^{30} much." She'll understand.
18. I'm sad. (　)^{31} host family is so busy. (　)^{32} don't take me anywhere.
19. Nana's host (　)^{33} always takes her to interesting (　)^{34}.
20. Carlo, you mustn't compare host families.
21. (　)^{35} can find interesting things around (　)^{36} home.
22. Look around and make (　)^{37} friends.

23. Mike, Kumi broke her arm! She's (　)^{38} the hospital.
24. Let's visit her (　)^{39} you have time.
25. If you (　)^{40} go with me to the (　)^{41}, please call me.

26. A New (　)^{42} Area for Bikes. Midori Park will (　)^{43} a parking area
27. for bikes. (　)^{44} complained when a bike fell (　)^{45}
28. a little girl (Ishii Kumi) near the (　)^{46}.
29. They asked the city for (　)^{47} new parking area.
30. But some (　)^{48} are against the plan. They (　)^{49} we should keep the park.
31. (　)^{50} park or a parking area— (　)^{51} is the question.

32. I read (　)^{52} the new parking area plan. (　)^{53} is bad news.
33. I am (　)^{54} the plan because we need (　)^{55} parks.
34. I know we have (　)^{56} problem with bikes. But we (　)^{57} keep our parks
35. if we (　)^{58} our habits. Remember that the (　)^{59} taught us
36. an important thing. (　)^{60} can do two things: (1) Walk (　)^{61} we don't
37. have to ride (　)^{62} bikes. (2) Be careful when we (　)^{63} our bikes.

jMET NH2 は，6つのダイアローグで構成され，合計63問からなり，jMET NH2作成規則も，jMET NH3と同様，(5) の2点のみである．

(5) jMET NH2作成規則
    a. 6単語目ごとに，空所が設けられる．
    b. 空所を設ける際，固有名詞，ハイフンで繋がれた長い語，数字，日本語，年，括弧の中にある発音されない語は，除外される．

Hasebe et al. (2010) は，jMET NH2 と jMET NH3 を，*New Horizon English Course 2* と *New Horizon English Course 3* をそれぞれ使用している中学2年生と3年生に実施した．その中学生は，すでに2学期期末テストを受けていた．それぞれの2学期期末テストは，読解問題と聴解問題からなり，それぞれ，45問と5問で，満点は，100点であった．被験者の情報は，表1に示される．

表1 被験者の情報

			中学2年生	中学3年生
被験者数（男性：女性）			245 (123:122)	232 (130:102)
平均得点		jMET	24.28 (NH2)	24.41 (NH3)
	2学期期末テスト	聴解	5.96	4.75
		読解	50.73	37.73
		総合	56.69	42.48

中学2年生の jMET NH2 の得点と2学期期末テストの得点の単回帰分析結果は，表2に示される．

表2 中学2年生の jMET NH2 の得点と2学期期末テストの得点の単回帰分析結果

	総合	読解	聴解
被験者数	245		
相関係数	.88	.87	.62
近似直線	y = .52x-5.10	y = .55x-3.45	y = 3.76x + 1.88
p 値	$p < .001$	$p < .001$	$p < .001$

jMET NH2 の得点と，2学期期末テスト総合得点との間には，強い相関（$n =$

245, $r = .88$, $p < .001$) があった.

続いて，中学 3 年生の jMET NH3 の得点と 2 学期期末テストの得点の単回帰分析結果は，表 3 に示される.

表 3　中学 3 年生の jMET NH3 の得点と 2 学期期末テストの得点の単回帰分析結果

	総合	読解	聴解
被験者数		232	
相関係数	.90	.89	.60
近似直線	y = .57x + .30	y = .60x + 1.84	y = 3.85x + 6.13
p 値	$p < .001$	$p < .001$	$p < .001$

jMET NH3 の得点と，2 学期期末テスト総合得点との間には，極めて強い相関 ($n = 232$, $r = .90$, $p < .001$) があった.

これらの結果より，jMET NH3 も jMET NH2 も，それぞれ，中学 3 年生の期末テスト総合得点と中学 2 年生の期末テスト総合得点を予測する力が，極めて強いことが明らかになった.

Maki et al. (2012d) は，さらに，jMET を改良し，笠島ほか (2006a, b, c) を使用し，中学 1 年から 3 年までの材料を 1 つの jMET に入れ込み，中学生全体の英語能力を測定する jMET を開発し，The junior Minimal English Test (H) (jMET (H)) と名付けた. jMET (H) も，(6) の規則にしたがって作成された.

(6)　jMET (H) 作成規則
    a.　6 単語目ごとに，空所が設けられる.
    b.　空所を設ける際，固有名詞，ハイフンで繋がれた長い語，数字，日本語，年，括弧の中にある発音されない語は，除外される.

jMET (H) は，9 つのダイアローグからなり，最も最初の版は，合計 68 の空所を含んでいた. その後，(7) に示すように，67 の空所を含むよう，修正された.

(7) The junior Minimal English Test H (jMET (H))

CDを聞きながら，空いている（　）の中に英単語を書き入れて下さい．

01. This is my family. This (　)¹ my sister Lisa.
02. She lives in (　)². She likes Japan very much. (　)³ husband Koji teaches Japanese.
03. Happy New (　)⁴! How are you doing? Are (　)⁵ enjoying your first *oshogatsu*?
04. We're having (　)⁶ great time in Canada. Yesterday (　)⁷ walked across
05. the Rainbow Bridge to America. (　)⁸ really enjoyed the view. See (　)⁹ soon!
06. At night I went (　)¹⁰ the shrine with Ms. Sato, the English (　)¹¹.
07. We saw a lot of (　)¹² there. I got home at (　)¹³.
08. Then I called my family (　)¹⁴ Canada. I went to bed (　)¹⁵ two.
09. I read about the (　)¹⁶ parking area plan. It is (　)¹⁷ news.
10. I am against the (　)¹⁸ because we need our parks.
11. (　)¹⁹ know we have a problem (　)²⁰ bikes.
12. But we can keep (　)²¹ parks if we change our (　)²².
13. Remember that the accident taught (　)²³ an important thing.
14. We can (　)²⁴ two things. One: Walk when (　)²⁵ don't have to ride
15. our (　)²⁶. Two: Be careful when we (　)²⁷ our bikes.
16. Look at this! (　)²⁸ so big. It's about eight (　)²⁹ tall and weighs seventy tons.
17. (　)³⁰ call it a *moai*. Easter Island is very (　)³¹.
18. But it has about one (　)³² *moais*. These *moais* are standing on the (　)³³.
19. They're looking at the sky. (　)³⁴ are they thinking about?
20. Communication (　)³⁵ important. You have to speak (　)³⁶.
21. But you don't have to (　)³⁷ perfect English.
22. You're a member (　)³⁸ the family. You have to (　)³⁹ with the housework.
23. Hello, everyone. (　)⁴⁰ is your reporter, Maria Jones. Today I'm (　)⁴¹ in a big park
24. in *Hirosaki*. (　)⁴² going to go to a *shamisen* (　)⁴³.
25. I've lived in Japan for (　)⁴⁴ years, and I've loved

26. Japanese ( )^{45} since I heard it for ( )^{46} first time.
27. When you want ( )^{47} order in Japanese restaurants, you ( )^{48} say,
28. "*Sumimasen*," in a loud voice. ( )^{49} in America, we just make ( )^{50} contact
29. or raise our hand. ( )^{51} I still have a hard ( )^{52}
30. in Japanese restaurants. I always ( )^{53}, "*Sumi* ... uh, uh, *sumimasen*," too quietly.
31. It's not easy ( )^{54} me to get food. So ( )^{55} get very hungry.
32. Thanks to ( )^{56} help, our village has another ( )^{57}. It is near my house.
33. ( )^{58} I have already started going ( )^{59} school again.
34. I have a ( )^{60} of things to learn. My ( )^{61} also go to
35. the same ( )^{62}. There is a class for ( )^{63}.
36. They are learning to read ( )^{64} write. We are very glad ( )^{65} have a chance
37. to study ( )^{66} at home. It is fun. ( )^{67} you all very much.

Maki et al. (2012d) は，68の空所を含む最初の版の jMET (H) を *New Horizon English Course 2* を使用している中学2年生74名と *New Horizon English Course 3* を使用している中学3年生71名に実施した．この中学生は，すでに，2学期期末テストを受けていた．その期末テストは，読解40点，聴解30点，書き30点からなる100点満点のテストであった．さらに，この同じ中学生は，*New Horizon English Course 2/New Horizon English Course 3* の内容とは全く独立して作られた業者による実力テストも受けていた．各学年の実力テストも，読解40点，聴解30点，書き30点からなる100点満点のテストであった．

まず，中学2年生の jMET (H) の得点と2学期期末テストの得点の単回帰分析結果は，表4に示される．

表4 中学2年生の jMET (H) の得点と2学期期末テストの得点の単回帰分析結果

	総合	読解	聴解	書き
相関係数	.83	.80	.69	.75
p 値	$p < .001$	$p < .001$	$p < .001$	$p < .001$

続いて，中学2年生のjMET（H）の得点と実力テストの得点の単回帰分析結果は，表5に示される．

表5　中学2年生のjMET（H）の得点と実力テストの得点の単回帰分析結果

	総合	読解	聴解	書き
相関係数	.80	.79	.62	.74
p 値	$p<.001$	$p<.001$	$p<.001$	$p<.001$

jMET（H）の得点と，2学期期末テスト総合得点との間には，強い相関（$n=74, r=.83, p<.001$）があり，jMET（H）の得点と，実力テスト総合得点との間にも，強い相関（$n=74, r=.80, p<.001$）があった．これらの結果より，jMET（H）は，中学2年生の期末テスト総合得点と実力テスト総合得点を予測する力が強いことが明らかになった．

次に，中学3年生のjMET（H）の得点と2学期期末テストの得点の単回帰分析結果は，表6に示される．

表6　中学3年生のjMET（H）の得点と2学期期末テストの得点の単回帰分析結果

	総合	読解	聴解	書き
相関係数	.82	.80	.77	.72
p 値	$p<.001$	$p<.001$	$p<.001$	$p<.001$

続いて，中学3年生のjMET（H）の得点と実力テストの得点の単回帰分析結果は，表7に示される．

表7　中学3年生のjMET（H）の得点と実力テストの得点の単回帰分析結果

	総合	読解	聴解	書き
相関係数	.79	.74	.62	.71
p 値	$p<.001$	$p<.001$	$p<.001$	$p<.001$

jMET（H）の得点と，2学期期末テスト総合得点との間には，強い相関（$n=$

71, $r = .82$, $p < .001$) があり，jMET (H) の得点と，実力テスト総合得点との間にも，強い相関 ($n = 71$, $r = .79$, $p < .001$) があった．これらの結果より，jMET (H) は，中学 3 年生の期末テスト総合得点と実力テスト総合得点についても，予測する力が強いことが明らかになった．

6.2　三省堂 New Crown 版

Maki et al. (2013c) は，jMET (H) を作成した後，さらに，日本の中学校で最も頻繁に使用されている教科書の別の 1 つ，斉藤ほか (2005a, b, c) の *New Crown English Series New Edition 1, 2, 3* に基づいて，新たな中学生版 junior Minimal English Test (C) (jMET (C)) を作成した．jMET (C) は，(8) に示される．

(8)　The junior Minimal English Test (C) (jMET (C))

CD を聞きながら，空いている（　）の中に英単語を書き入れて下さい．

01. This is Daichi. He is my (　)[1] in Okinawa.
02. He is a singer (　)[2] folk songs. This is Yuri. She (　)[3] my friend too.
03. She is (　)[4] *Eisa* dancer. She is in the (　)[5] club.
04. I study English. So (　)[6] can speak it a little.
05. Paul (　)[7] Japanese. So he can speak (　)[8] a little.
06. I teach Japanese (　)[9] Paul. He teaches English to me. (　)[10] help each other.
07. Hello, everyone. (　)[11] me tell you about my (　)[12] in Australia.
08. Like many people (　)[13] Australia, I love sports.
09. I (　)[14] netball every Saturday. It is (　)[15] among my friends.
10. Now it (　)[16] spring in Japan. The season (　)[17] different in Australia.
11. It is (　)[18] there. Why? Does anyone know?
12. (　)[19] want to be a tree (　)[20]. Why? First, I like trees.
13. (　)[21] spring, I go to the (　)[22] to see trees.
14. Fresh leaves (　)[23] the trees. The trees are (　)[24]. They are beautiful.
15. Second, some (　)[25] are sick. We must take (　)[26] of them.
16. Third, plants, animals, (　)[27] humans-all living things share (　)[28] earth.

第6章 中学生版 MET：jMET

17. We all live together. (　　)²⁹ must respect this idea.
18. We (　　)³⁰ many things to do, now (　　)³¹ in the future.
19. So, I (　　)³² to be a tree doctor. (　　)³³ I can spend time
20. with (　　)³⁴, I can save them, and (　　)³⁵ can save nature.
21. *Namaste!* This means '(　　)³⁶' and 'goodbye' in Hindi.
22. Hindi (　　)³⁷ the major language in India. (　　)³⁸ have many languages in India.
23. (　　)³⁹ use three of them. I (　　)⁴⁰ give you some examples.
24. I (　　)⁴¹ speaking Marathi with friends. I enjoy (　　)⁴² movies in Hindi.
25. And I (　　)⁴³ reading English books. I like (　　)⁴⁴ all of my languages.
26. I'll (　　)⁴⁵ you a trick. Let's do (　　)⁴⁶ together.
27. First, make two rings (　　)⁴⁷ the paper. Then, paste them (　　)⁴⁸ each other like this.
28. They're (　　)⁴⁹ at one point. Are you (　　)⁵⁰ me?
29. Good. Finally, cut along (　　)⁵¹ rings.
30. Start here and keep (　　)⁵². What will happen to the (　　)⁵³?
31. I'm studying sign language. Through (　　)⁵⁴ study, I learned signs. But (　　)⁵⁵
32. learned much more. I learned (　　)⁵⁶ sign language is not about (　　)⁵⁷ signs.
33. For example, my teacher (　　)⁵⁸ me how to sign the (　　)⁵⁹ 'happy'.
34. My hands were in (　　)⁶⁰ right place,
35. but other students (　　)⁶¹ understand me well. My teacher (　　)⁶²,
36. "Smile when you sign 'happy'. (　　)⁶³ people will understand you better." (　　)⁶⁴ this,
37. I learned that facial (　　)⁶⁵ and gestures are important for (　　)⁶⁶.

jMET（C）は，7つのダイアローグで構成され，合計66問からなり，jMET（C）作成規則も，jMET（H）と同様，(9)の2点のみである．

(9) jMET（C）作成規則
  a. 6単語目ごとに，空所が設けられる．
  b. 空所を設ける際，固有名詞，ハイフンで繋がれた長い語，数字，日本語，年，括弧の中にある発音されない語は，除外される．

Maki et al. (2013c) は，jMET (C) と jMET (H) を *New Horizon English Course 2* を使用している中学 2 年生 299 名に実施した．この中学生は，すでに，2 学期中間テストを受けていた．その中間テストは，読解，聴解，書きからなる 100 点満点のテストであった．さらに，この同じ中学生は，*New Horizon English Course 2* の内容とは全く独立して作られた業者による実力テストも受けていた．その実力テストも，読解，聴解，書きからなる 100 点満点のテストであった．

まず，被験者の jMET (C) の得点と jMET (H) の得点の相関は，(10) に示される．

(10) jMET (C) の得点と jMET (H) の得点の相関
 $n = 299$
 $r = .86$
 $p < .05$

次に，被験者の jMET (C) の得点と 2 学期中間テストの得点の相関は，(11) に示される．

(11) jMET (C) の得点と 2 学期中間テストの得点の相関
 $n = 299$
 $r = .70$
 $p < .05$

次に，被験者の jMET (C) の得点と実力テストの得点の相関は，(12) に示される．

(12) jMET (C) の得点と実力テストの得点の相関
 $n = 299$
 $r = .71$
 $p < .05$

さらに，被験者の jMET (H) の得点と 2 学期中間テストの得点の相関は，(13) に示される．

(13) jMET(H) の得点と 2 学期中間テストの得点の相関
$n = 299$
$r = .76$
$p < .05$

最後に，被験者の jMET (H) の得点と実力テストの得点の相関は，(14) に示される．

(14) jMET (H) の得点と実力テストの得点の相関
$n = 299$
$r = .75$
$p < .05$

Maki et al. (2013c) は，さらに，VassarStats: Web Site for Statistical Computation による Fisher r-to-z 変換を使用し，jMET (C) 得点と 2 学期中間テスト総合得点との間の相関係数と jMET (H) 得点と 2 学期中間テスト総合点との間の相関係数の間に，統計的有意な差があるかどうか，また，jMET (C) 得点と実力テスト総合得点との間の相関係数と jMET (H) 得点と実力テスト総合点との間の相関係数の間に，統計的有意な差があるかどうか，調査した．その結果は，(15) と (16) に示される．

(15) jMET (C) 得点と 2 学期中間テスト総合得点との間の相関係数と jMET (H) 得点と 2 学期中間テスト総合点との間の相関係数間の差の有意性

	jMET (C) と中間テスト	jMET (H) と中間テスト
相関係数 r	.70	.76
被験者数 n	299	299
z 値		-1.57
p 値（片側）		.06

(16) jMET (C) 得点と実力テスト総合得点との間の相関係数と jMET (H) 得点と実力テスト総合点との間の相関係数間の差の有意性

	jMET (C) と実力テスト	jMET (H) と実力テスト
相関係数 r	.71	.75
被験者数 n	299	299
z 値		-1.04
p 値 (片側)		.15

(15) より, jMET (C) 得点と2学期中間テスト総合得点との間の相関係数と jMET (H) 得点と2学期中間テスト総合点との間の相関係数の間には, 統計的有意な差がある傾向があることが分かった ($p < .06$). また, (16) より, jMET (C) 得点と実力テスト総合得点との間の相関係数と jMET (H) 得点と実力テスト総合点との間の相関係数の間に, 統計的有意な差がないことが分かった ($p < .15$).

これによって, jMET (C) は, jMET (H) と同程度に, 実力テストの得点を予測する能力があることが, 明確になった.

さらに, Maki et al. (2014c) は, jMET (H) と jMET (C) の得点が, 日本英語検定協会による実用英語技能検定 (英検) の合格級との間に, 相関があるかどうか調査した. 英検は, (17) に示すように, 7段階の級がある.

(17) 英検の級と受験推奨目安

級	難易度
1	大学上級程度
準1	大学中級程度
2	高校卒業程度
準2	高校中級程度
3	中学卒業程度
4	中学中級程度
5	中学初級程度

本調査では, 英検の級とそれに対応する得点を, (18) のように設定した.

第 6 章　中学生版 MET：jMET

(18)　英検の級と対応する得点

級	得点
1	7
準 1	6
2	5
準 2	4
3	3
4	2
5	1

Maki et al.（2014c）は，2010 年 10 月から 2012 年 1 月までの間に，合計 358 名の中学 2 年生と 3 年生に対して，jMET（H）と jMET（C）を実施し，同時に，その時点で，すでに合格している英検の最高級についても調査した．そして，jMET（H）の得点と（18）に示す英検最高級の得点との間に，また，jMET（C）の得点と（18）に示す英検最高級の得点との間の相関を調査した．その結果は，(19) に示される．

(19)　jMET（H）/jMET（C）の得点と英検最高級の得点との間の相関

	jMET（H）得点	jMET（C）得点
英検最高級の得点	$n = 358$ $r = .58$ $p < .001$	$n = 358$ $r = .64$ $p < .001$

その結果，jMET（H）の得点と英検最高級の得点との間に，また，jMET（C）の得点と英検最高級の得点との間に，相関があることが明らかになった．

Maki et al.（2014c）は，さらに，VassarStats: Web Site for Statistical Computation による Fisher r-to-z 変換を使用し，jMET（H）の得点と英検最高級の得点との間の相関係数と jMET（C）の得点と英検最高級の得点との間の相関係数の間に，統計的有意な差があるかどうか調査した．その結果は，(20) に示される．

(20) jMET (H) の得点と英検最高級の得点との間の相関係数と jMET (C) の得点と英検最高級の得点との間の相関係数の差の有意性

	jMET (H) と英検最高級	jMET (C) と英検最高級
相関係数 r	.58	.64
被験者数 n	358	358
z 値		−1.28
p 値（片側）		.10

その結果，両相関係数間には，統計的有意な差がないことが明らかになった（p one-tail = .10）．

これらの結果より，jMET は，jMET (H) と jMET (C) のどちらでも，学習者が，その学習時点において，合格可能な英検の級をある程度予測できるということも明確になった．

第 7 章

MET：第二言語習得研究機能

　MET は，第二言語習得研究のための簡易的一道具として機能する．1 章で指摘されたように，第二言語習得調査のために，どの第二言語を調査する研究者も，基本データとして，被験者のその第二言語の能力を測定する必要があり，第二言語としての英語の習得調査であれば，(1) に示すような，何らかの英語能力測定試験が必要となる．

　(1)　英語能力測定試験
　　　a.　実用英語技能検定（英検）
　　　b.　大学入試センター試験英語
　　　c.　TOEIC
　　　d.　TOEFL
　　　e.　Paul Nation's Vocabulary Size Test

しかし，上記の試験は，最も短くても，30 分以上かかり，長ければ，2 時間かかる．そうなると，本調査の前に，被験者は，疲労を感じ，本調査の結果に影響を与えかねない．さらに，研究者も，その英語能力測定試験の採点のために，疲労を感じる．MET は，このような問題を回避しながら，被験者の第二言語としての英語の能力を測定することができる．

　本章では，MET を使用した第二言語習得研究の例として，7.1 節で，*That-Trace* 現象に関する調査結果，7.2 節で，中学生による Wh 疑問文習得に関する調査結果，そして，7.3 節で，大学生による関係節・Wh 疑問文習得に関す

る調査結果を報告する．

7.1 *That*-Trace 現象

That-Trace 効果は，Perlmutter (1971) が最初に指摘した．それが，何を意味するか，(2) の例を基に示す．

(2) *That*-Trace 効果
   a. Who do you think [that John saw *t*]?
   b. Who do you think [John saw *t*]?
   c. *Who do you think [that *t* saw Bill]?
   d. Who do you think [*t* saw Bill]?

(2) の例は，長距離 wh 移動をする際，埋め込み節の主語を *wh* 句に変えて文頭に移動させると，その埋め込み節が *that* を持つ場合のみ，非文となることを示している．生成文法研究の分野において，Lasnik and Saito (1984, 1992) や Rizzi (1990) は，*That*-Trace 効果を Chomsky (1981) が提案した空範疇原理 (Empty Category Principle (ECP)) によって説明している．第二言語習得の分野においても，White (1988) や Kanno (1996) は，ECP が初期の中間言語文法においても機能していると主張している．また，White (1989, 2003) は，第二言語習得と普遍文法の関係を調査しており，Pienemann et al. (1988) は，英語学習者の Wh 疑問文の習得における発展段階的連鎖を調査している．

Hasebe et al. (2012a) は，MET を使用して，168 名の日本人英語学習者（大学生）を上位・中位・下位グループに分け，被験者全員に文法性判断実験を行い，どのグループが，英語における *That*-Trace 効果を出すかについて調査した．その後，Hasebe et al. (2012a) は，その結果を分散分析と多重比較によって分析した．

まず，168 名の日本人英語学習者は，MET の得点の偏差値によって，表 1 のように 3 グループに分けられた．

表1　被験者の分類

	初級	中級	上級
偏差値（DV）	DV < 45	45 ≤ DV < 55	55 ≤ DV
観測数	50	60	58

次に，被験者全員に，(3) に示すような，Gould et al. (2001) によって提案された Visual Analogue Scaling(VAS) 評価法を用いた文法性判断テストを実施した．それに使用される評価線は，100mm である．

(3) 本研究における VAS 評価法

あなたは，以下に示される文を，英語としてどの程度自然だと判断しますか？ あなたが，その文が自然であると感じる度合いを，以下の直線上に縦線 [l] を引いて，示して下さい．

全く　　　　　　　　　　　　　　　　完全に
不自然 0　　　　　　　　　100 自然

最後に，テスト文として，以下の (4) の4つのタイプの文を，それぞれ，8文ずつ使用した．その文の中で使用される *that* 節内部の動詞は，人間主語と人間目的語を同時に取るものだけを使用した．これは，主語の Wh 移動と目的語の Wh 移動に対して，最小組（ミニマル・ペアー）を作るためである．

(4) テスト文の例
   a. Who do you think that Ron found [*t*]?
   b. Who do you think Ron found [*t*]?
   c. Who do you think that [*t*] found Pam?
   d. Who do you think [*t*] found Pam?

調査結果は，表2に示される．この結果を分散分析と多重比較によって分析した．

表2 *That*-Trace 現象に関する調査結果

		(A)	(B)	(C)	(D)	(E)
Type	平均値 (mm)	71.94	75.78	78.15	80.78	68.56
(4a)	標準偏差	22.06	25.75	23.56	23.33	28.58
Type	平均値 (mm)	96.66	76.93	78.25	79.54	73.10
(4b)	標準偏差	6.56	27.34	27.85	25.54	28.95
Type	**平均値 (mm)**	**44.90**	**66.37**	**61.63**	**72.74**	**63.87**
(4c)	**標準偏差**	**27.76**	**29.19**	**31.20**	**26.45**	**29.43**
Type	平均値 (mm)	96.40	70.17	66.48	71.18	72.31
(4d)	標準偏差	8.53	29.63	33.24	29.00	27.10

A：英語母語話者，B：全日本人被験者，C：初級学習者，D：中級学習者，E：上級学習者

まず，英語母語話者と日本人英語学習者全体で，*That*-Trace 効果において差があるかどうか調査するために，2×4分散分析（2タイプの被験者×4タイプの文）を行った．その結果，英語母語話者は，(4c) と (4d) の平均値の間に統計的有意な差を示した（つまり，*That*-Trace 効果を示した）($p < .01$) が，日本人英語学習者全体は，示さなかった ($p < .41$)．

続いて，日本人英語学習者における3グループの間に，*That*-Trace 効果において差があるかどうか調査するために，3×4分散分析（3タイプの被験者×4タイプの文）を行った．その結果，初級・中級英語学習者は，(4c) と (4d) の平均値の間に統計的有意な差を示さなかった（つまり，*That*-Trace 効果を示さなかった）($p < 1.00$) が，上級英語学習者は，(4c) と (4d) の平均値の間に，統計的有意傾向がある差を示した ($p < .09$)．

したがって，英語能力上位者のみが，*That*-Trace 効果を示す傾向があり，Lasnik and Saito (1992) 等の分析が正しければ，英語能力上位者においてのみ，その背後にある原理 ECP が，他の要因によって遮断されずに，機能していることが分かった．つまり，英語能力上位者は，英語母語話者と同様に，ECP が活性化しているのである．この調査結果は，極めて重要である．というのも，英語学習者は，(4c) が非文であるという事実を一度も学習していないにもかかわらず，それが非文であると判断しているからである．これは，明らかに，教えられていないのに知っていること，つまり，言語の知識（普遍文

法）を日本語母語話者も持っており，それを第二言語としての英語の習得においても，無意識のうちに利用しているということを意味している．

7.2 日本人中学生による Wh 疑問文習得

Hasebe and Maki (2014) は，Lee (2008) による韓国人英語学習者についての実験結果と Hasebe et al. (2012b) による日本人英語学習者についての実験結果が異なることに注目した．Lee (2008) は，英語における Wh 疑問文の文法性判断においては，項 Wh 疑問文（*what* など）のほうが，付加詞 Wh 疑問文（*why* など）よりも容易であると報告している．一方，Hasebe et al. (2012b) は，英語における Wh 疑問文の日本語からの翻訳実験においては，付加詞 Wh 疑問文（*why*）のほうが，項 Wh 疑問文の中の目的語 Wh 疑問文（*what*）よりも，junior Minimal English Test (jMET) によって分けられた上位・中位グループにおいて，容易であると報告している．そこで，Hasebe and Maki (2014) は，どちらの報告がより正確であるかを調査するために，日本人英語学習者（中学生）に，Wh 疑問文形成実験を行った．

Lee (2008) は，41 名の韓国人英語学習者に，Wh 疑問文における倒置の習得において，項 Wh 疑問文（*what* など）と付加詞 Wh 疑問文（*why* など）に，非対称性があるかどうか調査した．そのために，聴解テストとして，文法性判断テストを行い，各文の文法性を Likert スケール（−2（完全に誤っている）から +2（完全に正しい）まで）を用いて，判断させた．項 Wh 疑問文には，*who* と *what* を，付加詞 Wh 疑問文には，*how* と *why* を使用した．(5) と (6) は，テスト文の一部で，表 3 は，判断テストの結果を示している．

(5) 倒置された文法的文
   a. Who are you meeting in the cafeteria?
   b. What are you reading in the library?
   c. Why are you jumping on the bed?
   d. How are you going to the campground?

(6) 倒置されていない非文法的文
   a. Who you are meeting in the cafeteria?
   b. What you are reading in the library?

c. Why you are jumping on the bed?
　　d. How you are going to the campground?

表3　Lee（2008）の研究における平均値

	a. *who*	b. *what*	c. *why*	d. *how*
(5) 倒置あり	.74	1.27	.81	1.20
(6) 倒置なし	－.09	.00	－.48	－.54

　Lee（2008）の分析によれば，倒置された文法的文における項 Wh 疑問文・付加詞 Wh 疑問文の間には，統計的有意な差は，見られなかった．一方，倒置されていない非文法的文においては，両者の間に，統計的有意な差が見られた．つまり，韓国人英語学習者にとっては，倒置されていない項 Wh 疑問文の非文法性よりも，倒置されていない付加詞 Wh 疑問文の非文法性に気付くほうが，より困難であった．このことから，Lee（2008）は，韓国人英語学習者は，Wh 疑問文の習得において，項・付加詞 Wh 疑問文非対称性を示し，付加詞 Wh 疑問文における倒置よりも，項 Wh 疑問文における倒置のほうが容易であると結論付けている．

　Hasebe et al. (2012b) は，日本人英語学習者が，Wh 疑問文に関して，項・付加詞非対称性と主語・目的語非対称性を示すかどうか，彼らが作成した翻訳テストを用いて調査した．Hasebe et al. (2012b) は，191 名の大学生被験者にその翻訳テストを実施した．そのテストは，30 ある日本語文を英語文に翻訳するテストである．そのテストにおいては，主語 Wh 疑問文，目的語 Wh 疑問文，そして，付加詞 Wh 疑問文の3種類が含まれている．主語・目的語 Wh 疑問文には，*who* が，また，付加詞 Wh 疑問文には，*why* が選ばれている．(7) は，テスト文の例で，表4は，翻訳テストの結果を示している．

　　(7)　翻訳テストにおけるテスト文
　　　　a. 誰が　パムを　見つけましたか？
　　　　b. ロンは　誰を　見つけましたか？
　　　　c. なぜ　ロンは　パムを　見つけましたか？

表4 Hasebe et al. (2012b) の研究における平均値 (%)

	a. 主語 who	b. 目的語 who	c. 付加詞 why
初級 ($n=51$)	30.39	17.16	38.24
中級 ($n=76$)	27.30	47.04	63.16
上級 ($n=64$)	37.89	39.84	59.77

まず第一に，中級学習者と上級学習者にとっては，主語 Wh 疑問文と付加詞 Wh 疑問文の間に，統計的有意な差があり，付加詞 Wh 疑問文のほうが，主語 Wh 疑問文よりも容易であった．しかしながら，初級学習者にとっては，両者に統計的有意な差は，なかった．さらに，すべての学習者にとって，目的語 Wh 疑問文と付加詞疑問文の間に，統計的有意な差があり，付加詞 Wh 疑問文のほうが，目的語 Wh 疑問文よりも容易であった．したがって，中級・上級英語学習者は，Wh 疑問文の習得において，項・付加詞非対称性を示し，彼らにとっては，付加詞 Wh 疑問文のほうが，項 Wh 疑問文よりも容易であった．

第二に，日本人英語学習者は，Wh 疑問文における主語・目的語非対称性について，2つの異なる傾向を示した．初級英語学習者にとっては，主語 Wh 疑問文は，目的語 Wh 疑問文よりも容易である一方で，中級英語学習者にとっては，目的語 Wh 疑問文は，主語 Wh 疑問文よりも容易であった．

Hasebe and Maki (2014) は，これらの異なる2つの報告を受け，どちらの報告がより正確であるかを調査するために，259名の日本人英語学習者（中学生）に，Wh 疑問文形成実験を行った．まず，259名の日本人英語学習者に jMET を実施し，jMET 得点の偏差値によって，日本人英語学習者は，表5に示されるように，3グループに分けられた．

表5 被験者の分類

	初級	中級	上級
偏差値 (DV)	DV < 45	45 ≤ DV < 55	55 ≤ DV
観測数	81	93	85

その後，(8) に示された Wh 疑問文形成テストを実施した．

(8) Wh 疑問文形成テスト（部分）
与えられた文の下線部を尋ねる疑問文を作りなさい．
a. 主語 Wh 疑問文：Who
   文： Ron found Pam.
   正解： **Who** found Pam?
b. 目的語 Wh 疑問文：Who/What
   文： Ron found Pam.
   正解： **Who** did Ron find?
c. 擬似付加詞 Wh 疑問文：When
   文： Ron found Pam two days ago.
   正解： **When** did Ron find Pam?
d. 付加詞 Wh 疑問文：Why
   文： Ron found Pam because she rode the bus.
   正解： **Why** did Ron find Pam?

表 6 は，Wh 疑問文形成テストの結果を示している．

表 6　Wh 疑問文形成テストの結果（項・付加詞 Wh 疑問文）

		項 Wh タイプ (8a + 8b)	付加詞 Wh タイプ (8c + 8d)
全学習者	平均値（%）	25.39	30.28
(n = 259)	標準偏差	28.76	39.49
初級学習者	平均値（%）	9.26	4.63
(n = 81)	標準偏差	18.35	13.63
中級学習者	平均値（%）	21.24	26.88
(n = 93)	標準偏差	24.22	36.82
上級学習者	平均値（%）	45.29	58.43
(n = 85)	標準偏差	30.11	40.98

項・付加詞 Wh 疑問文非対称性があるかどうか調査するために，まず，3×2 分散分析（3 タイプの被験者×2 タイプの文）を行った．その結果，統計的有意な［文タイプ］要因に対する主効果（$F(1, 256) = 8.94, p < .003$）と，統計的有意な［EFL レベル］要因に対する主効果（$F(2, 256) = 61.64, p < .001$）を発見し，また，統計的有意な 2 要因間の相互作用（$F(2, 256) = 10.29, p$

第 7 章　MET：第二言語習得研究機能

< .001) も発見した.

続いて，多重比較を行い，以下を発見した．第一に，すべての学習者には，項 Wh 疑問文の平均値と付加詞 Wh 疑問文の平均値との間に，統計的有意な差があり ($F(1, 256) = 8.94, p < .003$)，付加詞 Wh 疑問文のほうが，項 Wh 疑問文よりも，容易であった．第二に，中級・上級学習者にも，同様に，項 Wh 疑問文の平均値と付加詞 Wh 疑問文の平均値との間に，統計的有意な差があり（中級学習者（$F(1, 256) = 4.58, p < .033$)・上級学習者（$F(1, 256) = 22.95, p < .001$）），付加詞 Wh 疑問文のほうが，項 Wh 疑問文よりも，容易であった．第三に，しかしながら，初級学習者には，項 Wh 疑問文の平均値と付加詞 Wh 疑問文の平均値との間に，統計的有意な差がなかった（$F(1, 256) = 2.71, p < .101$）.

Hasebe and Maki (2014) は，さらに，項 Wh 疑問文内部において，主語・目的語 Wh 疑問文非対称性があるかどうかも調査した．表 7 は，Wh 疑問文形成テストにおける主語・目的語 Wh 疑問文の結果を示している．

表 7　Wh 疑問文形成テストの結果（主語・目的語 Wh 疑問文）

		主語 Wh タイプ (8a)	目的語 Wh タイプ (8b)
全学習者 ($n = 259$)	平均値（%）	20.46	30.31
	標準偏差	34.31	39.11
初級学習者 ($n = 81$)	平均値（%）	13.99	4.53
	標準偏差	29.75	14.19
中級学習者 ($n = 93$)	平均値（%）	14.16	28.32
	標準偏差	27.47	36.60
上級学習者 ($n = 85$)	平均値（%）	33.53	57.06
	標準偏差	41.11	40.86

主語・目的語 Wh 疑問文非対称性があるかどうか調査するために，まず，3×2×2 分散分析（3 タイプの被験者×2 タイプの文（項・付加詞）×2 タイプの項（主語・目的語））を行った．その結果，統計的有意な［文タイプ］要因に対する主効果（$F(1, 256) = 8.94, p < .003$），統計的有意な［項タイプ］要因に対する主効果（$F(1, 256) = 18.19, p < .001$），そして，統計的有意な［EFL レベル］要因に対する主効果（$F(2, 256) = 61.64, p < .001$）を発見し，また，

統計的有意な3要因間の相互作用（$F(2, 256) = 10.31, p < .001$）も発見した.

続いて，多重比較を行い，以下を発見した．第一に，すべての学習者には，主語 Wh 疑問文の平均値と目的語 Wh 疑問文の平均値との間に，統計的有意な差があり（$F(1, 256) = 11.72, p < .001$），目的語 Wh 疑問文のほうが，主語 Wh 疑問文よりも，容易であった．第二に，中級・上級学習者にも，同様に，主語 Wh 疑問文の平均値と目的語 Wh 疑問文の平均値との間に，統計的有意な差があり（中級学習者（$F(1, 256) = 4.18, p < .042$）・上級学習者（$F(1, 256) = 22.99, p < .001$）），目的語 Wh 疑問文のほうが，主語 Wh 疑問文よりも，容易であった．第三に，初級学習者にも，主語 Wh 疑問文の平均値と目的語 Wh 疑問文の平均値との間に，統計的有意な差があった（$F(1, 256) = 4.82, p < .029$）が，中級・上級学習者と異なり，主語 Wh 疑問文のほうが，目的語 Wh 疑問文よりも，容易であった．

以上の結果より，jMET によって分けられた上位・中位グループにおいて，付加詞 Wh 疑問文（why）のほうが，項 Wh 疑問文（主語 Wh 疑問文と目的語 Wh 疑問文）よりも，容易であることが明らかになった．したがって，この調査結果は，Hasebe et al. (2012b) の調査結果を支持することになる．

この調査結果は，さらに，中等教育における英語教育において，どのような教材をどの順番で提示すべきかも示唆してくれる．本調査によって，jMET によって分けられた上位・中位グループに関して，付加詞 Wh 疑問文（why）のほうが，項 Wh 疑問文（主語 Wh 疑問文と目的語 Wh 疑問文）よりも，容易であることが明らかになったことから，英語疑問文の導入に関して，より容易なものから導入することが好ましいのであれば，(9) に示すように，付加詞 Wh 疑問文（why）を，項 Wh 疑問文（主語 Wh 疑問文と目的語 Wh 疑問文）よりも先に導入すべきであるということになる．

(9) a. **Why** did Ron find Pam?
↓
b. **Who** found Pam?
Who did Ron find?

(9b) における主語 Wh 疑問文と目的語 Wh 疑問文の容易さに関しては，複雑な要因が関与しているため，導入の順番に関しては，熟考が必要である．というのは，Hasebe and Maki (2014) が明らかにしたように，初級学習者にとっ

ては，主語 Wh 疑問文のほうが，目的語 Wh 疑問文よりも容易であるが，中級・上級学習者にとっては，逆転しているからである．

7.3 日本人大学生による関係節・Wh 疑問文習得

Hasebe et al. (2015) は，Hasebe and Maki (2014) が中学生英語学習者に対して行った Wh 疑問文の習得の実験結果が，大学生英語学習者にも同様の結果が出るかどうか調査し，さらに，新たに，大学生英語学習者の関係節の習得に関しても，調査した．

英語と日本語には，Wh 疑問文形成に関して，決定的な相違が 1 つある．(10) に示されるように，英語においては，目的語 Wh 句は，文頭に移動されなければならないが，日本語においては，Wh 句は，移動する必要がない．

(10) a. Who did John find [t]?　　　　　（英語）
　　 b. ジョンは，誰を見つけましたか？　　（日本語）

Hasebe and Maki (2014) は，日本人中学生英語学習者が，項・付加詞 Wh 疑問文非対称性と，2 種類の主語・目的語 Wh 疑問文非対称性（初級学習者にとっては，主語 Wh 疑問文のほうが，目的語 Wh 疑問文よりも容易であるが，中級・上級学習者にとっては，目的語 Wh 疑問文のほうが，主語 Wh 疑問文よりも容易であること）を示すことを明らかにした．

関係節に関しては，(11) で示されるように，英語と日本語には，いくつかの相違点がある．

(11) a. Paul saw the man [who John found [t]].　　（英語）
　　 b. ポールは，[ジョンが [t] みつけた] 人を見た．　（日本語）

英語文 (11a) は，目的語の領域に，目的語関係節を含んでいる．関係節の主要部 [the man] は，関係節内部の動詞の論理的目的語で，関係代名詞 [who] が，関係節の左端に出現する．一方，日本語文 (11b) は，関係節は，主要部 [人] の前に置かれ，関係代名詞を持たない．O'Grady et al. (2003) は，韓国語を学ぶ英語母語話者による韓国語の関係節の習得状況を調査し，主語・目的語関係節非対称性があることを発見した．

Hasebe et al. (2015) は，これらの先行研究に基づき，日本人大学生英語学

習者に，Wh 疑問文習得に関して，中学生英語学習者と同様の非対称性を示すかどうか，また，関係節習得に関して，O'Grady et al. (2003) の被験者と同様の非対称性を示すかどうか調査した．ここで注意すべき重要な点は，Wh 疑問文も関係節も，英語においては，明らかに，Wh 句の移動が生じているという点である．

Hasebe et al. (2015) は，178 名の大学生英語学習者に，(12) と (13) に示す翻訳テストを実施した．

(12) 翻訳テスト（Wh 疑問文）（部分）
以下の日本語文を，英語文に翻訳しなさい．
a. 主語 Wh 疑問文： (項$_{(主語)}$, *who*)
問題： 誰がパム [Pam] を見つけましたか？
解答： Who found Pam?
b. 目的語 Wh 疑問文： (項$_{(目的語)}$, *who / what*)
問題： ロン [Ron] は，誰を見つけましたか？
解答： Who did Ron find?
c. 擬似付加詞 Wh 疑問文： (付加詞$_{(時間／日付)}$, *when*)
問題： いつロン [Ron] は，パム [Pam] を見つけましたか？
解答： When did Ron find Pam?
d. 付加詞 Wh 疑問文： (付加詞$_{(理由)}$, *why*)
問題： なぜロン [Ron] は，パム [Pam] を見つけましたか？
解答： Why did Ron find Pam?

(13) 翻訳テスト（関係節）（部分）
以下の日本語文を，英語文に翻訳しなさい．
a. 主語領域における主語 Wh 疑問文
問題： パム [Pam] を見つけた人は，リチャード [Richard] を助けた．
解答： The man who found Pam helped Richard.
b. 主語領域における目的語 Wh 疑問文
問題： ロン [Ron] が見つけた人は，リチャード [Richard] を助けた．
解答： The man who Ron found helped Richard.

第 7 章　MET：第二言語習得研究機能　　109

c. 目的語領域における主語語 Wh 疑問文
    問題：　リチャード［Richard］は，パム［Pam］を見つけた人を助けた．
    解答：　Richard helped the man who found Pam.
d. 目的語領域における目的語 Wh 疑問文
    問題：　リチャード［Richard］は，ロン［Ron］が見つけた人を助けた．
    解答：　Richard helped the man who Ron found.

Hasebe et al.（2015）は，178 名の大学生英語学習者に，MET を実施し，表 8 に示すように，3 グループに分類した．

表 8　被験者の分類

	初級	中級	上級
偏差値（DV）	DV < 45	45 ≤ DV < 55	55 ≤ DV
観測数	46	73	59

大学生英語学習者においても，項・付加詞 Wh 疑問文非対称性，また，主語・目的語 Wh 疑問文非対称性があるかどうか調査するために実施された Wh 疑問文翻訳テストの結果は，表 9 に示される．表 9 は，Wh 疑問文翻訳テストにおける正解率の平均値と標準偏差を示している．

表 9　Wh 疑問文翻訳テストにおける正解率の平均値と標準偏差

		主語	目的語	項	時間	理由	付加詞
初級	平均値	.33	.12	.22	.33	.34	.34
	標準偏差	.36	.23	.23	.39	.40	.38
中級	平均値	.27	.47	.37	.62	.62	.62
	標準偏差	.38	.41	.29	.35	.38	.34
上級	平均値	.40	.41	.40	.60	.61	.61
	標準偏差	.41	.42	.29	.39	.41	.38

まず，3×2×2 分散分析（3 タイプの被験者×2 タイプの文（項・付加詞）×2 タイプの項（主語・目的語））を行った．その結果，統計的有意な［文タイプ］要因に対する主効果（$F(1, 175) = 41.60, p < .001$），統計的有意な［EFL レベ

ル］要因に対する主効果（$F(2, 175) = 12.20, p < .001$），そして，統計的有意な 3 要因間の相互作用（$F(2, 175) = 7.68, p < .001$）を発見した．しかしながら，［項タイプ］要因に対する主効果（$F(1, 175) = .025, p < .874$）には，統計的有意性がなかった．

続いて，多重比較を行い，項・付加詞 Wh 疑問文非対称性に関して，以下を発見した．初級学習者には，項 Wh 疑問文の正解率と付加詞 Wh 疑問文の正解率との間に，統計的有意な差（$n = 46, F(1, 175) = 4.05, p < .046$）があった．また，中級学習者においても，項 Wh 疑問文の正解率と付加詞 Wh 疑問文の正解率との間に，統計的有意な差（$n = 73, F(1, 175) = 30.87, p < .001$）があった．さらに，上級学習者においても，項 Wh 疑問文の正解率と付加詞 Wh 疑問文の正解率との間に，統計的有意な差（$n = 59, F(1, 175) = 27.36, p < .001$）があった．これらは，図 1 によって，より明確に示される．

図 1　項 Wh 疑問文と付加詞 Wh 疑問文の比較

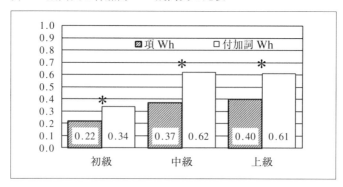

したがって，日本人大学生英語学習者は，項・付加詞 Wh 疑問文非対称性を示すことが明らかになった．彼らにとっては，項 Wh 疑問文の習得は，付加詞 Wh 疑問文の習得よりも，より困難であった．この結果は，Hasebe and Maki (2014) の中学生学習者から得られた結果を支持している．

次に，多重比較を行い，主語・目的語 Wh 疑問文非対称性に関して，以下を発見した．初級学習者には，主語 Wh 疑問文の正解率と目的語 Wh 疑問文の正解率との間に，統計的有意な差（$n = 46, F(1, 175) = 7.01, p < .009$）があった．また，中級学習者においても，主語 Wh 疑問文の正解率と目的語 Wh 疑問文の正解率との間に，統計的有意な差（$n = 73, F(1, 175) = 9.94, p <$

.002）があった．これらは，図 2 によって，より明確に示される．

図 2　主語 Wh 疑問文と目的語 Wh 疑問文の比較

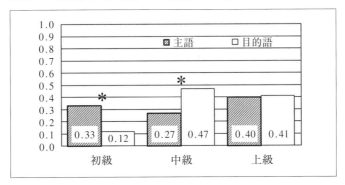

したがって，日本人大学生英語学習者は，主語・目的語 Wh 疑問文の習得に関して，2 種類の非対称性を示している．つまり，初級学習者にとっては，目的語 Wh 疑問文の習得は，主語 Wh 疑問文の習得よりも，より困難であるが，その反対に，中級学習者にとっては，主語 Wh 疑問文の習得は，目的語 Wh 疑問文の習得よりも，より困難であるということである．この結果も，Hasebe and Maki (2014) の中学生学習者から得られた結果を支持している．

次に，大学生英語学習者において，関係節の習得において，主語・目的語非対称性があるかどうか調査するために実施された関係節翻訳テストの結果は，表 10 に示される．表 10 は，関係節翻訳テストにおける正解率の平均値と標準偏差を示している．

表 10　関係節翻訳テストにおける正解率の平均値と標準偏差

		主語領域		目的語領域	
		主語	目的語	主語	目的語
初級	平均値	.24	.17	.37	.22
	標準偏差	.36	.32	.36	.34
中級	平均値	.40	.29	.49	.33
	標準偏差	.41	.40	.39	.38
上級	平均値	.56	.36	.69	.33
	標準偏差	.41	.40	.32	.36

まず、3×2×2分散分析（3タイプの被験者×2タイプの文（項・付加詞）×2タイプの項（主語・目的語））を行った。その結果、統計的有意な［領域タイプ］要因に対する主効果（$F(1,175) = 13.40$, $p < .001$）、統計的有意な［項タイプ］要因に対する主効果（$F(1,175) = 42.27$, $p < .001$）、そして、統計的有意な［EFLレベル］要因に対する主効果（$F(2,175) = 8.22$, $p < .001$）を発見した。しかしながら、統計3要因間の相互作用（$F(2, 175) = 1.43$, $p < .242$）には、統計的有意性がなかった。

続いて、多重比較を行い、主語・目的語関係節非対称性に関して、以下を発見した。(14)には、主語領域の関係節における主語・目的語関係節非対称性、(15)には、目的語領域における主語・目的語関係節非対称性が要約されている。

(14) 主語領域関係節
    a. 中級学習者にとって、主語関係節の正解率と目的語関係節の正解率の間に、統計的有意な差（$n = 73$, $F(1, 175) = 6.00$, $p < .015$）があった。
    b. 上級学習者にとって、主語関係節の正解率と目的語関係節の正解率の間に、統計的有意な差（$n = 59$, $F(1, 175) = 15.05$, $p < .001$）があった。

(15) 目的語領域関係節
    a. 初級学習者にとって、主語関係節の正解率と目的語関係節の正解率の間に、統計的有意な差（$n = 46$, $F(1, 175) = 5.97$, $p < .016$）があった。
    b. 中級学習者にとって、主語関係節の正解率と目的語関係節の正解率の間に、統計的有意な差（$n = 73$, $F(1, 175) = 11.41$, $p < .001$）があった。
    c. 上級学習者にとって、主語関係節の正解率と目的語関係節の正解率の間に、統計的有意な差（$n = 59$, $F(1, 175) = 45.08$, $p < .001$）があった。

(14)の結果と(15)の結果は、それぞれ、図3と図4によって、より明確に示される。

図3　主語の領域からの主語・目的語関係節の比較

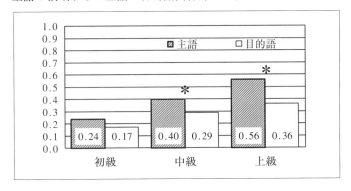

図4　目的語の領域からの主語・目的語関係節の比較

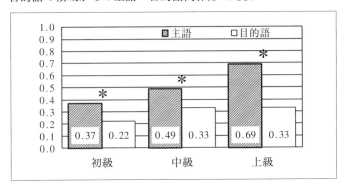

したがって，日本人大学生英語学習者は，学習レベルにかかわらず，関係節の習得において，主語・目的語非対称性を見せ，彼らにとっては，主語関係節のほうが，目的語関係節よりも，より容易であることが分かった．

このように，METを使用することで，被験者の英語能力の測定には，ほぼ時間をかけずに，被験者の分類を行うことができ，本来調査したい実験に関して，被験者に集中してもらうことができる点で，METは，第二言語習得研究において，極めて重要な役割を果たすことができると言える．

第 8 章

センター試験版 MET

2017 年 4 月に，大学入試センターより正式に許可を得，過去の大学入試センター試験英語聴解問題を利用して，新たなバージョンの MET を作成し始めた．これを始めた 1 つの理由は，今後，センター試験英語の体裁が大幅に変更され，最終的には，センター試験英語自体がなくなるという事実がある．センター試験英語の問題は，最良の問題の 1 つであると言えるため，今後，これまで蓄積されてきた音声問題をここで忘れ去るのではなく，再利用できないかと考え，MET という形で新たな役割を与えた．以下に，2013 年度から 2016 年度に実施された（つまり，2014 年 1 月から 2017 年 1 月に実施された）センター試験英語の聴解問題から作成した 4 バージョンの MET を提示し，その後，その MET の得点が，他の英語テストの得点をどの程度予測できるか，1 つずつ示していく．

センター試験英語の聴解問題に基づく MET を作成する規則は，MET E6 と同様であり，(1) の 2 点のみである．

(1) センター試験英語版 MET 作成規則
    a. 6 単語目ごとに，空所が設けられる．
    b. 空所を設ける際，固有名詞，ハイフンで繋がれた長い語，数字，日本語，年，括弧の中にある発音されない語は，除外される．

以下では，センター試験英語の聴解問題に基づいて作成された MET をそれが実施された年度ではなく，それが実施された年に基づいて，MET CT 2014

のように表記する．MET CT 2014 から MET CT 2017 は，それぞれ，(2)-(5) に示される．MET CT 2014 は，Xu (2018) が，MET CT 2015 と MET CT 2016 は，Morii (2018) が，そして，MET CT 2017 は，Wu (2018) が作成した．

(2) MET CT 2014

CD を聞きながら，空いている（　）の中に，英単語を入れて下さい．

01. Angora rabbits are soft and lovable (　)¹. There are different kinds in (　)² countries,
02. but Angoras originated in Ankara, Turkey, before (　)³ around the world.
03. One place (　)⁴ became popular was France. They were (　)⁵ by the French royal family
04. and (　)⁶ elites in the mid-18th century. Soon, Angoras (　)⁷ popular outside France
05. and could be (　)⁸ throughout Europe by the end of (　)⁹ century. Later, people in
06. the United States started (　)¹⁰ them as household pets in (　)¹¹ early 1900s:
07. Wherever you find them, (　)¹² long-haired rabbits live five to (　)¹³ years
08. when kept indoors and (　)¹⁴ for properly.
09. To make a (　)¹⁵ kimchi meat sauce, put some finely-chopped (　)¹⁶ into a pan
10. with two (　)¹⁷ of olive oil. Turn the (　)¹⁸ on, and when you smell (　)¹⁹
11. garlic cooking, add one chopped (　)²⁰ and cook for about two (　)²¹. After adding
12. 500 grams of ground (　)²², cook until light brown, then (　)²³ one can of
13. chopped tomatoes (　)²⁴ with about three tablespoons of (　)²⁵.
14. Before turning the heat down (　)²⁶ low and cooking everything
15. for (　)²⁷ thirty minutes, don't forget to add (　)²⁸ tablespoons
16. of kimchi base. This sauce (　)²⁹ great on either spaghetti or (　)³⁰!
17. Growing food locally in American cities (　)³¹ been getting more popular recently.

18. (　)^{32} fact, the vegetables you buy (　)^{33} the supermarket may be
19. grown (　)^{34} down the street. Shoppers may (　)^{35} surprised,
20. but actually urban farming (　)^{36} deep roots, especially in the northeastern US.
21. Before (　)^{37} had good highways and air (　)^{38}, fruits and vegetables
22. were often (　)^{39} in city greenhouses during the (　)^{40} instead of being shipped
23. in (　)^{41} faraway states or other countries. (　)^{42} it reduces transportation costs
24. and (　)^{43} people with fresh food more (　)^{44}, urban farming is
25. making a (　)^{45}.
26. There are many kinds of (　)^{46} and reasons why people build (　)^{47}.
27. People enjoy spending time and (　)^{48} gathering, organizing, and displaying
28. almost (　)^{49}. A serious collector can even (　)^{50} a career as a respected (　)^{51}.
29. Some people love certain musicians, (　)^{52}, or TV programs so much that (　)^{53} must
30. have any items associated (　)^{54} them. Collectors meet other fans, (　)^{55} information
31. online, and compete to (　)^{56} who has the biggest and (　)^{57} collection. Other people
32. may start (　)^{58} collection by accident. For example, (　)^{59} a friend gives you
33. a (　)^{60} whale souvenir and you keep (　)^{61} on your desk. Then, your (　)^{62}
34. notices it and gives you (　)^{63} umbrella with a whale design. (　)^{64} collection continues
35. to grow by (　)^{65} as others give you similar (　)^{66}. It may take over your (　)^{67}
36. if you aren't careful! Collecting may (　)^{68} have a deeper meaning. Some (　)^{69}
37. believe it begins with childhood (　)^{70} needs. They say we all (　)^{71}
38. uncertainty as children or wanted (　)^{72} we could not have, so (　)^{73} may give us
39. a greater (　)^{74} of control over our lives. (　)^{75} the motivation may be,
40. collecting (　)^{76} a satisfying and enjoyable hobby (　)^{77} many people.

(3) MET CT 2015

CDを聞きながら，空いている（　）の中に，英単語を入れて下さい．

01. If you're going to Machu Picchu in highland Peru, (　)¹ should consider visiting Cuzco,
02. at 3,400 meters (　)² sea level. You will enjoy (　)³ through the Plaza de Armas
03. and visiting (　)⁴ Temple of the Sun. You can also look at Cuzco's (　)⁵ museums
04. and beautiful houses as (　)⁶ as its magnificent churches. Remember, (　)⁷, that
05. these churches close for (　)⁸ few hours around noon. In (　)⁹, you can take advantage of
06. (　)¹⁰ hotels and restaurants, and at (　)¹¹ same time, see Cuzco's fascinating history
07. (　)¹² in its architecture, language, and (　)¹³ treasures.
08. When you start living (　)¹⁴, you might find it difficult (　)¹⁵ manage your money.
09. Here are (　)¹⁶ tips that you may find (　)¹⁷. One hint is first to (　)¹⁸
10. a detailed budget, or plan, (　)¹⁹ how much money you have (　)²⁰ what you are going to
11. (　)²¹ it on each month. Then, (　)²² at your budget and decide (　)²³
12. you can buy fewer items. (　)²⁴, use less electricity, water, or (　)²⁵ utilities
13. by turning off lights, (　)²⁶ example. Finally, before shopping, make (　)²⁷ list of
14. what you need (　)²⁸ compare prices on those items (　)²⁹ different shops.
15. Have you ever (　)³⁰ the phrase "It's all Greek to me"? (　)³¹ use it when we don't
16. understand (　)³² foreign language or a difficult (　)³³. If someone tries to
17. explain (　)³⁴ theory from physics or mathematics (　)³⁵ we cannot comprehend,
18. we could (　)³⁶, "It's all Greek to me." This phrase (　)³⁷ in William Shakespeare's

19. play *Julius Caesar*, where one Roman tells (   )³⁸ that he couldn't understand somebody
20. because (   )³⁹ spoke Greek. Although this phrase had (   )⁴⁰ used earlier by different
21. writers, Shakespeare's (   )⁴¹ of the phrase helped to (   )⁴² it popular,
22. and it continues (   )⁴³ be used even today.
23. Americans have (   )⁴⁴ wanted to live apart from (   )⁴⁵ parents, as personal
24. independence is (   )⁴⁶ thought to be very important. (   )⁴⁷, in most cases, the elderly
25. (   )⁴⁸ in their own homes, while (   )⁴⁹ grown children move away and
26. (   )⁵⁰ elsewhere. However, some elderly people (   )⁵¹ their grown-up children have
27. decided (   )⁵² combine households, and this trend (   )⁵³ been increasing in recent years.
28. (   )⁵⁴ certainly are benefits to living (   )⁵⁵ a multi-generational family
29. in the (   )⁵⁶ house. Grandparents take care of (   )⁵⁷ children while the parents go
30. (   )⁵⁸ work. Young children learn about (   )⁵⁹ family history, cooking, and household
31. (   )⁶⁰ skills from their grandparents. Senior (   )⁶¹ also get a lot
32. out (   )⁶² spending time with their grandchildren. (   )⁶³ stay in good health, hiking
33. (   )⁶⁴ playing sports with the grandchildren. (   )⁶⁵ grandchildren can teach their
34. grandparents (   )⁶⁶ to use computers and keep (   )⁶⁷ with the latest technology.
35. Parents (   )⁶⁸ teach their children proper manners (   )⁶⁹ older people through
36. their own (   )⁷⁰ toward their parents. Children learn (   )⁷¹ seeing their parents
37. interact with (   )⁷² grandparents. Parents can get the (   )⁷³ of the children
38. in watching (   )⁷⁴ for the safety of the (   )⁷⁵, thus sharing the burden
39. if (   )⁷⁶ state of their health becomes (   )⁷⁷ problem.

120

(4) MET CT 2016

CD を聞きながら，空いている（　）の中に，英単語を入れて下さい．

01. In some countries, silver gifts (　)¹ given for 25th wedding anniversaries
02. and (　)² gifts for 50th anniversaries. But in the United Kingdom,
03. (　)³ are also some traditional gifts (　)⁴ to celebrate other anniversaries.
04. Perhaps (　)⁵ are not so familiar with (　)⁶. For example, for third anniversaries,
05. (　)⁷ gifts are usually given. Three (　)⁸ later, gifts containing sugar are
06. (　)⁹. Six years after that, something (　)¹⁰ of silk is the expected (　)¹¹.
07. Some might be surprised to (　)¹² out that diamonds are given (　)¹³ only
08. for engagements, but also (　)¹⁴ 60th anniversaries.
09. Welcome to The Ocean Hotel. Our rooms (　)¹⁵ decorated in traditional French style,
10. but (　)¹⁶ can use the latest technology, (　)¹⁷ example, wireless Internet.
11. Every room (　)¹⁸ a splendid ocean view, so (　)¹⁹ can see the sunset.
12. Our (　)²⁰ has Chinese, Japanese, and Italian restaurants on the (　)²¹ floor
13. and three coffee shops (　)²² the first and second floors,
14. (　)²³ you can enjoy Asian and Western dishes. (　)²⁴ front of the hotel
15. we (　)²⁵ an outdoor swimming pool next (　)²⁶ the beach, and
16. you can (　)²⁷ enjoy an indoor swimming pool (　)²⁸ an exercise room.
17. Palau is a (　)²⁹ in the Pacific. It became an (　)³⁰ republic on October 1, 1994.
18. Palau's flag is (　)³¹ to Japan's because it features a (　)³² circle. However,
19. the circle is (　)³³, and the background is blue. (　)³⁴ is used to represent
20. the (　)³⁵, which the nation depends on (　)³⁶ food. Unlike the Japanese flag,
21. the (　)³⁷ on Palau's flag is a little off-center. (　)³⁸ of the sun,

22. as on ( )³⁹ Japanese flag, the circle represents the ( )⁴⁰, which is traditionally
23. thought to ( )⁴¹ important in the life cycle ( )⁴² customs of the people.
24. Helen Keller, admired ( )⁴³ her work on behalf of ( )⁴⁴ disabilities,
25. visited Japan three times. ( )⁴⁵ was unable to see or ( )⁴⁶, but she was
26. impressed with ( )⁴⁷ kindness of the Japanese people and ( )⁴⁸
27. and appreciation of Japan and its ( )⁴⁹. She first came to Japan in 1937,
28. ( )⁵⁰ she was invited by the Japanese ( )⁵¹ to make
29. a lecture tour ( )⁵² the country. While she was ( )⁵³, she was moved
30. by the ( )⁵⁴ about the faithful Akita dog, Hachiko, and ( )⁵⁵ if she could have
31. such ( )⁵⁶ dog. Ichiro Ogasawara, a police officer in Akita City, ( )⁵⁷ gave her
32. one of his ( )⁵⁸ puppies. She named this dog Kami. ( )⁵⁹ took Kami home with her,
33. which ( )⁶⁰ Kami the first Akita dog to ( )⁶¹ to the United States. In a letter
34. to ( )⁶² friend, she called Kami an "angel ( )⁶³ fur" and said that
35. he ( )⁶⁴ especially gentle and devoted. She ( )⁶⁵ this dog so much
36. that ( )⁶⁶ asked for another Akita dog, which ( )⁶⁷ sent to her in 1939.
37. This ( )⁶⁸ was Kami's brother, and she called ( )⁶⁹ Go-Go.
38. Helen Keller's dogs received a lot of ( )⁷⁰ in the United States,
39. which helped to introduce Akita ( )⁷¹ as popular pets for Americans.

(5) MET CT 2017

CDを聞きながら，空いている（　）の中に，英単語を入れて下さい．

01. Now let me tell you ( )¹ story. When we lived in Japan ( )² years ago,
02. my American friend Jane came ( )³ visit us with her Japanese boss,
03. ( )⁴ wanted to meet my husband. ( )⁵ he left, we decided to ( )⁶ the gift
04. that he had ( )⁷. Surprisingly, it was a neatly ( )⁸ live lobster.
05. I started laughing ( )⁹ shouting, "It's alive! It's alive!" But Jane, who'd just ( )¹⁰

06. to the bathroom, thought I ( )¹¹ yelling, "It's a lie! It's a lie!" ( )¹² thought we were
07. having an ( )¹³, so she was afraid to ( )¹⁴ back into the living room.
08. ( )¹⁵ she finally returned, she realized ( )¹⁶ we were not fighting,
09. but ( )¹⁷ at such an unexpected gift.
10. ( )¹⁸ had never cooked a lobster ( )¹⁹, so we didn't know what to ( )²⁰.
11. In those days there was ( )²¹ Internet to get information, so ( )²² went
12. and asked a neighbor. ( )²³, we had put the lobster ( )²⁴ a sink full of water.
13. ( )²⁵ we came home the lobster ( )²⁶ become so lively that
14. we ( )²⁷ longer had the heart to ( )²⁸ it. We managed to get ( )²⁹ back
15. into the box, and ( )³⁰ gave it to the neighbor ( )³¹.
16. So, Reina, what would you do ( )³² we had five million yen ( )³³ improve our school?
17. Hmm. I can ( )³⁴ of so many things, Ichiro. One ( )³⁵ would be
18. to put a ( )³⁶ over the bicycle parking area. Don't ( )³⁷ hate it
19. when it rains ( )³⁸ your bike gets wet?
20. We ( )³⁹ also put some picnic tables ( )⁴⁰ the grassy area over
21. by ( )⁴¹ bike stands. That would give ( )⁴² a place to have lunch
22. ( )⁴³ hang out after school. And ( )⁴⁴ could make the entrance
23. look ( )⁴⁵ lot nicer. What about painting ( )⁴⁶ a bright color
24. and buying ( )⁴⁷ plants and flowers?
25. Well, those ( )⁴⁸ all great ideas, Reina. I especially ( )⁴⁹ putting a roof
26. over the ( )⁵⁰. But to tell the truth, ( )⁵¹ we had that much money ( )⁵² spend,
27. I think it'd be better ( )⁵³ spend it on one big ( )⁵⁴ rather than a lot of
28. ( )⁵⁵ things. Oh, yeah. Good point, Ichiro.
29. ( )⁵⁶ think it'd be better if we ( )⁵⁷ free Wi-Fi everywhere in the school.
30. ( )⁵⁸ access would help us study ( )⁵⁹. We could get a lot ( )⁶⁰ information
31. that would help us ( )⁶¹ our homework, and there are ( )⁶²

32. many educational websites that are (　　)⁶³ free.
33. Best of all, we (　　)⁶⁴ chat with the students at (　　)⁶⁵ sister school in Australia.
34. Don't you (　　)⁶⁶, Mayuko?
35. Well, that's a pretty good idea, Ichiro, (　　)⁶⁷ the library has Internet access,
36. (　　)⁶⁸ most students already have smartphones (　　)⁶⁹ tablet PCs. I think it'd be
37. (　　)⁷⁰ to buy solar panels instead. (　　)⁷¹ electricity could be used
38. all (　　)⁷² the school - we could have (　　)⁷³ water in the winter
39. and (　　)⁷⁴ conditioning in the summer. Oh, (　　)⁷⁵ know!
40. We could make a (　　)⁷⁶ for the bicycles out of (　　)⁷⁷ solar panels.
41. That would kill (　　)⁷⁸ birds with one stone!

以下では，8.1 節で，日本において実施した調査結果を報告し，8.2 節で，中国において実施した調査結果を報告する．

8.1　日本：MET CT 2015 と MET CT 2016

Morii (2018) は，2017 年 5 月に The Test of English for International Communication Institutional Testing Program (TOEIC ITP) を受験した被験者 102 名に，MET CT 2015 と MET CT 2016 を実施し，MET の得点と TOEIC ITP の得点との相関を調査した．TOEIC ITP は，非公式なものであるが，その問題は，公式 TOEIC の問題と同じ構成であり，その試験内容は，(6) に示されるように，聴解問題と読解問題を含んでいる．

(6)　TOEIC / TOEIC ITP の試験内容

	聴解問題	読解問題	総合
問題数	100 問	100 問	200 問
最高点	495 点	495 点	990 点
制限時間	45 分	75 分	120 分

Morii (2018) の調査結果は，(7) と (8) に示される．

(7) MET CT 2015 の得点と TOEIC ITP の得点との相関
$n = 100$
$r = .62$
$p < .001$

(8) MET CT 2016 の得点と TOEIC ITP の得点との相関
$n = 100$
$r = .62$
$p < .001$

この結果，MET CT 2015 と MET CT 2016 の得点と TOEIC ITP の得点との間に，相関（$.4 < r < .7$）があることが明らかになった．したがって，センター試験英語聴解問題を基に作成された MET CT 2015 と MET CT 2016 は，TOEIC ITP によって測定される英語能力をある程度予測できることが分かった．

Morii (2018) は，さらに，同じ 100 名の被験者に，牧グループが一貫して使用している MET E6 と牧グループが中学生用に作成した jMET も実施した．これによって，MET CT 2015 と MET CT 2016 の TOEIC ITP によって測定される英語能力を予測する能力と MET E6 と jMET の TOEIC ITP によって測定される英語能力を予測する能力との間に，相違があるかどうか調査した．

Morii (2018) の調査結果は，(9) と (10) に示される．

(9) MET E6 の得点と TOEIC ITP の得点との相関
$n = 100$
$r = .58$
$p < .001$

(10) jMET の得点と TOEIC ITP の得点との相関
$n = 100$
$r = .62$
$p < .001$

Morii (2018) は，VassarStats: Web Site for Statistical Computation によ
る Fisher r-to-z 変換を使用し，各相関係数間に，統計的有意な差があるかど
うか調査した．その結果，4つの相関係数の中の，どの2つの相関係数の間に
も，統計的有意な差がなかった．したがって，MET CT 2015 と MET CT
2016 の TOEIC ITP によって測定される英語能力を予測する能力と MET E6
と jMET の TOEIC ITP によって測定される英語能力を予測する能力との間
には，相違がないことが分かった．このことは，Kawana and Walker (2002)
の大学1年生向け教科書だけでなく，センター試験英語の聴解問題も，同様
に，MET を作成する材料として適していることを示している．実際，セン
ター試験英語の聴解問題のスクリプトは，幾度も検討を経ているはずであるた
め，MET を含めた他のテストに利用するに当たっては，極めて安全であると
言える．

8.2　中国：MET CT 2014-MET CT 2017

8.2.1　MET CT 2014 と MET CT 2015

Xu (2018) は，2017年7月に，中国遼寧省の高校1年生274名に MET
CT 2014 と MET CT 2015 を実施した．この272名の高校生は，5月に2学
期の中間テストを受けていた．この中間テストは，読解問題（読解40点，文
法45点，作文35点）のみからなり，満点は，120点である．実施時間は，
100分である．

Xu (2018) の調査結果は，(11) と (12) に示される．

(11)　MET CT 2014 の得点と 2017年2学期中間テストの得点との相関
 $n = 274$
 $r = .24$
 $p < .001$

(12)　MET CT 2015 の得点と 2017年2学期中間テストの得点との相関
 $n = 274$
 $r = .47$
 $p < .001$

この結果，MET CT 2014 の得点と 2017 年 2 学期中間テストの得点との間に，相関がほぼない（$r < .4$）ことが明らかになった．一方，MET CT 2015 の得点と 2017 年 2 学期中間テストの得点との間には，相関がある（$.4 < r$）ことが明らかになった．

Xu（2018）は，さらに，この 274 名と同じ高校に通う別の 1 年生 304 名に，MET E6 を実施した．その結果は，(13) に示される．

(13) MET E6 の得点と 2017 年 2 学期中間テストの得点との相関
   $n = 304$
   $r = .49$
   $p < .001$

その結果，MET E6 の得点と 2017 年 2 学期中間テストの得点との間には，相関がある（$.4 < r$）ことが明らかになった．

8.2.2 MET CT 2016 と MET CT 2017

Wu（2018）は，2017 年 7 月に，中国河北省の高校 1 年生 145 名と 2 年生 147 名に MET CT 2016 と MET CT 2017 を実施した．この 292 名の高校生は，4 月に 2 学期の中間テストを受けていた．この中間テストは，聴解（30 点），読解（40 点），総合（内容と文法知識を同時に問う問題）（45 点）と作文・翻訳（35 点）からなり，満点は，150 点である．実施時間は，120 分である．Wu（2018）の調査結果は，(14)-(17) に示される．

(14) MET CT 2016 の得点と 2017 年 2 学期中間テストの得点との相関
   （1 年生）
   $n = 145$
   $r = .45$
   $p < .001$

(15) MET CT 2017 の得点と 2017 年 2 学期中間テストの得点との相関
   （1 年生）
   $n = 145$
   $r = .67$
   $p < .001$

(16) MET CT 2016 の得点と 2017 年 2 学期中間テストの得点との相関
（2 年生）
$n = 147$
$r = .38$
$p < .001$

(17) MET CT 2017 の得点と 2017 年 2 学期中間テストの得点との相関
（2 年生）
$n = 147$
$r = .53$
$p < .001$

この結果，調査に参加した中国河北省の高校 1 年生にとっては，MET CT 2016 の得点と 2017 年 2 学期中間テスト得点との間には，相関（$.4 < r < .7$）があり，また，MET CT 2017 の得点と 2017 年 2 学期中間テスト得点との間にも，相関（$.4 < r < .7$）があることが明らかになった．また，調査に参加した中国河北省の高校 2 年生にとっては，MET CT 2016 の得点と 2017 年 2 学期中間テスト得点との間には，相関がほぼなく（$r < .4$），MET CT 2017 の得点と 2017 年 2 学期中間テスト得点との間には，相関（$.4 < r < .7$）があることが明らかになった．

Wu (2018) は，さらに，同じ 292 名の被験者に，牧グループが一貫して使用している MET E6 と，牧グループが中学生用に作成した jMET も実施した．その結果は，(18)-(21) に示される．

(18) MET E6 の得点と 2017 年 2 学期中間テストの得点との相関（1 年生）
$n = 145$
$r = .65$
$p < .001$

(19) jMET の得点と 2017 年 2 学期中間テストの得点との相関（1 年生）
$n = 145$
$r = .50$
$p < .001$

(20) MET E6 の得点と 2017 年 2 学期中間テストの得点との相関 (2 年生)
$n = 147$
$r = .35$
$p < .001$

(21) jMET の得点と 2017 年 2 学期中間テストの得点との相関 (2 年生)
$n = 147$
$r = .53$
$p < .001$

この結果,調査に参加した中国河北省の高校 1 年生にとっては,MET E6 の得点と 2017 年 2 学期中間テスト得点との間には,相関 ($.4 < r < .7$) があり,また,jMET の得点と 2017 年 2 学期中間テスト得点との間にも,相関 ($.4 < r < .7$) があることが明らかになった.また,調査に参加した中国河北省の高校 2 年生にとっては,MET E6 の得点と 2017 年 2 学期中間テスト得点との間には,相関がほぼなく ($r < .4$),jMET の得点と 2017 年 2 学期中間テスト得点との間には,相関 ($.4 < r < .7$) があることが明らかになった.

Xu (2018) と Wu (2018) の調査は,日本のセンター試験英語聴解問題を基に作成された MET (MET CT 2014-MET CT 2017),MET E6,そして,jMET を中国の高校生に実施し,その得点と,高校における中間テストの得点との間の相関を示した初めての調査である.その結果は,あるグループにとっては,センター試験版 MET が,ある程度,中間テストの得点を予測することができ,また,あるグループにとっては,そうではないという,少々,不安定なものである.MET E6 についても,同様である.jMET に関しては,Wu (2018) の調査においては,一貫して,ある程度,中間テストの得点を予測することができると言える.これらの調査結果を踏まえて,今後も,継続して,同様の調査をすることで,センター試験英語版 MET の予測力を明らかにし,改良箇所を,明確にしていく必要がある.

第 9 章

中国版 MET

　Ma（in progress）は，これまで，MET がすべて日本人英語学習者に向けて作成されたテキストや試験を基に作成されているという事実を踏まえ，実際に，中国で使用されているテキストを用い，中国人英語学習者の英語能力をより正確に測定できる新たな中国版 MET を開発した．Ma（in progress）は，各出版社より使用許可を得た上で，中国における中学生向けに，Dawson（2001）の英語教科書を利用し，新たな MET を作成し（jMET-C），中国における高校生向けに，Kent（2003）の英語教科書を利用し，新たな MET を作成し（hMET-C），そして，中国における大学生向けに，李ほか（2013）の英語教科書を利用し，新たな MET を作成した（MET-C）．

　これらの中国版 MET を作成する規則は，牧グループによる MET E6 と同様であり，(1) の 2 点のみである．

(1) 中国版 MET 作成規則
    a. 6 単語目ごとに，空所が設けられる．
    b. 空所を設ける際，固有名詞，ハイフンで繋がれた長い語，数字，中国語，年，括弧の中にある発音されない語は，除外される．

以下に，jMET-C, hMET-C, そして，MET-C を示す．

(2) jMET-C（中学版）：問題

CD を聞きながら，空いている（　）の中に，英単語を入れて下さい．

01. October 25 Dear Millie, Thank you for (　)^1 me about the Mid-Autumn Festival.
02. We have (　)^2 festivals in the USA, and I (　)^3 Halloween best.
03. Halloween is on October 31. How (　)^4 we celebrate it?
04. Children have (　)^5 of fun on that day. (　)^6 dress up and wear masks.
05. (　)^7 we paint our faces. We (　)^8 make pumpkin lanterns.
06. It is (　)^9. When the evening comes,
07. we (　)^{10} houses and play a game (　)^{11} the people inside.
08. We knock (　)^{12} their doors and shout "trick (　)^{13} treat."
09. Usually they give us (　)^{14} candy as a treat.
10. If (　)^{15} do not give us a (　)^{16}, we play a trick on (　)^{17}.
11. We always have a party (　)^{18} the evening of October 31
12. and (　)^{19} nice food and drinks. It (　)^{20} really a special day.
13. Lots (　)^{21} love, Wendy
14. Hi! My name is Kitty. (　)^{22} love dancing. I dance for (　)^{23} an hour every day.
15. Healthy (　)^{24} is important for me. I (　)^{25} to keep fit.
16. I always (　)^{26} milk and bread for breakfast. (　)^{27} lunch and dinner,
17. I usually (　)^{28} fish and vegetables.
18. Sometimes I (　)^{29} hungry between meals,
19. so I (　)^{30} an apple or a pear. (　)^{31} seldom eat cakes or sweets.
20. (　)^{32} have too much sugar and (　)^{33} bad for my teeth.
21. Hello! (　)^{34} am Daniel. I like playing computer (　)^{35}.
22. I seldom exercise. I love (　)^{36} and cola, but they are (　)^{37} healthy.
23. I need to change (　)^{38} lifestyle now.
24. I plan to (　)^{39} more fruit and vegetables every (　)^{40}.
25. I love beef, but I (　)^{41} need to eat some fish.
26. (　)^{42} is a swimming pool near (　)^{43} home.
27. I plan to go (　)^{44} every week.
28. Good evening, ladies (　)^{45} gentlemen. Welcome to our fashion (　)^{46}.
29. I am Millie from Class 1, Grade 7.
30. Today we (　)^{47} going to show you different (　)^{48} of clothes.
31. Look at me. (　)^{49} am wearing sports clothes and (　)^{50} pair of trainers.

32. Trainers are (   )⁵¹ and comfortable and are popular (   )⁵² young people.
33. Here comes Simon. He (   )⁵³ wearing a purple shirt and (   )⁵⁴ pair of grey trousers.
34. His (   )⁵⁵ and grey tie matches his (   )⁵⁶. He looks smart.
35. Now Amy and Daniel (   )⁵⁷ coming. They look cool!
36. Amy is (   )⁵⁸ a yellow cotton blouse and (   )⁵⁹ blue scarf.
37. Daniel is wearing a (   )⁶⁰ T-shirt. Both of them are (   )⁶¹ blue jeans.
38. Young people really (   )⁶² jeans!
39. Look! Here comes Sandy. She (   )⁶³ wearing a red silk blouse,
40. (   )⁶⁴ black wool skirt and a (   )⁶⁵ of red boots. She looks (   )⁶⁶ and beautiful!
41. That's all for today's show. (   )⁶⁷ for coming.

(3)　jMET-C（中学版）：解答

01. October 25 Dear Millie, Thank you for (telling)¹ me about the Mid-Autumn Festival.
02. We have (some)² festivals in the USA, and I (like)³ Halloween best.
03. Halloween is on October 31. How (do)⁴ we celebrate it?
04. Children have (lots)⁵ of fun on that day. (We)⁶ dress up and wear masks.
05. (Sometimes)⁷ we paint our faces. We (also)⁸ make pumpkin lanterns.
06. It is (wonderful)⁹. When the evening comes,
07. we (visit)¹⁰ houses and play a game (with)¹¹ the people inside.
08. We knock (on)¹² their doors and shout "trick (or)¹³ treat."
09. Usually they give us (some)¹⁴ candy as a treat.
10. If (they)¹⁵ do not give us a (treat)¹⁶, we play a trick on (them)¹⁷.
11. We always have a party (on)¹⁸ the evening of October 31
12. and (enjoy)¹⁹ nice food and drinks. It (is)²⁰ really a special day.
13. Lots (of)²¹ love, Wendy

14. Hi! My name is Kitty. (I)²² love dancing. I dance for (half)²³ an hour every day.
15. Healthy (food)²⁴ is important for me. I (need)²⁵ to keep fit.
16. I always (have)²⁶ milk and bread for breakfast. (For)²⁷ lunch and dinner,
17. I usually (eat)²⁸ fish and vegetables.
18. Sometimes I (feel)²⁹ hungry between meals,
19. so I (eat)³⁰ an apple or a pear. (I)³¹ seldom eat cakes or sweets.
20. (They)³² have too much sugar and (are)³³ bad for my teeth.

21. Hello! (I)³⁴ am Daniel. I like playing computer (games)³⁵.
22. I seldom exercise. I love (hamburgers)³⁶ and cola, but they are (not)³⁷ healthy.
23. I need to change (my)³⁸ lifestyle now.
24. I plan to (eat)³⁹ more fruit and vegetables every (day)⁴⁰.
25. I love beef, but I (also)⁴¹ need to eat some fish.
26. (There)⁴² is a swimming pool near (my)⁴³ home.
27. I plan to go (swimming)⁴⁴ every week.
28. Good evening, ladies (and)⁴⁵ gentlemen. Welcome to our fashion (show)⁴⁶.
29. I am Millie from Class 1, Grade 7.
30. Today we (are)⁴⁷ going to show you different (styles)⁴⁸ of clothes.
31. Look at me. (I)⁴⁹ am wearing sports clothes and (a)⁵⁰ pair of trainers.
32. Trainers are (light)⁵¹ and comfortable and are popular (among)⁵² young people.
33. Here comes Simon. He (is)⁵³ wearing a purple shirt and (a)⁵⁴ pair of grey trousers.
34. His (red)⁵⁵ and grey tie matches his (clothes)⁵⁶. He looks smart.
35. Now Amy and Daniel (are)⁵⁷ coming. They look cool!
36. Amy is (wearing)⁵⁸ a yellow cotton blouse and (a)⁵⁹ blue scarf.
37. Daniel is wearing a (blue)⁶⁰ T-shirt. Both of them are (wearing)⁶¹ blue jeans.
38. Young people really (like)⁶² jeans!
39. Look! Here comes Sandy. She (is)⁶³ wearing a red silk blouse,
40. (a)⁶⁴ black wool skirt and a (pair)⁶⁵ of red boots. She looks (modern)⁶⁶ and beautiful!
41. That's all for today's show. (Thanks)⁶⁷ for coming.

(4) hMET-C（高校版）：問題

CD を聞きながら，空いている（　）の中に，英単語を入れて下さい．

01. Going to a British high school (　　)¹ one year was a very (　　)² and
02. exciting experience for me. (　　)³ was very happy with the (　　)⁴ hours in Britain
03. because school starts (　　)⁵ 9 a.m. And ends about 3.30 p.m. This means
04. (　　)⁶ could get up an hour (　　)⁷ than usual,
05. as schools in (　　)⁸ begin before 8 a.m.
06. On the first (　　)⁹, all of the new students (　　)¹⁰ an assembly in the school (　　)¹¹.

07. I sat next to a (　　)^{12} whose name was Diana. We soon (　　)^{13} best friends.
08. During the assembly, (　　)^{14} headmaster told us about the (　　)^{15} of the school.
09. He also (　　)^{16} us that the best way (　　)^{17} earn respect was to devote (　　)^{18}
10. to study and achieve high (　　)^{19}. This sounded like my school (　　)^{20} China.
11. I had many teachers in (　　)^{21} past year. Mr. Heywood, my class teacher,
12. (　　)^{22} very helpful. My favorite teacher (　　)^{23} Miss Burke—
13. I loved the lessons that (　　)^{24} gave in English Literature. In (　　)^{25} class
14. there were 28 students. This (　　)^{26} about the average size for British (　　)^{27}.
15. We had to move to (　　)^{28} classrooms for different classes. We (　　)^{29} had different students
16. in some (　　)^{30}, so it was a struggle (　　)^{31} me to remember all the (　　)^{32} and names.
17. I found that (　　)^{33} homework was not as heavy (　　)^{34} what I used to get (　　)^{35}
18. my old school. However, it (　　)^{36} a bit challenging for me (　　)^{37} first, because all the
19. homework (　　)^{38} in English. I felt lucky, (　　)^{39} all my teachers gave me (　　)^{40}
20. encouragement and I enjoyed all (　　)^{41} subjects: English, History,
21. English Literature, (　　)^{42} Science, Maths, Science, PE, Art, Cooking (　　)^{43} French.
22. My English improved a (　　)^{44}, as I used English every (　　)^{45} and spent an hour
23. each (　　)^{46} reading English books in the (　　)^{47}. I usually went to the (　　)^{48} Club
24. during the lunch break. (　　)^{49} I could send e-mails to (　　)^{50} family and friends back home
25. (　　)^{51} free. I also had an (　　)^{52} French class on Tuesday evenings. (　　)^{53} was
26. really fun as I (　　)^{54} how to buy, prepare and (　　)^{55} food. At the end of (　　)^{56}
27. we held a class party (　　)^{57} we all had to cook (　　)^{58}.

28. I was glad that all (　　)⁵⁹ classmates were fond of the (　　)⁶⁰ that I made.
29. Students at (　　)⁶¹ school have to study Maths, (　　)⁶² and Science, but can stop
30. (　　)⁶³ some subjects if they do (　　)⁶⁴ like them, for example, History (　　)⁶⁵ French.
31. They can choose other (　　)⁶⁶ like Art and Computer Science,
32. (　　)⁶⁷ languages such as Spanish and (　　)⁶⁸. In the Art class that (　　)⁶⁹ took,
33. I made a small (　　)⁷⁰. Though it did not look (　　)⁷¹ beautiful when it was finished,
34. (　　)⁷² still liked it very much.
35. (　　)⁷³ missed Chinese food a lot (　　)⁷⁴ lunch. British food is very different.
36. British (　　)⁷⁵ like eating dessert at the (　　)⁷⁶ of their main meal.
37. After (　　)⁷⁷, we usually played on the (　　)⁷⁸ field. Sometimes I played football
38. (　　)⁷⁹ the boys. Sometimes I just (　　)⁸⁰ under a tree or sat (　　)⁸¹ the grass.
39. I was very (　　)⁸² to experience this different way (　　)⁸³ life.
40. I look back on (　　)⁸⁴ time in the UK with satisfaction,
41. (　　)⁸⁵ I really hope to go (　　)⁸⁶ and study in Manchester again.

（5） hMET-C（高校版）：解答

01. Going to a British high school (for)¹ one year was a very (enjoyable)² and
02. exciting experience for me. (I)³ was very happy with the (school)⁴ hours in Britain
03. because school starts (around)⁵ 9 a.m. And ends about 3.30 p.m. This means
04. (I)⁶ could get up an hour (later)⁷ than usual,
05. as schools in (China)⁸ begin before 8 a.m.
06. On the first (day)⁹, all of the new students (attended)¹⁰ an assembly in the school (hall)¹¹.
07. I sat next to a (girl)¹² whose name was Diana. We soon (became)¹³ best friends.
08. During the assembly, (the)¹⁴ headmaster told us about the (rules)¹⁵ of the school.

09. He also (told)[16] us that the best way (to)[17] earn respect was to devote (ourselves)[18]
10. to study and achieve high (grades)[19]. This sounded like my school (in)[20] China.
11. I had many teachers in (the)[21] past year. Mr. Heywood, my class teacher,
12. (was)[22] very helpful. My favorite teacher (was)[23] Miss Burke—
13. I loved the lessons that (she)[24] gave in English Literature. In (our)[25] class
14. there were 28 students. This (is)[26] about the average size for British (schools)[27].
15. We had to move to (different)[28] classrooms for different classes. We (also)[29] had different students
16. in some (classes)[30], so it was a struggle (for)[31] me to remember all the (faces)[32] and names.
17. I found that (the)[33] homework was not as heavy (as)[34] what I used to get (in)[35]
18. my old school. However, it (was)[36] a bit challenging for me (at)[37] first, because all the
19. homework (was)[38] in English. I felt lucky, (as)[39] all my teachers gave me (much)[40]
20. encouragement and I enjoyed all (my)[41] subjects: English, History,
21. English Literature, (Computer)[42] Science, Maths, Science, PE, Art, Cooking (and)[43] French.
22. My English improved a (lot)[44], as I used English every (day)[45] and spent an hour
23. each (day)[46] reading English books in the (library)[47]. I usually went to the (Computer)[48] Club
24. during the lunch break. (So)[49] I could send e-mails to (my)[50] family and friends back home
25. (for)[51] free. I also had an (extra)[52] French class on Tuesday evenings. (Cooking)[53] was
26. really fun as I (learnt)[54] how to buy, prepare and (cook)[55] food. At the end of (term)[56]
27. we held a class party (and)[57] we all had to cook (something)[58].
28. I was glad that all (my)[59] classmates were fond of the (cake)[60] that I made.
29. Students at (that)[61] school have to study Maths, (English)[62] and Science, but can stop

30. (studying)⁶³ some subjects if they do (not)⁶⁴ like them, for example, History (and)⁶⁵ French.
31. They can choose other (subjects)⁶⁶ like Art and Computer Science,
32. (or)⁶⁷ languages such as Spanish and (German)⁶⁸. In the Art class that (I)⁶⁹ took,
33. I made a small (sculpture)⁷⁰. Though it did not look (very)⁷¹ beautiful when it was finished,
34. (I)⁷² still liked it very much.
35. (I)⁷³ missed Chinese food a lot (at)⁷⁴ lunch. British food is very different.
36. British (people)⁷⁵ like eating dessert at the (end)⁷⁶ of their main meal.
37. After (lunch)⁷⁷, we usually played on the (school)⁷⁸ field. Sometimes I played football
38. (with)⁷⁹ the boys. Sometimes I just (relaxed)⁸⁰ under a tree or sat (on)⁸¹ the grass.
39. I was very (lucky)⁸² to experience this different way (of)⁸³ life.
40. I look back on (my)⁸⁴ time in the UK with satisfaction,
41. (and)⁸⁵ I really hope to go (back)⁸⁶ and study in Manchester again.

(6) MET-C (大学版)：問題

CD を聞きながら，空いている（　）の中に，英単語を入れて下さい.

01. Whether we like it or ( )¹, the world we live in ( )² changed a great deal in ( )³
02. last hundred years, and it ( )⁴ likely to change even more ( )⁵ the next hundred.
03. Some people ( )⁶ like to stop these changes ( )⁷ go back to what they ( )⁸
04. as a purer and simpler ( )⁹. But as history shows, the ( )¹⁰ was not that wonderful.
05. It ( )¹¹ not so bad for a ( )¹² minority, though even they had ( )¹³ do
06. without modern medicine, and ( )¹⁴ was highly risky for women.
07. ( )¹⁵ for the vast majority of ( )¹⁶ population, life was nasty, brutish, ( )¹⁷ short.
08. Anyway, even if one ( )¹⁸ to, one couldn't put the clock ( )¹⁹ to an earlier age.

09. Knowledge (   )²⁰ techniques can't just be forgotten. Nor (   )²¹ one prevent
10. further advances in (   )²² future. Even if all government (   )²³
11. for research were cut off ((   )²⁴ the present government is doing (   )²⁵ best),
12. the force of competition (   )²⁶ still bring about advances in (   )²⁷.
13. Moreover, one cannot stop inquiring (   )²⁸ from thinking about basic science, (   )²⁹ or
14. not they are paid (   )³⁰ it. The only way to (   )³¹ further developments would be
15. a (   )³² state that suppressed anything new, (   )³³ human initiative and inventiveness are
16. (   )³⁴ that even this wouldn't succeed. All (   )³⁵ would do is slow down
17. (   )³⁶ rate of change. If we (   )³⁷ that we cannot prevent science (   )³⁸ technology
18. from changing our world, (   )³⁹ can at least try to (   )⁴⁰ that the changes
19. they make (   )⁴¹ in the right directions. In (   )⁴² democratic society, this means that
20. (   )⁴³ public needs to have a (   )⁴⁴ understanding of science, so that
21. (   )⁴⁵ can make informed decisions and (   )⁴⁶ leave them in the hands (   )⁴⁷ experts.
22. At the moment, the (   )⁴⁸ is in two minds about (   )⁴⁹. It has come to expect
23. (   )⁵⁰ steady increase in the standard (   )⁵¹ living that new developments in (   )⁵²
24. and technology have brought to (   )⁵³, but it also distrusts science
25. (   )⁵⁴ it doesn't understand it. This distrust (   )⁵⁵ evident
26. in the cartoon figure (   )⁵⁶ the mad scientist working in (   )⁵⁷ laboratory
27. to produce a Frankenstein. (   )⁵⁸ is also an important element (   )⁵⁹ support
28. for the Green Parties. But the (   )⁶⁰ also has a great interest (   )⁶¹ science,
29. particularly astronomy, as is (   )⁶² by the large audiences for (   )⁶³ series
30. such as The Sky at Night and for (   )⁶⁴ fiction.
31. What can be done (   )⁶⁵ harness this interest and give (   )⁶⁶ public

32. the scientific background it ( )^{67} to make informed decisions on ( )^{68}
33. like acid rain, the greenhouse ( )^{69}, nuclear weapons, and genetic engineering?
34. ( )^{70}, the basis must lie in ( )^{71} is taught in schools. But ( )^{72} schools
35. science is often presented ( )^{73} a dry and uninteresting manner. ( )^{74} learn it
36. by rote to ( )^{75} examinations, and they don't see its ( )^{76} to the world
37. around them. ( )^{77}, science is often taught in ( )^{78} of equations.
38. Although equations are ( )^{79} brief and accurate way of ( )^{80} mathematical ideas,
39. they frighten most ( )^{81}. When I wrote a popular ( )^{82} recently,
40. I was advised that ( )^{83} equation I included would halve ( )^{84} sales.
41. I included one equation, Einstein's ( )^{85} equation, E=mc2.
42. Maybe I would have ( )^{86} twice as many copies without ( )^{87}.

(7) MET-C (大学版)：解答

01. Whether we like it or (not)^{1}, the world we live in (has)^{2} changed a great deal in (the)^{3}
02. last hundred years, and it (is)^{4} likely to change even more (in)^{5} the next hundred.
03. Some people (would)^{6} like to stop these changes (and)^{7} go back to what they (see)^{8}
04. as a purer and simpler (age)^{9}. But as history shows, the (past)^{10} was not that wonderful.
05. It (was)^{11} not so bad for a (privileged)^{12} minority, though even they had (to)^{13} do
06. without modern medicine, and (childbirth)^{14} was highly risky for women.
07. (But)^{15} for the vast majority of (the)^{16} population, life was nasty, brutish, (and)^{17} short.
08. Anyway, even if one (wanted)^{18} to, one couldn't put the clock (back)^{19} to an earlier age.
09. Knowledge (and)^{20} techniques can't just be forgotten. Nor (can)^{21} one prevent
10. further advances in (the)^{22} future. Even if all government (money)^{23}

11. for research were cut off ((and)^{24} the present government is doing (its)^{25} best),
12. the force of competition (would)^{26} still bring about advances in (technology)^{27}.
13. Moreover, one cannot stop inquiring (minds)^{28} from thinking about basic science, (whether)^{29} or
14. not they are paid (for)^{30} it. The only way to (prevent)^{31} further developments would be
15. a (global)^{32} state that suppressed anything new, (and)^{33} human initiative and inventiveness are
16. (such)^{34} that even this wouldn't succeed. All (it)^{35} would do is slow down
17. (the)^{36} rate of change. If we (accept)^{37} that we cannot prevent science (and)^{38} technology
18. from changing our world, (we)^{39} can at least try to (ensure)^{40} that the changes
19. they make (are)^{41} in the right directions. In (a)^{42} democratic society, this means that
20. (the)^{43} public needs to have a (basic)^{44} understanding of science, so that
21. (it)^{45} can make informed decisions and (not)^{46} leave them in the hands (of)^{47} experts.
22. At the moment, the (public)^{48} is in two minds about (science)^{49}. It has come to expect
23. (the)^{50} steady increase in the standard (of)^{51} living that new developments in (science)^{52}
24. and technology have brought to (continue)^{53}, but it also distrusts science
25. (because)^{54} it doesn't understand it. This distrust (is)^{55} evident
26. in the cartoon figure (of)^{56} the mad scientist working in (his)^{57} laboratory
27. to produce a Frankenstein. (It)^{58} is also an important element (behind)^{59} support
28. for the Green Parties. But the (public)^{60} also has a great interest (in)^{61} science,
29. particularly astronomy, as is (shown)^{62} by the large audiences for (television)^{63} series
30. such as The Sky at Night and for (science)^{64} fiction.
31. What can be done (to)^{65} harness this interest and give (the)^{66} public
32. the scientific background it (needs)^{67} to make informed decisions on (subjects)^{68}
33. like acid rain, the greenhouse (effect)^{69}, nuclear weapons, and genetic engineering?

34. (Clearly)[70], the basis must lie in (what)[71] is taught in schools. But (in)[72] schools
35. science is often presented (in)[73] a dry and uninteresting manner. (Children)[74] learn it
36. by rote to (pass)[75] examinations, and they don't see its (relevance)[76] to the world
37. around them. (Moreover)[77], science is often taught in (terms)[78] of equations.
38. Although equations are (a)[79] brief and accurate way of (describing)[80] mathematical ideas,
39. they frighten most (people)[81]. When I wrote a popular (book)[82] recently,
40. I was advised that (each)[83] equation I included would halve (the)[84] sales.
41. I included one equation, Einstein's (famous)[85] equation, $E = mc^2$.
42. Maybe I would have (sold)[86] twice as many copies without (it)[87].

以下に，これらの中国版 MET を利用した調査の結果を提示する．9.1 節で，中国における中学生に実施した調査結果を報告し，9.2 節で，中国における高校生に実施した調査結果を報告し，9.3 節で，中国における大学生に実施した調査結果を報告する．

9.1　中学生

Ma (in progress) は，2017 年 9 月に，中国江蘇州省の中学 2 年生 147 名に jMET-C と牧グループが作成した jMET (C) を実施した．この 147 名の中学生は，4 月に 2 学期の中間テストを受けていた．この中間テストは，読解問題（100 点）と聴解問題（20 点）からなり，満点は，120 点である．実施時間は，120 分である．

Ma (in progress) の調査結果は，(8) と (9) に示される．

(8)　jMET-C の得点と中間テストの得点との相関
　　$n = 147$
　　$r = .89$
　　$p < .001$

(9) jMET（C）の得点と中間テストの得点との相関
$n = 147$
$r = .83$
$p < .001$

この結果，jMET-C と jMET（C）の得点と中間テスト得点との間に，強い相関（$.7 < r$）があることが明らかになった．実際，jMET-C 得点と中間テスト得点との間の相関係数は，$r = .89$ であるので，両者には，ほぼ，極めて強い相関（$.9 < r$）があると言える．したがって，中国の中学生向けに作成された教科書を基に作成された jMET-C は，本調査における中学 2 年の中間テストによって測定される英語能力を適確に予測できることが分かった．同時に，相関係数において劣るものの，牧グループによって作成された jMET（C）も，本調査における中学 2 年の中間テストによって測定される英語能力を適確に予測できることが分かった．

Ma（in progress）は，VassarStats: Web Site for Statistical Computation による Fisher r-to-z 変換を使用し，各相関係数間に，統計的有意な差があるかどうか調査した．その結果，(10) に示すように，jMET-C 得点と中間テスト得点の相関係数と jMET（C）得点と中間テスト得点の相関係数の間に，統計的有意な差があった．

(10) jMET-C 得点と中間テスト得点の相関係数と jMET（C）得点と中間テスト得点の相関係数間の差の有意性

	jMET-C	jMET（C）
相関係数 r	.89	.83
被験者数 n	147	147
z 値		1.98
p 値（片側）		.02

このことから，jMET-C の中間テストによって測定される英語能力を予測する能力のほうが，jMET（C）の中間テストによって測定される英語能力を予測する能力よりも，高いことが明らかになった．したがって，Ma（in progress）の当初の目論見，すなわち，中国人英語学習者の英語能力をより正確に測定できる新たな中国版 MET を開発するという計画は，中学生版 MET において成

功したと言える．

9.2 高校生

Ma（in progress）は，2017 年 9 月に，中国江蘇州省の高校 3 年生 168 名に jMET-C，hMET-C，そして，牧グループによる jMET（C）を実施した．この 168 名の高校生は，4 月に 2 学期の中間テストを受けていた．この中間テスト は，読解問題（100 点）と聴解問題（20 点）からなり，満点は，120 点である．実施時間は，120 分である．

Ma（in progress）の調査結果は，(11)–(13) に示される．

(11) jMET-C の得点と中間テストの得点との相関
$n = 168$
$r = .85$
$p < .001$

(12) hMET-C の得点と中間テストの得点との相関
$n = 168$
$r = .85$
$p < .001$

(13) jMET（C）の得点と中間テストの得点との相関
$n = 168$
$r = .78$
$p < .001$

この結果，jMET-C，hMET-C，そして，jMET（C）の得点と中間テスト得点 との間に，強い相関（$.7 < r$）があることが明らかになった．したがって，中 国の中学生向けに，また，中国の高校生向けに作成された教科書を基に作成さ れた jMET-C と hMET-C は，本調査における高校 3 年の中間テストによって 測定される英語能力を適確に予測できることが分かった．同時に，相関係数に おいて劣るものの，牧グループによって作成された jMET（C）も，本調査に おける高校 3 年の中間テストによって測定される英語能力を適確に予測でき ることが分かった．

Ma（in progress）は，VassarStats: Web Site for Statistical Computation による Fisher *r*-to-*z* 変換を使用し，各相関係数間に，統計的有意な差があるかどうか調査した．その結果，（14）に示すように，jMET-C 得点/hMET-C 得点と中間テスト得点の相関係数と jMET（C）得点と中間テスト得点の相関係数の間に，統計的有意な差があった．

(14) jMET-C 得点/hMET-C 得点と中間テスト得点の相関係数と jMET（C）得点と中間テスト得点の相関係数間の差の有意性

	jMET-C/hMET-C	jMET（C）
相関係数 *r*	.85	.78
被験者数 *n*	168	168
z 値		1.91
p 値（片側）		.03

このことから，jMET-C/hMET-C の中間テストによって測定される英語能力を予測する能力のほうが，jMET（C）の中間テストによって測定される英語能力を予測する能力よりも，高いことが明らかになった．したがって，Ma（in progress）の当初の目論見，すなわち，中国人英語学習者の英語能力をより正確に測定できる新たな中国版 MET を開発するという計画は，高校生版 MET においても，成功したと言える．

9.3 大学生

Ma（in progress）は，2017 年 9 月に，中国江蘇州省の大学 2 年生 126 名に jMET-C，hMET-C，そして，MET-C を実施した．彼らの専門は，旅行とメディアである．時間的な制約があり，牧グループによる日本人大学生向け MET（MET 6）は，実施することができなかった．この 126 名の大学生は，2016 年 6 月に大学入試英語を受けていた．また，2016 年 12 月に，その大部分の学生が，大学英語考試 4 級（College English Test Band 4 = CET 4）を受けていた．大学入試英語の得点は読解問題（100 点）と聴解問題（20 点）からなり，満点は，120 点で，実施時間は，120 分である．CET 4 は日本の英検 2 級とほぼ同じレベルで，聴解（35％），読解（35％），総合（内容と文法知識を同時に問う問題）（10％）と作文・翻訳（20％）からなり，満点は 710 点であ

る．合格得点は設けられていないが，425点（60％）以上であるとされている．試験の時間は130分で，年に二回，6月と12月に実施される．

　Ma（in progress）の調査結果は，(15)-(20) に示される．以下では，大学入試英語と CET 4 の得点と，3つのバージョンの MET の得点との相関を提示する．その際，大学入試英語と3つのバージョンの MET をすべて受けた学生は，126名中80名，CET 4 と4つのバージョンの MET をすべて受けた学生は，126名中80名であったが，この2グループの80名は，完全同一被験者ではない．

(15) MET-C の得点と大学入試英語の得点との相関
$n = 80$
$r = .53$
$p < .001$

(16) hMET-C の得点と大学入試英語の得点との相関
$n = 80$
$r = .48$
$p < .001$

(17) jMET-C の得点と大学入試英語の得点との相関
$n = 80$
$r = .49$
$p < .001$

(18) MET-C の得点と CET 4 の得点との相関
$n = 80$
$r = .53$
$p < .001$

(19) hMET-C の得点と CET 4 の得点との相関
$n = 80$
$r = .43$
$p < .001$

(20) jMET-C の得点と CET 4 の得点との相関
$n = 80$
$r = .53$
$p < .001$

この結果，jMET-C，hMET-C，そして，MET-C の得点と中国における大学入試英語の得点との間に，相関（$.4 < r < .7$）があることが明らかになった．さらに，jMET-C，hMET-C，そして，MET-C の得点と CET 4 の得点との間にも，相関（$.4 < r < .7$）があることが明らかになった．したがって，中国の大学生向けに作成された教科書を基に作成された MET-C は，大学入試英語と CET 4 によって測定される英語能力をある程度適確に予測できることが分かった．

ただし，大学生の実験において得られた相関係数が，中学生・高校生の実験において得られた相関係数よりも低く，強い相関が見られないことに注意する必要がある．これについては，日本においても，同様の状況が見られる．したがって，どの国においても，大学生の英語能力を測定する簡易型英語テストは，まだ知られていない要因を明らかにしつつ，慎重に作成されなければならいことが，本調査で，さらに明確になった．

第 10 章

MET：実際の問題と解答

　本章では，実際にこれまで調査に使用されてきた MET の問題と解答を提示する．10.1 節では，Kawana and Walker（2002）に基づいたオリジナルの成美堂版（4 文字以下版）を 10 題提示し，10.2 節では，それの修正版である成美堂版（6 単語目ごと版）を 10 題提示し，最後に，10.3 節では，センター試験英語聴解問題に基づいたセンター試験版を 10 題提示する．成美堂版（4 文字以下版／6 単語目ごと版）の作成には，長谷部めぐみ氏が，また，センター試験版の作成には，呉姝静氏（MET CT 2017），森井那奈美氏，(MET CT 2016/MET CT 2015)，徐子崴氏（MET CT 2014），呉文亮氏（MET CT 2013/MET CT 2012），劉怡氏（MET CT 2011/MET CT 2010）が貢献している．添付の CD には，20 トラック入っている．最初の 10 トラックは，Kawana and Walker（2002）より，また，最後の 10 トラックは，センター試験英語聴解問題 2017-2008 に基づいている．

　ただし，複写して実際に利用していただくために，一部，一行に入る語数において，オリジナルとは，微妙に異なっているものもあるが，テストの本質には，影響を与えない．

　その利用方法は，いろいろ考えられるが，まず第一に，第二言語習得における調査の基礎データとして，被験者の英語能力の測定をすることが挙げられる．第二に，自分が担当する学生の英語能力を伸ばすために，同じタイプの MET を 10 回与え，11 回目に，再度，一番初めに与えた MET を実施することが挙げられる．そして，第三に，小学校で英語教育に携わる方であれば，こ

れらの MET の形式を基盤として，小学校版の MET (eMET) の作成を工夫してみることが挙げられる．

いずれにせよ，どのような使い方であっても，MET がさまざまな段階の英語教育と第二言語習得調査に，効果的な形で寄与することを願っている．

10.1 成美堂版（4文字以下版）
CD Track 01

MET 01 問題：4 文字以下

CD を聞きながら，空いている（　）の中に，4 文字以下（最大で 4 文字）の英単語を入れて下さい．

01. The majority of people have at least one pet at (　)^1 time in their (　)^2.
02. Sometimes the relationship between a pet (　)^3 or cat and its owner is (　)^4 close
03. that (　)^5 begin to resemble (　)^6 other in their appearance and behavior.
04. On the other (　)^7, owners of unusual pets (　)^8 as tigers or snakes
05. sometimes (　)^9 to protect themselves (　)^{10} their own pets.
06. Thirty years (　)^{11} the idea of an inanimate (　)^{12} first arose.
07. This was the pet (　)^{13}, which became a craze (　)^{14} the United States and
08. spread (　)^{15} other countries as (　)^{16}.
09. People (　)^{17} large sums of money for ordinary rocks and assigned (　)^{18} names.
10. They tied a leash around the rock and pulled (　)^{19} down the street just (　)^{20} a dog.
11. The rock owners (　)^{21} talked (　)^{22} their pet rocks.
12. Now (　)^{23} we have entered the computer age, (　)^{24} have virtual pets.
13. The Japanese Tamagotchi — (　)^{25} imaginary chicken (　)^{26} —
14. (　)^{27} the precursor of (　)^{28} virtual pets.
15. Now there (　)^{29} an ever-increasing number of such virtual (　)^{30}
16. which mostly young people are adopting (　)^{31} their (　)^{32}.
17. And (　)^{33} your virtual pet (　)^{34},
18. you (　)^{35} reserve a permanent resting place (　)^{36} the Internet in a virtual pet cemetery.

第 10 章　MET：実際の問題と解答

19. Sports are big business. Whereas Babe Ruth, the ( )³⁷ famous athlete of ( )³⁸ day,
20. was well-known ( )³⁹ earning as ( )⁴⁰ as the President of the United States, the average
21. salary ( )⁴¹ today's professional baseball players is ( )⁴² times that of the President.
22. ( )⁴³ a handful of sports superstars earn 100 times ( )⁴⁴ through their contracts
23. ( )⁴⁵ manufacturers of clothing, ( )⁴⁶, and sports equipment.
24. But every generation produces ( )⁴⁷ or two legendary athletes ( )⁴⁸ rewrite
25. the record books, and whose ability and achievements ( )⁴⁹ remembered ( )⁵⁰
26. generations. ( )⁵¹ the current generation Tiger Woods and Michael Jordan are two ( )⁵²
27. legendary figures, ( )⁵³ of whom ( )⁵⁴ achieved almost mythical status.
28. The ( )⁵⁵ that a large number of professional athletes ( )⁵⁶ huge incomes
29. has ( )⁵⁷ to increased competition throughout ( )⁵⁸ sports world.
30. Parents ( )⁵⁹ their children to sports training camps ( )⁶⁰ an early age.
31. Such ( )⁶¹ typically practice three to ( )⁶² hours a day,
32. ( )⁶³ weekend ( )⁶⁴ during their school vacations
33. in order ( )⁶⁵ better their chances of eventually obtaining ( )⁶⁶ well-paid position
34. on a professional ( )⁶⁷ when they grow ( )⁶⁸.
35. As for the ( )⁶⁹ young aspirants who do ( )⁷⁰ succeed,
36. one wonders if they ( )⁷¹ regret having ( )⁷² their childhood.

CD Track 02

MET 02 問題：4 文字以下

CD を聞きながら，空いている（　　）の中に，4 文字以下（最大で 4 文字）の英単語を入れて下さい．

01. Many people (   )¹ experienced the (   )² of standing on a
02. moving (   )³ and watching a group (   )⁴ dolphins swim alongside.
03. Dolphins are (   )⁵ only playful animals (   )⁶ they are also highly
04. intelligent. They (   )⁷ mammals that can be found in (   )⁸ of
05. the world's oceans (   )⁹ well as (   )¹⁰ fresh water.
06. Dolphins (   )¹¹ swim at speeds of (   )¹² to
07. 56 k.p.h., and (   )¹³ can dive (   )¹⁴ depths of 200 meters
08. and (   )¹⁵ under water (   )¹⁶ 5-8 minutes without resurfacing
09. for (   )¹⁷. They are well-known for (   )¹⁸ unique
10. clicking sound they (   )¹⁹ like sonar to locate (   )²⁰ as
11. well (   )²¹ obstacles. Every dolphin (   )²² has
12. its (   )²³ individual whistling sound (   )²⁴ for communication.
13. (   )²⁵ dolphins sleep, they sleep in (   )²⁶ semi-alert
14. state (   )²⁷ resting one side of their brain (   )²⁸ a time.
15. They (   )²⁹ help sick or injured dolphins as (   )³⁰ as
16. they can, and they (   )³¹ as a team (   )³² there is danger.
17. It (   )³³ because of these (   )³⁴ other human-like
18. qualities (   )³⁵ people have a special feeling (   )³⁶ dolphins.

19. Everybody seems to (   )³⁷ or be interested (   )³⁸ the ostrich.
20. This (   )³⁹ be because it is unique (   )⁴⁰ appearance and
21. character. The ostrich is a (   )⁴¹, but it cannot (   )⁴².
22. It (   )⁴³ the tallest and heaviest bird in (   )⁴⁴ world,
23. and (   )⁴⁵ it is the fastest two-legged creature (   )⁴⁶ Earth,
24. (   )⁴⁷ the ability to reach a speed (   )⁴⁸ 70 k.p.h.
25. Ostriches (   )⁴⁹ been successfully domesticated and are (   )⁵⁰
26. farmed throughout the world (   )⁵¹ meat, feathers (   )⁵² leather.
27. Ostrich (   )⁵³, although red, (   )⁵⁴ fewer calories and less
28. cholesterol (   )⁵⁵ chicken (   )⁵⁶ turkey meat.
29. There (   )⁵⁷ several myths about ostriches. Perhaps the (   )⁵⁸
30. enduring myth about (   )⁵⁹ ostrich is (   )⁶⁰ it hides
31. its (   )⁶¹ in the sand (   )⁶² in danger.
32. Although (   )⁶³ can read (   )⁶⁴ myth in stories
33. written (   )⁶⁵ ancient Romans 2000 years (   )⁶⁶, it is not at
34. all (   )⁶⁷. But people continue to believe this (   )⁶⁸ and
35. think (   )⁶⁹ the ostrich is (   )⁷⁰ stupid animal. Maybe people
36. think this (   )⁷¹ because ostriches' eyes are larger (   )⁷² their brains.

CD Track 03

MET 03 問題：4 文字以下

CD を聞きながら，空いている（　）の中に，4 文字以下（最大で4 文字）の英単語を入れて下さい．

01. Levi Straus (　)¹ a German immigrant (　)² arrived in San Francisco
02. in 1853. (　)³ was the (　)⁴ of the California Gold Rush.
03. He planned to (　)⁵ a business similar (　)⁶ the clothing
04. business owned (　)⁷ his brothers (　)⁸ New York. Levi
05. built (　)⁹ a very successful business (　)¹⁰ San Francisco over the
06. (　)¹¹ 20 years. In 1873, (　)¹² and a tailor named Jacob Davis
07. patented (　)¹³ process of putting rivets in pants (　)¹⁴ strength,
08. and Levi's jeans (　)¹⁵ we know (　)¹⁶ today were born.
09. (　)¹⁷ the beginning, jeans (　)¹⁸ popular.
10. Working people, (　)¹⁹ usually worked (　)²⁰ outside, were
11. especially happy (　)²¹ the strength (　)²² jeans.
12. (　)²³ the next 29 years, the Levi Strauss jeans business (　)²⁴ into
13. a (　)²⁵ successful and very (　)²⁶ company.
14. When Levi Strauss (　)²⁷ in 1902, his (　)²⁸ nephews
15. inherited (　)²⁹ successful company. Since Levi Strauss' death jeans (　)³⁰ gone
16. from (　)³¹ clothes to (　)³² fashion.
17. Today it seems (　)³³ almost everybody (　)³⁴ at least
18. one (　)³⁵ of jeans. In (　)³⁶, some young people wear only jeans.
19. The average citizen (　)³⁷ the United States has (　)³⁸ little personal
20. contact (　)³⁹ the police. Contacts (　)⁴⁰ frequently occur
21. in (　)⁴¹ contexts: Americans sometimes approach a policeman to (　)⁴² street
22. directions; and police sometimes (　)⁴³ a motorist (　)⁴⁴ speeding or
23. (　)⁴⁵ other traffic violation. Neither (　)⁴⁶ these
24. situations (　)⁴⁷ usually violent (　)⁴⁸ life-threatening.
25. However, the (　)⁴⁹ of a policeman in a large American (　)⁵⁰
26. can be (　)⁵¹ violent and life-threatening almost (　)⁵² a daily basis.
27. This is especially (　)⁵³ for police assigned (　)⁵⁴ patrol the poorest sections
28. of the city where (　)⁵⁵ violent crimes take place. (　)⁵⁶ police routinely

29. come in contact with ( )⁵⁷ dealers, armed robbers, muggers and the ( )⁵⁸.
30. If a policeman is exposed ( )⁵⁹ too long a period of ( )⁶⁰ to these types
31. of people ( )⁶¹ the lowest level of society, they run the ( )⁶² of
32. being injured or ( )⁶³ developing a prejudice against ( )⁶⁴ the residents of
33. the ( )⁶⁵ districts of the city. For ( )⁶⁶ reason, the police chief
34. regularly changes policemen's assignments ( )⁶⁷ that they ( )⁶⁸ escape from
35. the tension ( )⁶⁹ danger of patrols ( )⁷⁰ the ghetto. These other
36. assignments might ( )⁷¹ deskwork ( )⁷² controlling traffic.

CD Track 04

MET 04 問題：4文字以下

CD を聞きながら，空いている（　　）の中に，4文字以下（最大で4文字）の英単語を入れて下さい．

01. Extreme sports are ( )¹ a billion-dollar-a-year business throughout ( )² world.
02. The credit ( )³ popularizing such sports ( )⁴ usually
03. given ( )⁵ A. J. Hackett, the New Zealander ( )⁶ developed bungee jumping.
04. ( )⁷ 1986 Hackett ( )⁸ a video of some young
05. English thrill seekers doing ( )⁹ couple of jumps ( )¹⁰ England
06. in the ( )¹¹ seventies. The video caught ( )¹²
07. imagination, and ( )¹³ and his friend ( )¹⁴ about
08. developing a ( )¹⁵, standardized method ( )¹⁶ jumping
09. from bridges in New Zealand. ( )¹⁷ 1990 Hackett ( )¹⁸ established
10. bungee jumping ( )¹⁹ the world's first extreme sport ( )²⁰ ordinary people.
11. There ( )²¹ always ( )²² a select group
12. ( )²³ people in the world ( )²⁴ enjoy
13. flirting ( )²⁵ danger and ( )²⁶ death.
14. But in the ( )²⁷ decade, extreme sports ( )²⁸ gained
15. ( )²⁹ appeal. Hobbies such ( )³⁰ in-line skating, windsurfing and

第 10 章　MET：実際の問題と解答　　　　　　　　　　　153

16. skateboarding now ( )³¹ extreme versions and ( )³² world
17. competitions, ( )³³ which participants ( )³⁴ to defy
18. gravity ( )³⁵ doing somersaults, twists ( )³⁶ spins.
19. Special delivery mail is ( )³⁷ delivered especially ( )³⁸.
20. Although ( )³⁹ America the concept has ( )⁴⁰ changed over the years,
21. the methods ( )⁴¹. The most interesting ( )⁴² innovative
22. method ( )⁴³ special delivery mail ( )⁴⁴ probably the pony express.
23. The ( )⁴⁵ express consisted of a series of ( )⁴⁶ stations located
24. equidistant ( )⁴⁷ each other stretching ( )⁴⁸ St. Louis, Missouri, westward.
25. Expert horsemen, usually adventurous ( )⁴⁹ young, ( )⁵⁰ their
26. horses ( )⁵¹ breakneck speed between the stations. ( )⁵² arriving
27. at ( )⁵³ station, ( )⁵⁴ rider would transfer
28. his ( )⁵⁵ of special delivery mail ( )⁵⁶ a fresh horse and
29. start ( )⁵⁷ for a ( )⁵⁸ station. Riders became
30. tired quickly, ( )⁵⁹ they would ( )⁶⁰ replaced
31. ( )⁶¹ a well-rested rider after about three hours ( )⁶² riding.
32. Not ( )⁶³ was the pony express ( )⁶⁴, but
33. it ( )⁶⁵ captured the imagination ( )⁶⁶ the American public.
34. Unfortunately, the ( )⁶⁷ express had a short ( )⁶⁸,
35. for ( )⁶⁹ introduction ( )⁷⁰ the telegraph
36. ( )⁷¹ the 1860's led to ( )⁷² sudden decline.

CD Track 05

MET 05 問題：4 文字以下

CD を聞きながら，空いている (　　) の中に，4 文字以下（最大で 4 文字）の英単語を入れて下さい．

01. Not so long ago the ( )¹ "women's work" referred to ( )² traditionally
02. performed ( )³ by women—cooking, cleaning, caring ( )⁴ children and
03. ( )⁵ elderly—which basically served the needs ( )⁶ others.
04. Women ( )⁷ the working world ( )⁸ usually restricted to jobs
05. such ( )⁹ office and sales clerks, nurses, teachers, waitresses ( )¹⁰ stewardesses.
06. The 1960's ( )¹¹ the appearance in the ( )¹² of the women's liberation

07. movement ( )¹³ the birth control pill ( )¹⁴ about the
08. ( )¹⁵ time, which together dramatically altered the work scene ( )¹⁶ women.
09. The women's liberation movement fought ( )¹⁷ equal rights for women ( )¹⁸ a broad
10. front including the workplace. The Pill, ( )¹⁹ the birth control ( )²⁰ became
11. known, enabled women to ( )²¹ the birth of their children and ( )²² devote
12. enough ( )²³ before marriage and children ( )²⁴ establishing
13. ( )²⁵ career so that they could resume ( )²⁶ career after their children
14. reached school age. By the ( )²⁷ of the millennium women ( )²⁸ made
15. great progress ( )²⁹ gaining job equality ( )³⁰
16. in ( )³¹ male-dominated fields as the ( )³².
17. This ( )³³ meant better job choice, ( )³⁴ job
18. satisfaction ( )³⁵ higher pay for ( )³⁶ women.
19. The dog is man's ( )³⁷ friend, it is ( )³⁸.
20. We ( )³⁹ see from cave paintings ( )⁴⁰ early human beings
21. 20,000 years ( )⁴¹ that man and ( )⁴² have had
22. a ( )⁴³ relationship. Presumably, primitive ( )⁴⁴ was
23. attracted ( )⁴⁵ the dog's ( )⁴⁶ sense of smell
24. and hearing ( )⁴⁷ its speed—all of which ( )⁴⁸
25. useful ( )⁴⁹ protecting early man from ( )⁵⁰ dangerous animals.
26. ( )⁵¹ the millennia, man has taught ( )⁵² dogs
27. to perform ( )⁵³ functions besides guarding the ( )⁵⁴.
28. For example, sheepdogs ( )⁵⁵ famous for their ability ( )⁵⁶
29. control the movements ( )⁵⁷ a flock of hundreds ( )⁵⁸ sheep.
30. Dogs have ( )⁵⁹ used to aid disabled people ( )⁶⁰ centuries.
31. There ( )⁶¹ even a picture of a guide ( )⁶² and
32. ( )⁶³ blind owner in the ancient ( )⁶⁴ of Pompeii.
33. Nowadays, ( )⁶⁵ can be taught to ( )⁶⁶ on light switches,
34. ( )⁶⁷ refrigerator doors and activate ( )⁶⁸ telephone for their
35. disabled owners. ( )⁶⁹ the majority of people, however, dogs ( )⁷⁰
36. simply ( )⁷¹ and friends for both young and ( )⁷² members of the family.

CD Track 06

MET 06 問題：4 文字以下

CD を聞きながら，空いている（　）の中に，4 文字以下（最大で 4 文字）の英単語を入れて下さい．

01. From an American's perspective it seems (　)¹ Japanese students (　)² always
02. cramming for (　)³ kind of exam. Japanese even (　)⁴ private cram schools,
03. called *juku*, where students (　)⁵ elementary school (　)⁶
04. high school study after (　)⁷ regular school (　)⁸.
05. (　)⁹ American parents would consider a *juku* almost (　)¹⁰ child abuse.
06. They think children (　)¹¹ to play or (　)¹² some physical activity after school to provide
07. balance (　)¹³ their lives. A proverb in English (　)¹⁴,
08. "All (　)¹⁵ and no play makes Jack a (　)¹⁶ boy."
09. For both Japanese parents (　)¹⁷ their children, the (　)¹⁸ of the *juku* makes sense.
10. Because the (　)¹⁹ of the school one graduates from is much (　)²⁰ important
11. in Japan (　)²¹ in the United States, Japanese parents (　)²² great financial sacrifices
12. and (　)²³ their children to study (　)²⁴ to enter such schools.
13. The competitive atmosphere created (　)²⁵ this kind of society (　)²⁶ great pressure on
14. children (　)²⁷ study as hard as they (　)²⁸.
15. Although Americans might think (　)²⁹ overemphasis (　)³⁰ studying damages children
16. (　)³¹ physically (　)³² psychologically,
17. Japanese children often (　)³³ their parents to allow (　)³⁴
18. to attend (　)³⁵ neighborhood *juku* because their friends attend (　)³⁶.
19. Throughout history people (　)³⁷ over the world have (　)³⁸ to special places
20. where mineral-rich (　)³⁹ springs flow (　)⁴⁰ beneath the earth's surface.

21. Countries ( )⁴¹ much volcanic activity such as Japan have ( )⁴² such hot springs
22. and have established ( )⁴³ time many customs related ( )⁴⁴ taking baths
23. ( )⁴⁵ these special waters. But many other countries, especially in Europe, ( )⁴⁶ have
24. centuries-old traditions associated with visiting springs to ( )⁴⁷ certain types ( )⁴⁸
25. illnesses. One of the oldest ( )⁴⁹ places in the world ( )⁵⁰ located in present-day
26. Jordan and Israel. Actually, it is ( )⁵¹ a spring, ( )⁵² rather a sea, the Dead Sea.
27. ( )⁵³ ancient Greek philosopher Aristotle wrote about the wonders ( )⁵⁴ the Dead Sea
28. 2500 years ( )⁵⁵. It is also ( )⁵⁶ that the Egyptian
29. Queen Cleopatra ( )⁵⁷ water from the Dead Sea to ( )⁵⁸ her skin beautiful.
30. The Dead Sea, which ( )⁵⁹ a 33 percent concentration of salts ( )⁶⁰ minerals
31. (compared to ( )⁶¹ 3 percent in ocean water), is located ( )⁶² the lowest point on Earth,
32. 390 meters below ( )⁶³ level. Because of ( )⁶⁴ unique location, certain atmospheric,
33. thermal, chemical and optical characteristics ( )⁶⁵ found which occur nowhere ( )⁶⁶
34. in the world. Of course, no ( )⁶⁷ can ( )⁶⁸ in the Dead Sea, but no one can
35. drown there either. The ( )⁶⁹ concentration of ( )⁷⁰ allows a person to float on the
36. surface of the water and ( )⁷¹ a newspaper without getting it ( )⁷².

CD Track 07

MET 07 問題：4 文字以下

CD を聞きながら，空いている（　）の中に，4 文字以下（最大で 4 文字）の英単語を入れて下さい．

01. Forty years ago, Americans planning a ( )¹ trip overwhelmingly chose ( )² travel

02. by car or train, or (　)³ going overseas, by (　)⁴. Air travel was still a relatively
03. expensive (　)⁵ of transportation favored by (　)⁶ wealthy Americans.
04. These (　)⁷ air travel is an integral (　)⁸ of the lives of the large
05. majority (　)⁹ travelers in the United States. The (　)¹⁰ of
06. an air ticket has (　)¹¹ changed (　)¹² since 1960, while the average
07. American's buying power (　)¹³ increased (　)¹⁴ times.
08. Even in the (　)¹⁵ ten years, (　)¹⁶ travel
09. by Americans (　)¹⁷ increased (　)¹⁸ 37 percent.
10. Unfortunately (　)¹⁹ construction of (　)²⁰ airports and the
11. training of personnel (　)²¹ not kept pace (　)²² the
12. demand for (　)²³ flights. These shortfalls, along with (　)²⁴
13. usual, frequent occurrences of (　)²⁵ weather, have resulted (　)²⁶
14. a large number (　)²⁷ delays in (　)²⁸ departures and arrivals of airplanes
15. across the country. In (　)²⁹, delays affected 40 percent of (　)³⁰ domestic
16. flights during the past (　)³¹. These delays (　)³² contributed
17. (　)³³ increased frustration among travelers (　)³⁴ outbreaks of violent
18. behavior during flights, a (　)³⁵ phenomenon known (　)³⁶ "air rage."
19. No one can deny (　)³⁷ technology is transforming the (　)³⁸
20. we live (　)³⁹ a breathtaking rate. It is (　)⁴⁰ to believe that only
21. a (　)⁴¹ years ago the great majority of people (　)⁴² still
22. communicating (　)⁴³ letter and traditional telephones. (　)⁴⁴ e-mail
23. and (　)⁴⁵ phones are rapidly replacing the (　)⁴⁶ forms of communication.
24. And (　)⁴⁷ around the corner are robot vacuum cleaners and (　)⁴⁸ which
25. automatically (　)⁴⁹ a safe distance (　)⁵⁰ the car ahead.
26. (　)⁵¹ these technological advances (　)⁵² our lives
27. increasingly (　)⁵³ comfortable (　)⁵⁴ convenient.
28. Just (　)⁵⁵ the dishwasher, clothes washer (　)⁵⁶ dryer and microwave oven
29. made (　)⁵⁷ easier and created more leisure (　)⁵⁸ for our parents'
30. generation, (　)⁵⁹ technological advances of the future (　)⁶⁰ create
31. an (　)⁶¹ more leisurely life (　)⁶² the future generation.
32. (　)⁶³ worries some people, however, (　)⁶⁴ that the technological
33. devices which (　)⁶⁵ transforming our lives are at the (　)⁶⁶ time
34. leading to (　)⁶⁷ human interaction. (　)⁶⁸ the future people
35. will (　)⁶⁹ to be watchful to prevent technology (　)⁷⁰ diminishing
36. (　)⁷¹ personal contacts (　)⁷² our fellow human beings.

CD Track 08

MET 08 問題：4 文字以下

CD を聞きながら，空いている（　）の中に，4 文字以下（最大で4 文字）の英単語を入れて下さい．

01. The computer and the automobile, (　)¹ mainstays on modern (　)², share
02. similar pasts. The computer, which (　)³ only recently become (　)⁴ common
03. feature of (　)⁵ people's homes and offices, (　)⁶ its beginnings
04. (　)⁷ the 1830's. At that (　)⁸, the British mathematician, Charles Babbage,
05. developed (　)⁹ mechanical computer. In the (　)¹⁰ way,
06. the first (　)¹¹ of automobile (　)¹² a steam-powered vehicle
07. invented (　)¹³ 1769. The gas-powered (　)¹⁴ was not mass-produced until
08. Henry Ford's Model T (　)¹⁵ 1915, and (　)¹⁶ not become
09. (　)¹⁷ common possession (　)¹⁸ Americans until several decades later.
10. Although (　)¹⁹ the computer and the automobile (　)²⁰ a long time to
11. become integral parts (　)²¹ most people's lives, (　)²² they did,
12. (　)²³ revolutionized the whole world. Today (　)²⁴ people would rather drive
13. their (　)²⁵ to the office in the city (　)²⁶ take public transportation, even though the
14. latter (　)²⁷ be cheaper, more convenient and safer. The reason (　)²⁸ this is
15. the sense of freedom, independence (　)²⁹ privacy afforded (　)³⁰ car travel.
16. In the same (　)³¹, people will (　)³² spend a large amount of money to own
17. a computer which allows (　)³³ to communicate by e-mail instead of by (　)³⁴, and
18. which allows them (　)³⁵ obtain information (　)³⁶ the Internet instead of the library.
19. Commercial advertising, especially (　)³⁷ television, lies (　)³⁸ the heart of any
20. business undertaking these (　)³⁹. The effectiveness (　)⁴⁰ an advertising
21. campaign (　)⁴¹ a product (　)⁴² make or

第 10 章　MET：実際の問題と解答　　　　　　　　　　　　159

22. break (　　)⁴³. For (　　)⁴⁴ reason, manufacturers' advertising budgets sometimes
23. exceed their budgets (　　)⁴⁵ research (　　)⁴⁶ development.
24. The primary (　　)⁴⁷ of a television advertisement (　　)⁴⁸ to catch the
25. audience's attention. And, (　　)⁴⁹ course, the larger (　　)⁵⁰ audience the better.
26. (　　)⁵¹, business leaders are keen to (　　)⁵² advertising time during
27. especially popular television shows, (　　)⁵³ the Super Bowl, (　　)⁵⁴ final professional
28. American football contest (　　)⁵⁵ the season. Every January, American people (　　)⁵⁶
29. the tens of millions arrange their schedules (　　)⁵⁷ in advance (　　)⁵⁸ that
30. they will be (　　)⁵⁹ to be seated comfortably (　　)⁶⁰ front
31. of their TV (　　)⁶¹ on the (　　)⁶² of the Super Bowl.
32. Knowing (　　)⁶³, advertising managers (　　)⁶⁴ all year
33. producing their (　　)⁶⁵ creative, most attractive (　　)⁶⁶ most
34. persuasive commercials to (　　)⁶⁷ shown on the day (　　)⁶⁸ the Super Bowl.
35. In (　　)⁶⁹, many people say that they (　　)⁷⁰ forward to seeing
36. the TV commercials on (　　)⁷¹ day as much as the football (　　)⁷² itself.

CD Track 09

MET 09 問題：4 文字以下

CD を聞きながら，空いている (　　) の中に，4 文字以下（最大で 4 文字）の英単語を入れて下さい．

01. Life isn't (　　)¹ for disabled people, but it (　　)² improved
02. during the (　　)³ 25 years. Until recently, (　　)⁴ disabled
03. people were (　　)⁵ in hospitals and other (　　)⁶ institutions,
04. or (　　)⁷ they stayed inside their (　　)⁸ homes.
05. But (　　)⁹ things changed. (　　)¹⁰ disabled people,
06. especially those (　　)¹¹ were (　　)¹² severely
07. disabled, thought (　　)¹³ should be (　　)¹⁴
08. to (　　)¹⁵ a normal life (　　)¹⁶ other people.
09. (　　)¹⁷ they needed (　　)¹⁸. So around 1970 disabled people formed
10. organizations, explained their demands (　　)¹⁹ the public, and (　　)²⁰ pressure

11. on local institutions, (   )²¹ private and public, to help (   )²².
12. Today we (   )²³ see the (   )²⁴ results
13. of (   )²⁵ movement: specially designed toilets; ramps (   )²⁶ to
14. stairs (   )²⁷ wheelchairs; elevators (   )²⁸ subways;
15. loudspeakers (   )²⁹ crosswalks for (   )³⁰ blind;
16. special areas in concert halls (   )³¹ wheelchairs; and (   )³² more.
17. (   )³³ these conveniences for disabled people increase, (   )³⁴ should
18. the understanding (   )³⁵ acceptance (   )³⁶ the general public.
19. There is a proverb (   )³⁷ English, "Behind every great (   )³⁸, there is
20. a great woman." In the context (   )³⁹ American presidents, (   )⁴⁰ proverb
21. underlines (   )⁴¹ importance of a president's (   )⁴²
22. for (   )⁴³ success in winning election (   )⁴⁴ the nation's highest office.
23. A great (   )⁴⁵ is known and has (   )⁴⁶ written about the lives of U.S.
24. presidents, including their formative years. (   )⁴⁷ mothers of these (   )⁴⁸ since
25. World (   )⁴⁹ II might deserve (   )⁵⁰ credit than the wives for molding
26. their special characters. Almost (   )⁵¹ presidents' mothers in the modern
    (   )⁵² have
27. been strong-willed, independent women, often (   )⁵³ more (   )⁵⁴ average
28. education for their (   )⁵⁵. They raised their sons with great (   )⁵⁶ and
29. great (   )⁵⁷ and instilled in (   )⁵⁸ a feeling that they could do
30. anything (   )⁵⁹ put their minds (   )⁶⁰. Invariably they ensure that
31. their (   )⁶¹ developed a strong self-image (   )⁶² great self-confidence.
32. Former President Bill Clinton (   )⁶³ such a mother, and he (   )⁶⁴
33. married (   )⁶⁵ woman, Hillary Rodham, who (   )⁶⁶ great intelligence,
34. ambition and self-confidence. (   )⁶⁷ people predict (   )⁶⁸ someday
35. Hillary Clinton (   )⁶⁹ become the first woman (   )⁷⁰ American history
36. to (   )⁷¹ for the office of President (   )⁷² the United States.

CD Track 10

MET 10 問題：4 文字以下

CD を聞きながら，空いている (   ) の中に，4 文字以下（最大で 4 文字）の英単語を入れて下さい．

01. The human mouth (   )¹ three major functions. (   )² of them—eating
02. and breathing— (   )³ shared by members (   )⁴ the animal kingdom.

第 10 章　MET：実際の問題と解答

03. (　　)⁵ third function—speaking—is (　　)⁶ of the principal features which
04. distinguishes human beings (　　)⁷ the rest (　　)⁸ living creatures.
05. Although primitive (　　)⁹ must have (　　)¹⁰ a spoken language,
06. social scientists (　　)¹¹ no evidence of language as (　　)¹² until the
07. appearance (　　)¹³ written records (　　)¹⁴ ancient Mesopotamia and Egypt
08. 5-6000 years (　　)¹⁵. Present-day linguists can identify (　　)¹⁶ 1500
09. spoken languages, (　　)¹⁷ Mandarin Chinese being spoken by more (　　)¹⁸ three-quarters
10. of (　　)¹⁹ billion people. After Mandarin Chinese, English is the (　　)²⁰ widely spoken first
11. language, and (　　)²¹ become the language of choice (　　)²² international communication.
12. English has (　　)²³ always been the international language. (　　)²⁴ hundred years ago
13. French (　　)²⁵ the dominant language. (　　)²⁶ ancient times, Aramaic, Greek and Latin
14. (　　)²⁷ international languages (　　)²⁸ different points in time. Efforts have
15. (　　)²⁹ made throughout history (　　)³⁰ adopt a common universal language for
16. (　　)³¹ peoples of the world. The most successful such effort to (　　)³² was Esperanto
17. which was spoken (　　)³³ about 750,000 people at one (　　)³⁴ in the mid-20th century.
18. However, such universal languages always (　　)³⁵ because of the absence (　　)³⁶ a cultural foundation.
19. Hinduism, the primary religion (　　)³⁷ India, has produced a wealth of (　　)³⁸,
20. customs and rituals since (　　)³⁹ origins in prehistory. (　　)⁴⁰ of its more colorful
21. aspects (　　)⁴¹ the large number (　　)⁴² wandering beggars called *sadhus*.
22. Traditionally a *sadhu* renounces (　　)⁴³ comforts of ordinary (　　)⁴⁴ and leads
23. a life (　　)⁴⁵ a begging nomad. He travels (　　)⁴⁶ one holy
24. place to another on (　　)⁴⁷, often barefoot with hardly (　　)⁴⁸ clothes,
25. carrying a begging (　　)⁴⁹ and perhaps a walking stick. In (　　)⁵⁰ way,
26. he hopes (　　)⁵¹ escape from the evils (　　)⁵² a materialistic life.
27. Indian people believe (　　)⁵³ giving food, shelter (　　)⁵⁴
28. money (　　)⁵⁵ *sadhus* improves their chances of escaping (　　)⁵⁶ reincarnation.

29. Reincarnation ( )⁵⁷ the belief that one's ( )⁵⁸ is repeatedly
30. reborn in a different ( )⁵⁹. For Hindus, never-ending rebirth ( )⁶⁰
31. equivalent ( )⁶¹ the Christian idea of ( )⁶². Hindus believe that by
32. performing ( )⁶³ good actions (such ( )⁶⁴ giving
33. to *sadhus*), ( )⁶⁵ can enter ( )⁶⁶ Hindu heaven.
34. Some *sadhus* ( )⁶⁷ truly holy people with ( )⁶⁸ minds and hearts.
35. Others ( )⁶⁹ that they can ( )⁷⁰ through their whole life without working simply
36. ( )⁷¹ pretending to be a holy ( )⁷² and living off the kindness of others.

CD Track 01

MET 01 解答：4 文字以下

01. The majority of people have at least one pet at (some)¹ time in their (life)².
02. Sometimes the relationship between a pet (dog)³ or cat and its owner is (so)⁴ close
03. that (they)⁵ begin to resemble (each)⁶ other in their appearance and behavior.
04. On the other (hand)⁷, owners of unusual pets (such)⁸ as tigers or snakes
05. sometimes (have)⁹ to protect themselves (from)¹⁰ their own pets.
06. Thirty years (ago)¹¹ the idea of an inanimate (pet)¹² first arose.
07. This was the pet (rock)¹³, which became a craze (in)¹⁴ the United States and
08. spread (to)¹⁵ other countries as (well)¹⁶.
09. People (paid)¹⁷ large sums of money for ordinary rocks and assigned (them)¹⁸ names.
10. They tied a leash around the rock and pulled (it)¹⁹ down the street just (like)²⁰ a dog.
11. The rock owners (even)²¹ talked (to)²² their pet rocks.
12. Now (that)²³ we have entered the computer age, (we)²⁴ have virtual pets.
13. The Japanese Tamagotchi— (the)²⁵ imaginary chicken (egg)²⁶—
14. (was)²⁷ the precursor of (many)²⁸ virtual pets.
15. Now there (are)²⁹ an ever-increasing number of such virtual (pets)³⁰
16. which mostly young people are adopting (as)³¹ their (own)³².
17. And (if)³³ your virtual pet (dies)³⁴,
18. you (can)³⁵ reserve a permanent resting place (on)³⁶ the Internet in a virtual pet cemetery.

19. Sports are big business. Whereas Babe Ruth, the (most)^37 famous athlete of (his)^38 day,
20. was well-known (for)^39 earning as (much)^40 as the President of the United States,
21. the average salary (of)^41 today's professional baseball players is (ten)^42 times that of the President.
22. (And)^43 a handful of sports superstars earn 100 times (more)^44 through their contracts
23. (with)^45 manufacturers of clothing, (food)^46, and sports equipment.
24. But every generation produces (one)^47 or two legendary athletes (who)^48 rewrite
25. the record books, and whose ability and achievements (are)^49 remembered (for)^50
26. generations. (In)^51 the current generation Tiger Woods and Michael Jordan are two (such)^52
27. legendary figures, (both)^53 of whom (have)^54 achieved almost mythical status.
28. The (fact)^55 that a large number of professional athletes (earn)^56 huge incomes
29. has (led)^57 to increased competition throughout (the)^58 sports world.
30. Parents (send)^59 their children to sports training camps (at)^60 an early age.
31. Such (kids)^61 typically practice three to (four)^62 hours a day,
32. (all)^63 weekend (and)^64 during their school vacations
33. in order (to)^65 better their chances of eventually obtaining (a)^66 well-paid position
34. on a professional (team)^67 when they grow (up)^68.
35. As for the (many)^69 young aspirants who do (not)^70 succeed,
36. one wonders if they (will)^71 regret having (lost)^72 their childhood.

CD Track 02

MET 02 解答：4文字以下

01. Many people (have)^1 experienced the (joy)^2 of standing on a
02. moving (ship)^3 and watching a group (of)^4 dolphins swim alongside.
03. Dolphins are (not)^5 only playful animals (but)^6 they are also highly
04. intelligent. They (are)^7 mammals that can be found in (most)^8 of
05. the world's oceans (as)^9 well as (in)^10 fresh water.

06. Dolphins (can)[11] swim at speeds of (up)[12] to
07. 56 k.p.h., and (they)[13] can dive (to)[14] depths of 200 meters
08. and (stay)[15] under water (for)[16] 5-8 minutes without resurfacing
09. for (air)[17]. They are well-known for (the)[18] unique
10. clicking sound they (use)[19] like sonar to locate (food)[20] as
11. well (as)[21] obstacles. Every dolphin (also)[22] has
12. its (own)[23] individual whistling sound (used)[24] for communication.
13. (When)[25] dolphins sleep, they sleep in (a)[26] semi-alert
14. state (by)[27] resting one side of their brain (at)[28] a time.
15. They (will)[29] help sick or injured dolphins as (much)[30] as
16. they can, and they (act)[31] as a team (if)[32] there is danger.
17. It (is)[33] because of these (and)[34] other human-like
18. qualities (that)[35] people have a special feeling (for)[36] dolphins.
19. Everybody seems to (like)[37] or be interested (in)[38] the ostrich.
20. This (may)[39] be because it is unique (in)[40] appearance and
21. character. The ostrich is a (bird)[41], but it cannot (fly)[42].
22. It (is)[43] the tallest and heaviest bird in (the)[44] world,
23. and (yet)[45] it is the fastest two-legged creature (on)[46] Earth,
24. (with)[47] the ability to reach a speed (of)[48] 70 k.p.h.
25. Ostriches (have)[49] been successfully domesticated and are (now)[50]
26. farmed throughout the world (for)[51] meat, feathers (and)[52] leather.
27. Ostrich (meat)[53], although red, (has)[54] fewer calories and less
28. cholesterol (than)[55] chicken (or)[56] turkey meat.
29. There (are)[57] several myths about ostriches. Perhaps the (most)[58]
30. enduring myth about (the)[59] ostrich is (that)[60] it hides
31. its (head)[61] in the sand (when)[62] in danger.
32. Although (we)[63] can read (this)[64] myth in stories
33. written (by)[65] ancient Romans 2000 years (ago)[66], it is not at
34. all (true)[67]. But people continue to believe this (myth)[68] and
35. think (that)[69] the ostrich is (a)[70] stupid animal. Maybe people
36. think this (way)[71] because ostriches' eyes are larger (than)[72] their brains.

CD Track 03

MET 03 解答：4 文字以下

01. Levi Straus (was)[1] a German immigrant (who)[2] arrived in San Francisco

02. in 1853. (It)³ was the (time)⁴ of the California Gold Rush.
03. He planned to (open)⁵ a business similar (to)⁶ the clothing
04. business owned (by)⁷ his brothers (in)⁸ New York. Levi
05. built (up)⁹ a very successful business (in)¹⁰ San Francisco over the
06. (next)¹¹ 20 years. In 1873, (he)¹² and a tailor named Jacob Davis
07. patented (the)¹³ process of putting rivets in pants (for)¹⁴ strength,
08. and Levi's jeans (as)¹⁵ we know (them)¹⁶ today were born.
09. (From)¹⁷ the beginning, jeans (were)¹⁸ popular.
10. Working people, (who)¹⁹ usually worked (hard)²⁰ outside, were
11. especially happy (with)²¹ the strength (of)²² jeans.
12. (For)²³ the next 29 years, the Levi Strauss jeans business (grew)²⁴ into
13. a (very)²⁵ successful and very (big)²⁶ company.
14. When Levi Strauss (died)²⁷ in 1902, his (four)²⁸ nephews
15. inherited (his)²⁹ successful company. Since Levi Strauss' death jeans (have)³⁰ gone
16. from (work)³¹ clothes to (high)³² fashion.
17. Today it seems (that)³³ almost everybody (owns)³⁴ at least
18. one (pair)³⁵ of jeans. In (fact)³⁶, some young people wear only jeans.
19. The average citizen (in)³⁷ the United States has (very)³⁸ little personal
20. contact (with)³⁹ the police. Contacts (most)⁴⁰ frequently occur
21. in (two)⁴¹ contexts: Americans sometimes approach a policeman to (ask)⁴² street
22. directions; and police sometimes (stop)⁴³ a motorist (for)⁴⁴ speeding or
23. (some)⁴⁵ other traffic violation. Neither (of)⁴⁶ these
24. situations (is)⁴⁷ usually violent (or)⁴⁸ life-threatening.
25. However, the (life)⁴⁹ of a policeman in a large American (city)⁵⁰
26. can be (both)⁵¹ violent and life-threatening almost (on)⁵² a daily basis.
27. This is especially (true)⁵³ for police assigned (to)⁵⁴ patrol the poorest sections
28. of the city where (most)⁵⁵ violent crimes take place. (Here)⁵⁶ police routinely
29. come in contact with (drug)⁵⁷ dealers, armed robbers, muggers and the (like)⁵⁸.
30. If a policeman is exposed (for)⁵⁹ too long a period of (time)⁶⁰ to these types
31. of people (from)⁶¹ the lowest level of society, they run the (risk)⁶² of
32. being injured or (of)⁶³ developing a prejudice against (all)⁶⁴ the residents of
33. the (poor)⁶⁵ districts of the city. For (this)⁶⁶ reason, the police chief
34. regularly changes policemen's assignments (so)⁶⁷ that they (can)⁶⁸ escape from

35. the tension (and)⁶⁹ danger of patrols (in)⁷⁰ the ghetto. These other
36. assignments might (be)⁷¹ deskwork (or)⁷² controlling traffic.

CD Track 04

MET 04 解答：4 文字以下

01. Extreme sports are (now)¹ a billion-dollar-a-year business throughout (the)² world.
02. The credit (for)³ popularizing such sports (is)⁴ usually
03. given (to)⁵ A. J. Hackett, the New Zealander (who)⁶ developed bungee jumping.
04. (In)⁷ 1986 Hackett (saw)⁸ a video of some young
05. English thrill seekers doing (a)⁹ couple of jumps (in)¹⁰ England
06. in the (late)¹¹ seventies. The video caught (his)¹²
07. imagination, and (he)¹³ and his friend (set)¹⁴ about
08. developing a (safe)¹⁵, standardized method (of)¹⁶ jumping
09. from bridges in New Zealand. (By)¹⁷ 1990 Hackett (had)¹⁸ established
10. bungee jumping (as)¹⁹ the world's first extreme sport (for)²⁰ ordinary people.
11. There (has)²¹ always (been)²² a select group
12. (of)²³ people in the world (who)²⁴ enjoy
13. flirting (with)²⁵ danger and (even)²⁶ death.
14. But in the (past)²⁷ decade, extreme sports (have)²⁸ gained
15. (mass)²⁹ appeal. Hobbies such (as)³⁰ in-line skating, windsurfing and
16. skateboarding now (have)³¹ extreme versions and (also)³² world
17. competitions, (in)³³ which participants (seem)³⁴ to defy
18. gravity (by)³⁵ doing somersaults, twists (and)³⁶ spins.
19. Special delivery mail is (mail)³⁷ delivered especially (fast)³⁸.
20. Although (in)³⁹ America the concept has (not)⁴⁰ changed over the years,
21. the methods (have)⁴¹. The most interesting (and)⁴² innovative
22. method (for)⁴³ special delivery mail (was)⁴⁴ probably the pony express.
23. The (pony)⁴⁵ express consisted of a series of (way)⁴⁶ stations located
24. equidistant (from)⁴⁷ each other stretching (from)⁴⁸ St. Louis, Missouri, westward.
25. Expert horsemen, usually adventurous (and)⁴⁹ young, (rode)⁵⁰ their
26. horses (at)⁵¹ breakneck speed between the stations. (Upon)⁵² arriving

第10章 MET：実際の問題と解答

27. at (one)⁵³ station, (the)⁵⁴ rider would transfer
28. his (bag)⁵⁵ of special delivery mail (onto)⁵⁶ a fresh horse and
29. start (out)⁵⁷ for a (new)⁵⁸ station. Riders became
30. tired quickly, (so)⁵⁹ they would (be)⁶⁰ replaced
31. (by)⁶¹ a well-rested rider after about three hours (of)⁶² riding.
32. Not (only)⁶³ was the pony express (fast)⁶⁴, but
33. it (also)⁶⁵ captured the imagination (of)⁶⁶ the American public.
34. Unfortunately, the (pony)⁶⁷ express had a short (life)⁶⁸,
35. for (the)⁶⁹ introduction (of)⁷⁰ the telegraph
36. (in)⁷¹ the 1860's led to (its)⁷² sudden decline.

CD Track 05

MET 05 解答：4文字以下

01. Not so long ago the (term)¹ "women's work" referred to (work)² traditionally
02. performed (only)³ by women—cooking, cleaning, caring (for)⁴ children and
03. (the)⁵ elderly—which basically served the needs (of)⁶ others.
04. Women (in)⁷ the working world (were)⁸ usually restricted to jobs
05. such (as)⁹ office and sales clerks, nurses, teachers, waitresses (and)¹⁰ stewardesses.
06. The 1960's (saw)¹¹ the appearance in the (West)¹² of the women's liberation
07. movement (and)¹³ the birth control pill (at)¹⁴ about the
08. (same)¹⁵ time, which together dramatically altered the work scene (for)¹⁶ women.
09. The women's liberation movement fought (for)¹⁷ equal rights for women (on)¹⁸ a broad
10. front including the workplace. The Pill, (as)¹⁹ the birth control (pill)²⁰ became
11. known, enabled women to (plan)²¹ the birth of their children and (to)²² devote
12. enough (time)²³ before marriage and children (to)²⁴ establishing
13. (a)²⁵ career so that they could resume (that)²⁶ career after their children
14. reached school age. By the (end)²⁷ of the millennium women (had)²⁸ made
15. great progress (in)²⁹ gaining job equality (even)³⁰
16. in (such)³¹ male-dominated fields as the (army)³².
17. This (has)³³ meant better job choice, (more)³⁴ job
18. satisfaction (and)³⁵ higher pay for (many)³⁶ women.

19. The dog is man's (best)³⁷ friend, it is (said)³⁸.
20. We (can)³⁹ see from cave paintings (of)⁴⁰ early human beings
21. 20,000 years (ago)⁴¹ that man and (dog)⁴² have had
22. a (long)⁴³ relationship. Presumably, primitive (man)⁴⁴ was
23. attracted (to)⁴⁵ the dog's (keen)⁴⁶ sense of smell
24. and hearing (and)⁴⁷ its speed—all of which (were)⁴⁸
25. useful (in)⁴⁹ protecting early man from (more)⁵⁰ dangerous animals.
26. (Over)⁵¹ the millennia, man has taught (his)⁵² dogs
27. to perform (many)⁵³ functions besides guarding the (home)⁵⁴.
28. For example, sheepdogs (are)⁵⁵ famous for their ability (to)⁵⁶
29. control the movements (of)⁵⁷ a flock of hundreds (of)⁵⁸ sheep.
30. Dogs have (been)⁵⁹ used to aid disabled people (for)⁶⁰ centuries.
31. There (is)⁶¹ even a picture of a guide (dog)⁶² and
32. (its)⁶³ blind owner in the ancient (city)⁶⁴ of Pompeii.
33. Nowadays, (dogs)⁶⁵ can be taught to (turn)⁶⁶ on light switches,
34. (open)⁶⁷ refrigerator doors and activate (the)⁶⁸ telephone for their
35. disabled owners. (For)⁶⁹ the majority of people, however, dogs (are)⁷⁰
36. simply (pets)⁷¹ and friends for both young and (old)⁷² members of the family.

CD Track 06

MET 06 解答：4文字以下

01. From an American's perspective it seems (that)¹ Japanese students (are)² always
02. cramming for (some)³ kind of exam. Japanese even (have)⁴ private cram schools,
03. called *juku*, where students (from)⁵ elementary school (to)⁶
04. high school study after (the)⁷ regular school (day)⁸.
05. (Most)⁹ American parents would consider a *juku* almost (like)¹⁰ child abuse.
06. They think children (need)¹¹ to play or (do)¹² some physical activity after school to provide
07. balance (in)¹³ their lives. A proverb in English (says)¹⁴,
08. "All (work)¹⁵ and no play makes Jack a (dull)¹⁶ boy."
09. For both Japanese parents (and)¹⁷ their children, the (idea)¹⁸ of the *juku* makes sense.

10. Because the (name)[19] of the school one graduates from is much (more)[20] important
11. in Japan (than)[21] in the United States, Japanese parents (make)[22] great financial sacrifices
12. and (push)[23] their children to study (hard)[24] to enter such schools.
13. The competitive atmosphere created (by)[25] this kind of society (puts)[26] great pressure on
14. children (to)[27] study as hard as they (can)[28].
15. Although Americans might think (this)[29] overemphasis (on)[30] studying damages children
16. (both)[31] physically (and)[32] psychologically,
17. Japanese children often (beg)[33] their parents to allow (them)[34]
18. to attend (a)[35] neighborhood *juku* because their friends attend (it)[36].
19. Throughout history people (all)[37] over the world have (gone)[38] to special places
20. where mineral-rich (hot)[39] springs flow (from)[40] beneath the earth's surface.
21. Countries (with)[41] much volcanic activity such as Japan have (many)[42] such hot springs
22. and have established (over)[43] time many customs related (to)[44] taking baths
23. (in)[45] these special waters. But many other countries, especially in Europe, (also)[46] have
24. centuries-old traditions associated with visiting springs to (cure)[47] certain types (of)[48]
25. illnesses. One of the oldest (such)[49] places in the world (is)[50] located in present-day
26. Jordan and Israel. Actually, it is (not)[51] a spring, (but)[52] rather a sea, the Dead Sea.
27. (The)[53] ancient Greek philosopher Aristotle wrote about the wonders (of)[54] the Dead Sea
28. 2500 years (ago)[55]. It is also (said)[56] that the Egyptian
29. Queen Cleopatra (used)[57] water from the Dead Sea to (keep)[58] her skin beautiful.
30. The Dead Sea, which (has)[59] a 33 percent concentration of salts (and)[60] minerals
31. (compared to (only)[61] 3 percent in ocean water), is located (at)[62] the lowest point on Earth,

32. 390 meters below (sea)⁶³ level. Because of (this)⁶⁴ unique location, certain atmospheric,
33. thermal, chemical and optical characteristics (are)⁶⁵ found which occur nowhere (else)⁶⁶
34. in the world. Of course, no (fish)⁶⁷ can (live)⁶⁸ in the Dead Sea, but no one can
35. drown there either. The (high)⁶⁹ concentration of (salt)⁷⁰ allows a person to float on the
36. surface of the water and (read)⁷¹ a newspaper without getting it (wet)⁷².

CD Track 07

MET 07 解答：4文字以下

01. Forty years ago, Americans planning a (long)¹ trip overwhelmingly chose (to)² travel
02. by car or train, or (if)³ going overseas, by (ship)⁴. Air travel was still a relatively
03. expensive (mode)⁵ of transportation favored by (more)⁶ wealthy Americans.
04. These (days)⁷ air travel is an integral (part)⁸ of the lives of the large
05. majority (of)⁹ travelers in the United States. The (cost)¹⁰ of
06. an air ticket has (not)¹¹ changed (much)¹² since 1960, while the average
07. American's buying power (has)¹³ increased (ten)¹⁴ times.
08. Even in the (past)¹⁵ ten years, (air)¹⁶ travel
09. by Americans (has)¹⁷ increased (by)¹⁸ 37 percent.
10. Unfortunately (the)¹⁹ construction of (new)²⁰ airports and the
11. training of personnel (have)²¹ not kept pace (with)²² the
12. demand for (more)²³ flights. These shortfalls, along with (the)²⁴
13. usual, frequent occurrences of (bad)²⁵ weather, have resulted (in)²⁶
14. a large number (of)²⁷ delays in (both)²⁸ departures and arrivals of airplanes
15. across the country. In (fact)²⁹, delays affected 40 percent of (all)³⁰ domestic
16. flights during the past (year)³¹. These delays (have)³² contributed
17. (to)³³ increased frustration among travelers (and)³⁴ outbreaks of violent
18. behavior during flights, a (new)³⁵ phenomenon known (as)³⁶ "air rage."
19. No one can deny (that)³⁷ technology is transforming the (way)³⁸
20. we live (at)³⁹ a breathtaking rate. It is (hard)⁴⁰ to believe that only
21. a (few)⁴¹ years ago the great majority of people (were)⁴² still

22. communicating (by)⁴³ letter and traditional telephones. (Now)⁴⁴ e-mail
23. and (cell)⁴⁵ phones are rapidly replacing the (old)⁴⁶ forms of communication.
24. And (just)⁴⁷ around the corner are robot vacuum cleaners and (cars)⁴⁸ which
25. automatically (keep)⁴⁹ a safe distance (from)⁵⁰ the car ahead.
26. (All)⁵¹ these technological advances (make)⁵² our lives
27. increasingly (more)⁵³ comfortable (and)⁵⁴ convenient.
28. Just (as)⁵⁵ the dishwasher, clothes washer (and)⁵⁶ dryer and microwave oven
29. made (life)⁵⁷ easier and created more leisure (time)⁵⁸ for our parents'
30. generation, (the)⁵⁹ technological advances of the future (will)⁶⁰ create
31. an (even)⁶¹ more leisurely life (for)⁶² the future generation.
32. (What)⁶³ worries some people, however, (is)⁶⁴ that the technological
33. devices which (are)⁶⁵ transforming our lives are at the (same)⁶⁶ time
34. leading to (less)⁶⁷ human interaction. (In)⁶⁸ the future people
35. will (have)⁶⁹ to be watchful to prevent technology (from)⁷⁰ diminishing
36. (our)⁷¹ personal contacts (with)⁷² our fellow human beings.

CD Track 08

MET 08 解答：4 文字以下

01. The computer and the automobile, (the)¹ mainstays on modern (life)², share
02. similar pasts. The computer, which (has)³ only recently become (a)⁴ common
03. feature of (most)⁵ people's homes and offices, (had)⁶ its beginnings
04. (in)⁷ the 1830's. At that (time)⁸, the British mathematician, Charles Babbage,
05. developed (the)⁹ mechanical computer. In the (same)¹⁰ way,
06. the first (type)¹¹ of automobile (was)¹² a steam-powered vehicle
07. invented (in)¹³ 1769. The gas-powered (car)¹⁴ was not mass-produced until
08. Henry Ford's Model T (in)¹⁵ 1915, and (did)¹⁶ not become
09. (a)¹⁷ common possession (for)¹⁸ Americans until several decades later.
10. Although (both)¹⁹ the computer and the automobile (took)²⁰ a long time to
11. become integral parts (of)²¹ most people's lives, (once)²² they did,
12. (they)²³ revolutionized the whole world. Today (most)²⁴ people would rather drive

13. their (car)^{25} to the office in the city (than)^{26} take public transportation, even though the
14. latter (may)^{27} be cheaper, more convenient and safer. The reason (for)^{28} this is
15. the sense of freedom, independence (and)^{29} privacy afforded (by)^{30} car travel.
16. In the same (way)^{31}, people will (now)^{32} spend a large amount of money to own
17. a computer which allows (them)^{33} to communicate by e-mail instead of by (post)^{34}, and
18. which allows them (to)^{35} obtain information (from)^{36} the Internet instead of the library.
19. Commercial advertising, especially (for)^{37} television, lies (at)^{38} the heart of any
20. business undertaking these (days)^{39}. The effectiveness (of)^{40} an advertising
21. campaign (for)^{41} a product (can)^{42} make or
22. break (it)^{43}. For (this)^{44} reason, manufacturers' advertising budgets sometimes
23. exceed their budgets (for)^{45} research (and)^{46} development.
24. The primary (aim)^{47} of a television advertisement (is)^{48} to catch the
25. audience's attention. And, (of)^{49} course, the larger (the)^{50} audience the better.
26. (Thus)^{51}, business leaders are keen to (gain)^{52} advertising time during
27. especially popular television shows, (like)^{53} the Super Bowl, (the)^{54} final professional
28. American football contest (of)^{55} the season. Every January, American people (by)^{56}
29. the tens of millions arrange their schedules (far)^{57} in advance (so)^{58} that
30. they will be (sure)^{59} to be seated comfortably (in)^{60} front
31. of their TV (sets)^{61} on the (day)^{62} of the Super Bowl.
32. Knowing (this)^{63}, advertising managers (work)^{64} all year
33. producing their (most)^{65} creative, most attractive (and)^{66} most
34. persuasive commercials to (be)^{67} shown on the day (of)^{68} the Super Bowl.
35. In (fact)^{69}, many people say that they (look)^{70} forward to seeing
36. the TV commercials on (that)^{71} day as much as the football (game)^{72} itself.

CD Track 09

MET 09 解答：4 文字以下

01. Life isn't (easy)¹ for disabled people, but it (has)² improved
02. during the (past)³ 25 years. Until recently, (most)⁴ disabled
03. people were (kept)⁵ in hospitals and other (such)⁶ institutions,
04. or (else)⁷ they stayed inside their (own)⁸ homes.
05. But (then)⁹ things changed. (Some)¹⁰ disabled people,
06. especially those (who)¹¹ were (not)¹² severely
07. disabled, thought (they)¹³ should be (able)¹⁴
08. to (lead)¹⁵ a normal life (like)¹⁶ other people.
09. (But)¹⁷ they needed (help)¹⁸. So around 1970 disabled people formed
10. organizations, explained their demands (to)¹⁹ the public, and (put)²⁰ pressure
11. on local institutions, (both)²¹ private and public, to help (them)²².
12. Today we (can)²³ see the (many)²⁴ results
13. of (this)²⁵ movement: specially designed toilets; ramps (next)²⁶ to
14. stairs (for)²⁷ wheelchairs; elevators (in)²⁸ subways;
15. loudspeakers (at)²⁹ crosswalks for (the)³⁰ blind;
16. special areas in concert halls (for)³¹ wheelchairs; and (many)³² more.
17. (As)³³ these conveniences for disabled people increase, (so)³⁴ should
18. the understanding (and)³⁵ acceptance (of)³⁶ the general public.
19. There is a proverb (in)³⁷ English, "Behind every great (man)³⁸, there is
20. a great woman." In the context (of)³⁹ American presidents, (this)⁴⁰ proverb
21. underlines (the)⁴¹ importance of a president's (wife)⁴²
22. for (his)⁴³ success in winning election (to)⁴⁴ the nation's highest office.
23. A great (deal)⁴⁵ is known and has (been)⁴⁶ written about the lives of U.S.
24. presidents, including their formative years. (The)⁴⁷ mothers of these (men)⁴⁸ since
25. World (War)⁴⁹ II might deserve (more)⁵⁰ credit than the wives for molding
26. their special characters. Almost (all)⁵¹ presidents' mothers in the modern (era)⁵² have
27. been strong-willed, independent women, often (with)⁵³ more (than)⁵⁴ average
28. education for their (day)⁵⁵. They raised their sons with great (care)⁵⁶ and
29. great (love)⁵⁷ and instilled in (them)⁵⁸ a feeling that they could do
30. anything (they)⁵⁹ put their minds (to)⁶⁰. Invariably they ensure that
31. their (sons)⁶¹ developed a strong self-image (and)⁶² great self-confidence.
32. Former President Bill Clinton (had)⁶³ such a mother, and he (also)⁶⁴

33. married (a)⁶⁵ woman, Hillary Rodham, who (had)⁶⁶ great intelligence,
34. ambition and self-confidence. (Many)⁶⁷ people predict (that)⁶⁸ someday
35. Hillary Clinton (will)⁶⁹ become the first woman (in)⁷⁰ American history
36. to (run)⁷¹ for the office of President (of)⁷² the United States.

CD Track 10

MET 10 解答：4 文字以下

01. The human mouth (has)¹ three major functions. (Two)² of them—eating
02. and breathing—(are)³ shared by members (of)⁴ the animal kingdom.
03. (The)⁵ third function—speaking—is (one)⁶ of the principal features which
04. distinguishes human beings (from)⁷ the rest (of)⁸ living creatures.
05. Although primitive (man)⁹ must have (had)¹⁰ a spoken language,
06. social scientists (have)¹¹ no evidence of language as (such)¹² until the
07. appearance (of)¹³ written records (in)¹⁴ ancient Mesopotamia and Egypt
08. 5-6000 years (ago)¹⁵. Present-day linguists can identify (over)¹⁶ 1500
09. spoken languages, (with)¹⁷ Mandarin Chinese being spoken by more (than)¹⁸ three-quarters
10. of (a)¹⁹ billion people. After Mandarin Chinese, English is the (most)²⁰ widely spoken first
11. language, and (has)²¹ become the language of choice (in)²² international communication.
12. English has (not)²³ always been the international language. (Two)²⁴ hundred years ago
13. French (was)²⁵ the dominant language. (In)²⁶ ancient times, Aramaic, Greek and Latin
14. (were)²⁷ international languages (at)²⁸ different points in time. Efforts have
15. (been)²⁹ made throughout history (to)³⁰ adopt a common universal language for
16. (all)³¹ peoples of the world. The most successful such effort to (date)³² was Esperanto
17. which was spoken (by)³³ about 750,000 people at one (time)³⁴ in the mid-20th century.
18. However, such universal languages always (fail)³⁵ because of the absence (of)³⁶ a cultural foundation.

19. Hinduism, the primary religion (of)³⁷ India, has produced a wealth of (gods)³⁸,
20. customs and rituals since (its)³⁹ origins in prehistory. (One)⁴⁰ of its more colorful
21. aspects (is)⁴¹ the large number (of)⁴² wandering beggars called *sadhus*.
22. Traditionally a *sadhu* renounces (the)⁴³ comforts of ordinary (life)⁴⁴ and leads
23. a life (as)⁴⁵ a begging nomad. He travels (from)⁴⁶ one holy
24. place to another on (foot)⁴⁷, often barefoot with hardly (any)⁴⁸ clothes,
25. carrying a begging (bowl)⁴⁹ and perhaps a walking stick. In (this)⁵⁰ way,
26. he hopes (to)⁵¹ escape from the evils (of)⁵² a materialistic life.
27. Indian people believe (that)⁵³ giving food, shelter (or)⁵⁴
28. money (to)⁵⁵ *sadhus* improves their chances of escaping (from)⁵⁶ reincarnation.
29. Reincarnation (is)⁵⁷ the belief that one's (soul)⁵⁸ is repeatedly
30. reborn in a different (body)⁵⁹. For Hindus, never-ending rebirth (is)⁶⁰
31. equivalent (to)⁶¹ the Christian idea of (hell)⁶². Hindus believe that by
32. performing (many)⁶³ good actions (such (as)⁶⁴ giving
33. to *sadhus*), (they)⁶⁵ can enter (the)⁶⁶ Hindu heaven.
34. Some *sadhus* (are)⁶⁷ truly holy people with (pure)⁶⁸ minds and hearts.
35. Others (know)⁶⁹ that they can (go)⁷⁰ through their whole life without working simply
36. (by)⁷¹ pretending to be a holy (man)⁷² and living off the kindness of others.

10.2　成美堂版（6単語目ごと版）

CD Track 01

MET 01 問題：6単語目ごと

01. The majority of people have (　　)¹ least one pet at some (　　)² in their life.
02. Sometimes the (　　)³ between a pet dog or (　　)⁴ and its owner
03. is so (　　)⁵ that they begin to resemble (　　)⁶ other in their appearance
04. and (　　)⁷. On the other hand, owners (　　)⁸ unusual pets
05. such as tigers (　　)⁹ snakes sometimes have to protect (　　)¹⁰ from their own pets.
06. Thirty (　　)¹¹ ago the idea of an (　　)¹² pet first arose.

07. This was ( )¹³ pet rock, which became a ( )¹⁴ in the United States
08. and ( )¹⁵ to other countries as well. ( )¹⁶ paid large sums of money
09. ( )¹⁷ ordinary rocks and assigned them ( )¹⁸.
10. They tied a leash around ( )¹⁹ rock and pulled it down ( )²⁰ street just like a dog.
11. ( )²¹ rock owners even talked to ( )²² pet rocks.
12. Now that we ( )²³ entered the computer age, we ( )²⁴ virtual pets.
13. The Japanese *Tamagotchi*—the ( )²⁵ chicken egg—
14. was the precursor ( )²⁶ many virtual pets.
15. Now there ( )²⁷ an ever-increasing number of such ( )²⁸ pets
16. which mostly young people ( )²⁹ adopting as their own.
17. And ( )³⁰ your virtual pet dies, you ( )³¹ reserve a permanent resting place
18. ( )³² the Internet in a virtual ( )³³ cemetery.
19. Sports are big business. ( )³⁴ Babe Ruth, the most famous athlete of ( )³⁵ day,
20. was well-known for earning ( )³⁶ much as the President of ( )³⁷ United States,
21. the average salary ( )³⁸ today's professional baseball players
22. is ( )³⁹ times that of the President. ( )⁴⁰ a handful of sports superstars
23. ( )⁴¹ one hundred times more through ( )⁴² contracts with manufacturers
24. of clothing, ( )⁴³, and sports equipment. But every ( )⁴⁴ produces
25. one or two legendary ( )⁴⁵ who rewrite the record books,
26. ( )⁴⁶ whose ability and achievements are ( )⁴⁷ for generations.
27. In the current ( )⁴⁸ Tiger Woods and Michael Jordan are two such legendary ( )⁴⁹,
28. both of whom have achieved ( )⁵⁰ mythical status.
29. The fact that ( )⁵¹ large number of professional athletes ( )⁵² huge incomes
30. has led to ( )⁵³ competition throughout the sports world.
31. ( )⁵⁴ send their children to sports ( )⁵⁵ camps at an early age.
32. ( )⁵⁶ kids typically practice three to ( )⁵⁷ hours a day,
33. all weekend ( )⁵⁸ during their school vacations in ( )⁵⁹ to better their chances
34. of ( )⁶⁰ obtaining a well-paid position on ( )⁶¹ professional team
35. when they grow ( )⁶². As for the many young ( )⁶³ who do not succeed,
36. one ( )⁶⁴ if they will regret having ( )⁶⁵ their childhood.

第 10 章　MET：実際の問題と解答

CD Track 02

MET 02 問題：6 単語目ごと

01. Many people have experienced the (　　)¹ of standing on a
02. moving (　　)² and watching a group of (　　)³ swim alongside.
03. Dolphins are not (　　)⁴ playful animals but they are (　　)⁵ highly
04. intelligent. They are mammals (　　)⁶ can be found in most (　　)⁷
05. the world's oceans as well as (　　)⁸ fresh water.
06. Dolphins can swim (　　)⁹ speeds of up to
07. 56 k.p.h., and (　　)¹⁰ can dive to depths of 200 (　　)¹¹
08. and stay under water for 5-8 (　　)¹² without resurfacing
09. for air. They (　　)¹³ well-known for the unique
10. clicking sound (　　)¹⁴ use like sonar to locate (　　)¹⁵ as
11. well as obstacles. Every (　　)¹⁶ also has
12. its own individual (　　)¹⁷ sound used for communication.
13. When (　　)¹⁸ sleep, they sleep in a semi-alert
14. (　　)¹⁹ by resting one side of (　　)²⁰ brain at a time.
15. They (　　)²¹ help sick or injured dolphins (　　)²² much as
16. they can, and (　　)²³ act as a team if (　　)²⁴ is danger.
17. It is because (　　)²⁵ these and other human-like
18. qualities that (　　)²⁶ have a special feeling for (　　)²⁷.
19. Everybody seems to like or (　　)²⁸ interested in the ostrich.
20. This (　　)²⁹ be because it is unique (　　)³⁰ appearance and
21. character. The ostrich (　　)³¹ a bird, but it cannot (　　)³².
22. It is the tallest and (　　)³³ bird in the world,
23. and (　　)³⁴ it is the fastest two-legged creature (　　)³⁵ Earth,
24. with the ability to (　　)³⁶ a speed of 70 k.p.h.
25. Ostriches have (　　)³⁷ successfully domesticated and are now
26. (　　)³⁸ throughout the world for meat, (　　)³⁹ and leather.
27. Ostrich meat, although (　　)⁴⁰, has fewer calories and less
28. (　　)⁴¹ than chicken or turkey meat.
29. (　　)⁴² are several myths about ostriches. (　　)⁴³ the most
30. enduring myth about (　　)⁴⁴ ostrich is that it hides
31. (　　)⁴⁵ head in the sand when (　　)⁴⁶ danger.
32. Although we can read (　　)⁴⁷ myth in stories
33. written by (　　)⁴⁸ Romans 2000 years ago, it is not (　　)⁴⁹
34. all true. But people continue (　　)⁵⁰ believe this myth and

35. think (   )⁵¹ the ostrich is a stupid (   )⁵². Maybe people
36. think this way (   )⁵³ ostriches' eyes are larger than their (   )⁵⁴.

CD Track 03

MET 03 問題：6 単語目ごと

01. Levi Straus was a German immigrant who arrived (   )¹ San Francisco
02. in 1853. It was the time (   )² the California Gold Rush.
03. He planned to open (   )³ business similar to the clothing
04. (   )⁴ owned by his brothers in New York. Levi
05. (   )⁵ up a very successful business (   )⁶ San Francisco over the
06. next 20 years. In 1873, (   )⁷ and a tailor named Jacob Davis
07. patented (   )⁸ process of putting rivets in (   )⁹ for strength,
08. and Levi's jeans as (   )¹⁰ know them today were born.
09. (   )¹¹ the beginning, jeans were popular.
10. (   )¹² people, who usually worked hard (   )¹³, were
11. especially happy with the (   )¹⁴ of jeans.
12. For the next 29 (   )¹⁵, the Levi Strauss jeans business grew into
13. (   )¹⁶ very successful and very big (   )¹⁷.
14. When Levi Strauss died in 1902, his four (   )¹⁸
15. inherited his successful company. Since Levi Strauss' (   )¹⁹ jeans have gone
16. from work (   )²⁰ to high fashion.
17. Today it (   )²¹ that almost everybody owns at (   )²²
18. one pair of jeans. In (   )²³, some young people wear only (   )²⁴.

19. The average citizen in the United States (   )²⁵ very little personal
20. contact with (   )²⁶ police. Contacts most frequently occur
21. (   )²⁷ two contexts: Americans sometimes approach a (   )²⁸ to ask street
22. directions; and (   )²⁹ sometimes stop a motorist for (   )³⁰ or
23. some other traffic violation. (   )³¹ of these
24. situations is usually (   )³² or life-threatening.
25. However, the life of (   )³³ policeman in a large American city
26. (   )³⁴ be both violent and life-threatening almost (   )³⁵ a daily basis.
27. This is (   )³⁶ true for police assigned to (   )³⁷ the poorest sections
28. of the (   )³⁸ where most violent crimes take (   )³⁹. Here police routinely
29. come in (   )⁴⁰ with drug dealers, armed robbers, (   )⁴¹ and the like.
30. If a (   )⁴² is exposed for too long (   )⁴³ period of time to these (   )⁴⁴

第 10 章　MET：実際の問題と解答　　　　　　　　　　　　　　　　179

31. of people from the lowest (　　)⁴⁵ of society, they run the (　　)⁴⁶ of
32. being injured or of (　　)⁴⁷ a prejudice against all the (　　)⁴⁸ of
33. the poor districts of (　　)⁴⁹ city. For this reason, the (　　)⁵⁰ chief
34. regularly changes policemen's assignments so (　　)⁵¹ they can escape from
35. the (　　)⁵² and danger of patrols in (　　)⁵³ ghetto. These other
36. assignments might be (　　)⁵⁴ or controlling traffic.

CD Track 04

MET 04 問題：6 単語目ごと

01. Extreme sports are now a billion-dollar-a-year (　　)¹ throughout the world.
02. The credit (　　)² popularizing such sports is usually
03. (　　)³ to A. J. Hackett, the New Zealander who developed bungee (　　)⁴.
04. In 1986 Hackett saw a video of (　　)⁵ young
05. English thrill seekers doing a (　　)⁶ of jumps in England
06. in the (　　)⁷ seventies. The video caught his
07. (　　)⁸, and he and his friend (　　)⁹ about
08. developing a safe, standardized (　　)¹⁰ of jumping
09. from bridges in New Zealand. (　　)¹¹ 1990 Hackett had established
10. bungee jumping as (　　)¹² world's first extreme sport for ordinary (　　)¹³.
11. There has always been a (　　)¹⁴ group
12. of people in the (　　)¹⁵ who enjoy
13. flirting with danger (　　)¹⁶ even death.
14. But in the (　　)¹⁷ decade, extreme sports have gained
15. (　　)¹⁸ appeal. Hobbies such as in-line skating, (　　)¹⁹ and
16. skateboarding now have extreme (　　)²⁰ and also world
17. competitions, in (　　)²¹ participants seem to defy
18. gravity (　　)²² doing somersaults, twists and spins.
19. (　　)²³ delivery mail is mail delivered (　　)²⁴ fast.
20. Although in America the concept (　　)²⁵ not changed over the years,
21. (　　)²⁶ methods have. The most interesting (　　)²⁷ innovative
22. method for special delivery (　　)²⁸ was probably the pony express.
23. (　　)²⁹ pony express consisted of a (　　)³⁰ of way stations located
24. equidistant (　　)³¹ each other stretching from St. Louis, Missouri, westward.
25. (　　)³² horsemen, usually adventurous and young, (　　)³³ their
26. horses at breakneck speed (　　)³⁴ the stations. Upon arriving

27. at (   )³⁵ station, the rider would transfer
28. (   )³⁶ bag of special delivery mail (   )³⁷ a fresh horse and
29. start (   )³⁸ for a new station. Riders (   )³⁹
30. tired quickly, so they would (   )⁴⁰ replaced
31. by a well-rested rider after (   )⁴¹ three hours of riding.
32. Not (   )⁴² was the pony express fast, (   )⁴³
33. it also captured the imagination (   )⁴⁴ the American public.
34. Unfortunately, the pony (   )⁴⁵ had a short life,
35. for (   )⁴⁶ introduction of the telegraph
36. in (   )⁴⁷ 1860's led to its sudden decline.

CD Track 05

MET 05 問題：6 単語目ごと

01. Not so long ago the (   )¹ "women's work" referred to work traditionally
02. (   )² only by women—cooking, cleaning, (   )³ for children and
03. the elderly— (   )⁴ basically served the needs of (   )⁵.
04. Women in the working world (   )⁶ usually restricted to jobs
05. such (   )⁷ office and sales clerks, nurses, (   )⁸, waitresses and stewardesses.
06. The 1960's saw (   )⁹ appearance in the West of (   )¹⁰ women's liberation
07. movement and the birth (   )¹¹ pill at about the
08. same (   )¹², which together dramatically altered the (   )¹³ scene for women.
09. The women's liberation (   )¹⁴ fought for equal rights for (   )¹⁵ on a broad
10. front including (   )¹⁶ workplace. The Pill, as the birth (   )¹⁷ pill became
11. known, enabled women (   )¹⁸ plan the birth of their (   )¹⁹ and to devote
12. enough time (   )²⁰ marriage and children to establishing (   )²¹ career
13. so that they could (   )²² that career after their children (   )²³ school age.
14. By the end (   )²⁴ the millennium women had made
15. (   )²⁵ progress in gaining job equality (   )²⁶
16. in such male-dominated fields as the (   )²⁷.
17. This has meant better job (   )²⁸, more job
18. satisfaction and higher (   )²⁹ for many women.

19. The dog (   )³⁰ man's best friend, it is said.
20. (   )³¹ can see from cave paintings (   )³² early human beings
21. 20,000 years ago (   )³³ man and dog have had

第 10 章　MET：実際の問題と解答

22. (　)³⁴ long relationship. Presumably, primitive man (　)³⁵
23. attracted to the dog's keen sense (　)³⁶ smell
24. and hearing and its speed—(　)³⁷ of which were
25. useful in (　)³⁸ early man from more dangerous (　)³⁹.
26. Over the millennia, man has taught (　)⁴⁰ dogs
27. to perform many functions (　)⁴¹ guarding the home.
28. For example, (　)⁴² are famous for their ability (　)⁴³
29. control the movements of a (　)⁴⁴ of hundreds of sheep.
30. Dogs (　)⁴⁵ been used to aid disabled (　)⁴⁶ for centuries.
31. There is even (　)⁴⁷ picture of a guide dog (　)⁴⁸
32. its blind owner in the (　)⁴⁹ city of Pompeii.
33. Nowadays, dogs can (　)⁵⁰ taught to turn on light (　)⁵¹,
34. open refrigerator doors and activate (　)⁵² telephone for their
35. disabled owners. (　)⁵³ the majority of people, however, (　)⁵⁴ are
36. simply pets and friends (　)⁵⁵ both young and old members (　)⁵⁶ the family.

CD Track 06

MET 06 問題：6 単語目ごと

01. From an American's perspective it seems (　)¹ Japanese students are always
02. cramming for (　)² kind of exam. Japanese even have (　)³ cram schools,
03. called juku, where students (　)⁴ elementary school to
04. high school (　)⁵ after the regular school day.
05. (　)⁶ American parents would consider a juku almost (　)⁷ child abuse.
06. They think children (　)⁸ to play or do some (　)⁹ activity after school to provide
07. (　)¹⁰ in their lives. A proverb (　)¹¹ English says,
08. "All work and no (　)¹² makes Jack a dull boy."
09. For (　)¹³ Japanese parents and their children, the (　)¹⁴ of the juku makes sense.
10. Because (　)¹⁵ name of the school one (　)¹⁶ from is much more important
11. (　)¹⁷ Japan than in the United States, Japanese parents make (　)¹⁸ financial sacrifices
12. and push their (　)¹⁹ to study hard to enter (　)²⁰ schools.

13. The competitive atmosphere created ( )²¹ this kind of society puts ( )²² pressure on
14. children to study ( )²³ hard as they can.
15. Although Americans ( )²⁴ think this overemphasis on studying ( )²⁵ children
16. both physically and psychologically,
17. Japanese ( )²⁶ often beg their parents to ( )²⁷ them
18. to attend a neighborhood juku ( )²⁸ their friends attend it.
19. Throughout ( )²⁹ people all over the world ( )³⁰ gone to special places
20. where mineral-rich ( )³¹ springs flow from beneath the earth's ( )³².
21. Countries with much volcanic activity ( )³³ as Japan have many such hot ( )³⁴
22. and have established over time ( )³⁵ customs related to taking baths
23. ( )³⁶ these special waters. But many ( )³⁷ countries, especially in Europe, also have
24. centuries-old ( )³⁸ associated with visiting springs to ( )³⁹ certain types of illnesses.
25. One ( )⁴⁰ the oldest such places in ( )⁴¹ world is located in present-day Jordan
26. and Israel. ( )⁴², it is not a spring, ( )⁴³ rather a sea, the Dead Sea.
27. The ( )⁴⁴ Greek philosopher Aristotle wrote about the wonders ( )⁴⁵ the Dead Sea
28. 2500 years ago. It is ( )⁴⁶ said that the Egyptian
29. Queen Cleopatra used water ( )⁴⁷ the Dead Sea to keep her skin ( )⁴⁸.
30. The Dead Sea, which has a 33 percent ( )⁴⁹ of salts and minerals (compared ( )⁵⁰
31. only 3 percent in ocean water), ( )⁵¹ located at the lowest point ( )⁵² Earth,
32. 390 meters below sea level. ( )⁵³ of this unique location, certain ( )⁵⁴,
33. thermal, chemical and optical characteristics ( )⁵⁵ found which occur nowhere else
34. ( )⁵⁶ the world. Of course, no ( )⁵⁷ can live in the Dead Sea, but ( )⁵⁸ one can
35. drown there either. ( )⁵⁹ high concentration of salt allows ( )⁶⁰ person to float on the
36. ( )⁶¹ of the water and read ( )⁶² newspaper without getting it wet.

CD Track 07

MET 07 問題：6 単語目ごと

01. Forty years ago, Americans planning a (　)¹ trip overwhelmingly chose to travel
02. (　)² car or train, or if (　)³ overseas, by ship. Air travel (　)⁴ still a relatively
03. expensive mode (　)⁵ transportation favored by more wealthy Americans.
04. (　)⁶ days air travel is an (　)⁷ part of the lives of (　)⁸ large
05. majority of travelers in (　)⁹ United States. The cost of
06. an air (　)¹⁰ has not changed much since 1960, (　)¹¹ the average
07. American's buying power has (　)¹² ten times.
08. Even in the (　)¹³ ten years, air travel
09. by Americans (　)¹⁴ increased by 37 percent.
10. Unfortunately the (　)¹⁵ of new airports and the
11. (　)¹⁶ of personnel have not kept (　)¹⁷ with the
12. demand for more (　)¹⁸. These shortfalls, along with the
13. (　)¹⁹, frequent occurrences of bad weather, (　)²⁰ resulted in
14. a large number (　)²¹ delays in both departures and (　)²² of airplanes
15. across the country. (　)²³ fact, delays affected 40 percent of (　)²⁴ domestic
16. flights during the past (　)²⁵. These delays have contributed
17. to (　)²⁶ frustration among travelers and outbreaks (　)²⁷ violent
18. behavior during flights, a (　)²⁸ phenomenon known as "air rage."
19. No one (　)²⁹ deny that technology is transforming (　)³⁰ way
20. we live at a (　)³¹ rate. It is hard to (　)³² that only
21. a few years (　)³³ the great majority of people (　)³⁴ still
22. communicating by letter and (　)³⁵ telephones. Now e-mail
23. and cell phones (　)³⁶ rapidly replacing the old forms (　)³⁷ communication.
24. And just around the (　)³⁸ are robot vacuum cleaners and (　)³⁹ which
25. automatically keep a safe (　)⁴⁰ from the car ahead.
26. All (　)⁴¹ technological advances make our lives
27. (　)⁴² more comfortable and convenient.
28. Just (　)⁴³ the dishwasher, clothes washer and (　)⁴⁴ and microwave oven
29. made life (　)⁴⁵ and created more leisure time (　)⁴⁶ our parents'
30. generation, the technological advances (　)⁴⁷ the future will create

31. an ( )⁴⁸ more leisurely life for the ( )⁴⁹ generation.
32. What worries some people, ( )⁵⁰, is that the technological
33. devices ( )⁵¹ are transforming our lives are ( )⁵² the same time
34. leading to ( )⁵³ human interaction. In the future ( )⁵⁴
35. will have to be watchful ( )⁵⁵ prevent technology from diminishing
36. our ( )⁵⁶ contacts with our fellow human ( )⁵⁷.

CD Track 08

MET 08 問題：6 単語目ごと

01. The computer and the automobile, ( )¹ mainstays on modern life, share
02. ( )² pasts. The computer, which has ( )³ recently become a common
03. feature ( )⁴ most people's homes and offices, had ( )⁵ beginnings
04. in the 1830's. At that ( )⁶, the British mathematician, Charles Babbage,
05. developed the mechanical ( )⁷. In the same way,
06. the ( )⁸ type of automobile was a steam-powered ( )⁹
07. invented in 1769. The gas-powered car was ( )¹⁰ mass-produced until
08. Henry Ford's Model T in 1915, and did not ( )¹¹
09. a common possession for Americans until ( )¹² decades later.
10. Although both the ( )¹³ and the automobile took a ( )¹⁴ time to
11. become integral parts ( )¹⁵ most people's lives, once they did,
12. ( )¹⁶ revolutionized the whole world. Today ( )¹⁷ people would rather drive
13. their ( )¹⁸ to the office in the ( )¹⁹ than take public transportation, even ( )²⁰
14. the latter may be cheaper, ( )²¹ convenient and safer. The reason ( )²² this is
15. the sense of ( )²³ ⋅ independence and privacy afforded by ( )²⁴ travel.
16. In the same way, ( )²⁵ will now spend a large ( )²⁶ of money to own
17. a ( )²⁷ which allows them to communicate ( )²⁸ e-mail instead of by post, and
18. ( )²⁹ allows them to obtain information ( )³⁰ the Internet instead of the ( )³¹.
19. Commercial advertising, especially for television, ( )³² at the heart of any
20. ( )³³ undertaking these days. The effectiveness ( )³⁴ an advertising
21. campaign for a ( )³⁵ can make or

第10章　MET：実際の問題と解答　　　　　　　　　　　　　　　　185

22. break it.　(　　)³⁶ this reason, manufacturers' advertising budgets sometimes
23. (　　)³⁷ their budgets for research and (　　)³⁸.
24. The primary aim of a (　　)³⁹ advertisement is to catch the
25. audience's (　　)⁴⁰. And, of course, the larger (　　)⁴¹ audience the better.
26. Thus, business (　　)⁴² are keen to gain advertising (　　)⁴³ during
27. especially popular television shows, (　　)⁴⁴ the Super Bowl, the final professional
28. American football (　　)⁴⁵ of the season. Every January, American (　　)⁴⁶ by the tens
29. of millions (　　)⁴⁷ their schedules far in advance (　　)⁴⁸ that
30. they will be sure (　　)⁴⁹ be seated comfortably in front
31. (　　)⁵⁰ their TV sets on the day (　　)⁵¹ the Super Bowl.
32. Knowing this, advertising managers (　　)⁵² all year
33. producing their most (　　)⁵³, most attractive and most
34. persuasive (　　)⁵⁴ to be shown on the (　　)⁵⁵ of the Super Bowl.
35. In fact, many (　　)⁵⁶ say that they look forward (　　)⁵⁷ seeing
36. the TV commercials on that (　　)⁵⁸ as much as the football (　　)⁵⁹ itself.

CD Track 09

MET 09 問題：6 単語目ごと

01. Life isn't easy for disabled people, (　　)¹ it has improved
02. during the (　　)² 25 years. Until recently, most disabled
03. (　　)³ were kept in hospitals and (　　)⁴ such institutions,
04. or else they (　　)⁵ inside their own homes.
05. But (　　)⁶ things changed. Some disabled people,
06. (　　)⁷ those who were not severely
07. (　　)⁸, thought they should be able
08. (　　)⁹ lead a normal life like (　　)¹⁰ people.
09. But they needed help. (　　)¹¹ around 1970 disabled people formed
10. organizations, (　　)¹² their demands to the public, (　　)¹³ put pressure
11. on local institutions, (　　)¹⁴ private and public, to help (　　)¹⁵.
12. Today we can see the (　　)¹⁶ results
13. of this movement: specially (　　)¹⁷ toilets; ramps next to
14. stairs (　　)¹⁸ wheelchairs; elevators in subways;
15. loudspeakers (　　)¹⁹ crosswalks for the blind;

16. special (   )²⁰ in concert halls for wheelchairs; (   )²¹ many more.
17. As these conveniences (   )²² disabled people increase, so should
18. (   )²³ understanding and acceptance of the (   )²⁴ public.
19. There is a proverb (   )²⁵ English, "Behind every great man, there (   )²⁶
20. a great woman." In the (   )²⁷ of American presidents, this proverb
21. underlines (   )²⁸ importance of a president's wife
22. for (   )²⁹ success in winning election to (   )³⁰ nation's highest office.
23. A great deal (   )³¹ known and has been written (   )³² the lives of U.S.
24. presidents, including (   )³³ formative years. The mothers of (   )³⁴ men since
25. World War II might deserve more (   )³⁵ than the wives for molding
26. (   )³⁶ special characters. Almost all presidents' mothers (   )³⁷ the modern era have
27. been strong-willed, (   )³⁸ women, often with more than (   )³⁹
28. education for their day. They (   )⁴⁰ their sons with great care (   )⁴¹
29. great love and instilled in (   )⁴² a feeling that they could (   )⁴³
30. anything they put their minds (   )⁴⁴. Invariably they ensure that
31. their (   )⁴⁵ developed a strong self-image and great self-confidence.
32. (   )⁴⁶ President Bill Clinton had such a mother, (   )⁴⁷ he also
33. married a woman, Hillary Rodham, (   )⁴⁸ had great intelligence,
34. ambition and self-confidence. (   )⁴⁹ people predict that someday
35. Hillary Clinton will (   )⁵⁰ the first woman in American history
36. (   )⁵¹ run for the office of (   )⁵² of the United States.

CD Track 10

MET 10 問題：6 単語目ごと

01. The human mouth has three (   )¹ functions. Two of them—eating
02. (   )² breathing—are shared by members (   )³ the animal kingdom.
03. The third (   )⁴—speaking—is one of the (   )⁵ features which
04. distinguishes human beings (   )⁶ the rest of living creatures.
05. (   )⁷ primitive man must have had (   )⁸ spoken language,
06. social scientists have (   )⁹ evidence of language as such (   )¹⁰ the
07. appearance of written records (   )¹¹ ancient Mesopotamia and Egypt
08. 5-6000 years ago. Present-day linguists (   )¹² identify over 1500
09. spoken languages, with Mandarin Chinese (   )¹³ spoken by more than three-quarters

10. of (　　)¹⁴ billion people. After Mandarin Chinese, English is the (　　)¹⁵ widely spoken first
11. language, and (　　)¹⁶ become the language of choice (　　)¹⁷ international communication.
12. English has not always (　　)¹⁸ the international language. Two hundred (　　)¹⁹ ago
13. French was the dominant language. (　　)²⁰ ancient times, Aramaic, Greek
14. and Latin were international (　　)²¹ at different points in time. (　　)²² have been
15. made throughout history (　　)²³ adopt a common universal language (　　)²⁴
16. all peoples of the world. (　　)²⁵ most successful such effort to (　　)²⁶ was Esperanto which
17. was spoken by (　　)²⁷ 750,000 people at one time in (　　)²⁸ mid-20th century. However,
18. such universal languages (　　)²⁹ fail because of the absence (　　)³⁰ a cultural foundation.
19. Hinduism, the primary (　　)³¹ of India, has produced a wealth (　　)³² gods,
20. customs and rituals since (　　)³³ origins in prehistory. One of (　　)³⁴ more colorful
21. aspects is the (　　)³⁵ number of wandering beggars called *sadhus*.
22. (　　)³⁶ a *sadhu* renounces the comforts of (　　)³⁷ life and leads
23. a life (　　)³⁸ a begging nomad. He travels (　　)³⁹ one holy
24. place to another (　　)⁴⁰ foot, often barefoot with hardly (　　)⁴¹ clothes,
25. carrying a begging bowl (　　)⁴² perhaps a walking stick. In (　　)⁴³ way,
26. he hopes to escape (　　)⁴⁴ the evils of a materialistic (　　)⁴⁵.
27. Indian people believe that giving food, (　　)⁴⁶ or
28. money to *sadhus* improves their (　　)⁴⁷ of escaping from reincarnation.
29. Reincarnation (　　)⁴⁸ the belief that one's soul is (　　)⁴⁹
30. reborn in a different body. (　　)⁵⁰ Hindus, never-ending rebirth is
31. equivalent to the Christian (　　)⁵¹ of hell. Hindus believe that by
32. (　　)⁵² many good actions (such as (　　)⁵³
33. to *sadhus*), they can enter the Hindu (　　)⁵⁴.
34. Some *sadhus* are truly holy people (　　)⁵⁵ pure minds and hearts.
35. Others (　　)⁵⁶ that they can go through (　　)⁵⁷ whole life without working simply
36. (　　)⁵⁸ pretending to be a holy (　　)⁵⁹ and living off the kindness (　　)⁶⁰ others.

CD Track 01

MET 01 解答：6 単語目ごと

01. The majority of people have (at)¹ least one pet at some (time)² in their life.
02. Sometimes the (relationship)³ between a pet dog or (cat)⁴ and its owner
03. is so (close)⁵ that they begin to resemble (each)⁶ other in their appearance
04. and (behavior)⁷. On the other hand, owners (of)⁸ unusual pets
05. such as tigers (or)⁹ snakes sometimes have to protect (themselves)¹⁰ from their own pets.
06. Thirty (years)¹¹ ago the idea of an (inanimate)¹² pet first arose.
07. This was (the)¹³ pet rock, which became a (craze)¹⁴ in the United States
08. and (spread)¹⁵ to other countries as well. (People)¹⁶ paid large sums of money
09. (for)¹⁷ ordinary rocks and assigned them (names)¹⁸.
10. They tied a leash around (the)¹⁹ rock and pulled it down (the)²⁰ street just like a dog.
11. (The)²¹ rock owners even talked to (their)²² pet rocks.
12. Now that we (have)²³ entered the computer age, we (have)²⁴ virtual pets.
13. The Japanese Tamagotchi—the (imaginary)²⁵ chicken egg—
14. was the precursor (of)²⁶ many virtual pets.
15. Now there (are)²⁷ an ever-increasing number of such (virtual)²⁸ pets
16. which mostly young people (are)²⁹ adopting as their own.
17. And (if)³⁰ your virtual pet dies, you (can)³¹ reserve a permanent resting place
18. (on)³² the Internet in a virtual (pet)³³ cemetery.
19. Sports are big business. (Whereas)³⁴ Babe Ruth, the most famous athlete of (his)³⁵ day,
20. was well-known for earning (as)³⁶ much as the President of (the)³⁷ United States,
21. the average salary (of)³⁸ today's professional baseball players
22. is (ten)³⁹ times that of the President. (And)⁴⁰ a handful of sports superstars
23. (earn)⁴¹ one hundered times more through (their)⁴² contracts with manufacturers
24. of clothing, (food)⁴³, and sports equipment. But every (generation)⁴⁴ produces
25. one or two legendary (athletes)⁴⁵ who rewrite the record books,
26. (and)⁴⁶ whose ability and achievements are (remembered)⁴⁷ for generations.
27. In the current (generation)⁴⁸ Tiger Woods and Michael Jordan are two such legendary (figures)⁴⁹,

28. both of whom have achieved (almost)⁵⁰ mythical status.
29. The fact that (a)⁵¹ large number of professional athletes (earn)⁵² huge incomes
30. Has led to (increased)⁵³ competition throughout the sports world.
31. (Parents)⁵⁴ send their children to sports (training)⁵⁵ camps at an early age.
32. (Such)⁵⁶ kids typically practice three to (four)⁵⁷ hours a day,
33. all weekend (and)⁵⁸ during their school vacations in (order)⁵⁹ to better their chances
34. of (eventually)⁶⁰ obtaining a well-paid position on (a)⁶¹ professional team
35. when they grow (up)⁶². As for the many young (aspirants)⁶³ who do not succeed,
36. one (wonders)⁶⁴ if they will regret having (lost)⁶⁵ their childhood.

CD Track 02

MET 02 解答：6 単語目ごと

01. Many people have experienced the (joy)¹ of standing on a
02. moving (ship)² and watching a group of (dolphins)³ swim alongside.
03. Dolphins are not (only)⁴ playful animals but they are (also)⁵ highly
04. intelligent. They are mammals (that)⁶ can be found in most (of)⁷
05. the world's oceans as well as (in)⁸ fresh water.
06. Dolphins can swim (at)⁹ speeds of up to
07. 56 k.p.h., and (they)¹⁰ can dive to depths of 200 (meters)¹¹
08. and stay under water for 5-8 (minutes)¹² without resurfacing
09. for air. They (are)¹³ well-known for the unique
10. clicking sound (they)¹⁴ use like sonar to locate (food)¹⁵ as
11. well as obstacles. Every (dolphin)¹⁶ also has
12. its own individual (whistling)¹⁷ sound used for communication.
13. When (dolphins)¹⁸ sleep, they sleep in a semi-alert
14. (state)¹⁹ by resting one side of (their)²⁰ brain at a time.
15. They (will)²¹ help sick or injured dolphins (as)²² much as
16. they can, and (they)²³ act as a team if (there)²⁴ is danger.
17. It is because (of)²⁵ these and other human-like
18. qualities that (people)²⁶ have a special feeling for (dolphins)²⁷.
19. Everybody seems to like or (be)²⁸ interested in the ostrich.
20. This (may)²⁹ be because it is unique (in)³⁰ appearance and

21. character. The ostrich (is)³¹ a bird, but it cannot (fly)³².
22. It is the tallest and (heaviest)³³ bird in the world,
23. and (yet)³⁴ it is the fastest two-legged creature (on)³⁵ Earth,
24. with the ability to (reach)³⁶ a speed of 70 k.p.h.
25. Ostriches have (been)³⁷ successfully domesticated and are now
26. (farmed)³⁸ throughout the world for meat, (feathers)³⁹ and leather.
27. Ostrich meat, although (red)⁴⁰, has fewer calories and less
28. (cholesterol)⁴¹ than chicken or turkey meat.
29. (There)⁴² are several myths about ostriches. (Perhaps)⁴³ the most
30. enduring myth about (the)⁴⁴ ostrich is that it hides
31. (its)⁴⁵ head in the sand when (in)⁴⁶ danger.
32. Although we can read (this)⁴⁷ myth in stories
33. written by (ancient)⁴⁸ Romans 2000 years ago, it is not (at)⁴⁹
34. all true. But people continue (to)⁵⁰ believe this myth and
35. think (that)⁵¹ the ostrich is a stupid (animal)⁵². Maybe people
36. think this way (because)⁵³ ostriches' eyes are larger than their (brains)⁵⁴.

CD Track 03

MET 03 解答：6 単語目ごと

01. Levi Straus was a German immigrant who arrived (in)¹ San Francisco
02. in 1853. It was the time (of)² the California Gold Rush.
03. He planned to open (a)³ business similar to the clothing
04. (business)⁴ owned by his brothers in New York. Levi
05. (built)⁵ up a very successful business (in)⁶ San Francisco over the
06. next 20 years. In 1873, (he)⁷ and a tailor named Jacob Davis
07. patented (the)⁸ process of putting rivets in (pants)⁹ for strength,
08. and Levi's jeans as (we)¹⁰ know them today were born.
09. (From)¹¹ the beginning, jeans were popular.
10. (Working)¹² people, who usually worked hard (outside)¹³, were
11. especially happy with the (strength)¹⁴ of jeans.
12. For the next 29 (years)¹⁵, the Levi Strauss jeans business grew into
13. (a)¹⁶ very successful and very big (company)¹⁷.
14. When Levi Strauss died in 1902, his four (nephews)¹⁸
15. inherited his successful company. Since Levi Strauss' (death)¹⁹ jeans have gone

16. from work (clothes)²⁰ to high fashion.
17. Today it (seems)²¹ that almost everybody owns at (least)²²
18. one pair of jeans. In (fact)²³, some young people wear only (jeans)²⁴.
19. The average citizen in the United States (has)²⁵ very little personal
20. contact with (the)²⁶ police. Contacts most frequently occur
21. (in)²⁷ two contexts: Americans sometimes approach a (policeman)²⁸ to ask street
22. directions; and (police)²⁹ sometimes stop a motorist for (speeding)³⁰ or
23. some other traffic violation. (Neither)³¹ of these
24. situations is usually (violent)³² or life-threatening.
25. However, the life of (a)³³ policeman in a large American city
26. (can)³⁴ be both violent and life-threatening almost (on)³⁵ a daily basis.
27. This is (especially)³⁶ true for police assigned to (patrol)³⁷ the poorest sections
28. of the (city)³⁸ where most violent crimes take (place)³⁹. Here police routinely
29. come in (contact)⁴⁰ with drug dealers, armed robbers, (muggers)⁴¹ and the like.
30. If a (policeman)⁴² is exposed for too long (a)⁴³ period of time to these (types)⁴⁴
31. of people from the lowest (level)⁴⁵ of society, they run the (risk)⁴⁶ of
32. being injured or of (developing)⁴⁷ a prejudice against all the (residents)⁴⁸ of
33. the poor districts of (the)⁴⁹ city. For this reason, the (police)⁵⁰ chief
34. regularly changes policemen's assignments so (that)⁵¹ they can escape from
35. the (tension)⁵² and danger of patrols in (the)⁵³ ghetto. These other
36. assignments might be (deskwork)⁵⁴ or controlling traffic.

CD Track 04

MET 04 解答：6 単語目ごと

01. Extreme sports are now a billion-dollar-a-year (business)¹ throughout the world.
02. The credit (for)² popularizing such sports is usually
03. (given)³ to A. J. Hackett, the New Zealander who developed bungee (jumping)⁴.
04. In 1986 Hackett saw a video of (some)⁵ young
05. English thrill seekers doing a (couple)⁶ of jumps in England
06. in the (late)⁷ seventies. The video caught his
07. (imagination)⁸, and he and his friend (set)⁹ about

08. developing a safe, standardized (method)[10] of jumping
09. from bridges in New Zealand. (By)[11] 1990 Hackett had established
10. bungee jumping as (the)[12] world's first extreme sport for ordinary (people)[13].
11. There has always been a (select)[14] group
12. of people in the (world)[15] who enjoy
13. flirting with danger (and)[16] even death.
14. But in the (past)[17] decade, extreme sports have gained
15. (mass)[18] appeal. Hobbies such as in-line skating, (windsurfing)[19] and
16. skateboarding now have extreme (versions)[20] and also world
17. competitions, in (which)[21] participants seem to defy
18. gravity (by)[22] doing somersaults, twists and spins.
19. (Special)[23] delivery mail is mail delivered (especially)[24] fast.
20. Although in America the concept (has)[25] not changed over the years,
21. (the)[26] methods have. The most interesting (and)[27] innovative
22. method for special delivery (mail)[28] was probably the pony express.
23. (The)[29] pony express consisted of a (series)[30] of way stations located
24. equidistant (from)[31] each other stretching from St. Louis, Missouri, westward.
25. (Expert)[32] horsemen, usually adventurous and young, (rode)[33] their
26. horses at breakneck speed (between)[34] the stations. Upon arriving
27. at (one)[35] station, the rider would transfer
28. (his)[36] bag of special delivery mail (onto)[37] a fresh horse and
29. start (out)[38] for a new station. Riders (became)[39]
30. tired quickly, so they would (be)[40] replaced
31. by a well-rested rider after (about)[41] three hours of riding.
32. Not (only)[42] was the pony express fast, (but)[43]
33. it also captured the imagination (of)[44] the American public.
34. Unfortunately, the pony (express)[45] had a short life,
35. for (the)[46] introduction of the telegraph
36. in (the)[47] 1860's led to its sudden decline.

CD Track 05

MET 05 解答：6 単語目ごと

01. Not so long ago the (term)[1] "women's work" referred to work traditionally
02. (performed)[2] only by women—cooking, cleaning, (caring)[3] for children and
03. the elderly—(which)[4] basically served the needs of (others)[5].

04. Women in the working world (were)⁶ usually restricted to jobs
05. such (as)⁷ office and sales clerks, nurses, (teachers)⁸, waitresses and stewardesses.
06. The 1960's saw (the)⁹ appearance in the West of (the)¹⁰ women's liberation
07. movement and the birth (control)¹¹ pill at about the
08. same (time)¹², which together dramatically altered the (work)¹³ scene for women.
09. The women's liberation (movement)¹⁴ fought for equal rights for (women)¹⁵ on a broad
10. front including (the)¹⁶ workplace. The Pill, as the birth (control)¹⁷ pill became
11. known, enabled women (to)¹⁸ plan the birth of their (children)¹⁹ and to devote
12. enough time (before)²⁰ marriage and children to establishing (a)²¹ career
13. so that they could (resume)²² that career after their children (reached)²³ school age.
14. By the end (of)²⁴ the millennium women had made
15. (great)²⁵ progress in gaining job equality (even)²⁶
16. in such male-dominated fields as the (army)²⁷.
17. This has meant better job (choice)²⁸, more job
18. satisfaction and higher (pay)²⁹ for many women.
19. The dog (is)³⁰ man's best friend, it is said.
20. (We)³¹ can see from cave paintings (of)³² early human beings
21. 20,000 years ago (that)³³ man and dog have had
22. (a)³⁴ long relationship. Presumably, primitive man (was)³⁵
23. attracted to the dog's keen sense (of)³⁶ smell
24. and hearing and its speed—(all)³⁷ of which were
25. useful in (protecting)³⁸ early man from more dangerous (animals)³⁹.
26. Over the millennia, man has taught (his)⁴⁰ dogs
27. to perform many functions (besides)⁴¹ guarding the home.
28. For example, (sheepdogs)⁴² are famous for their ability (to)⁴³
29. control the movements of a (flock)⁴⁴ of hundreds of sheep.
30. Dogs (have)⁴⁵ been used to aid disabled (people)⁴⁶ for centuries.
31. There is even (a)⁴⁷ picture of a guide dog (and)⁴⁸
32. its blind owner in the (ancient)⁴⁹ city of Pompeii.
33. Nowadays, dogs can (be)⁵⁰ taught to turn on light (switches)⁵¹,
34. open refrigerator doors and activate (the)⁵² telephone for their
35. disabled owners. (For)⁵³ the majority of people, however, (dogs)⁵⁴ are
36. simply pets and friends (for)⁵⁵ both young and old members (of)⁵⁶ the family.

CD Track 06

MET 06 解答：6 単語目ごと

01. From an American's perspective it seems (that)[1] Japanese students are always
02. cramming for (some)[2] kind of exam. Japanese even have (private)[3] cram schools,
03. called *juku*, where students (from)[4] elementary school to
04. high school (study)[5] after the regular school day.
05. (Most)[6] American parents would consider a *juku* almost (like)[7] child abuse.
06. They think children (need)[8] to play or do some (physical)[9] activity after school to provide
07. (balance)[10] in their lives. A proverb (in)[11] English says,
08. "All work and no (play)[12] makes Jack a dull boy."
09. For (both)[13] Japanese parents and their children, the (idea)[14] of the *juku* makes sense.
10. Because (the)[15] name of the school one (graduates)[16] from is much more important
11. (in)[17] Japan than in the United States, Japanese parents make (great)[18] financial sacrifices
12. and push their (children)[19] to study hard to enter (such)[20] schools.
13. The competitive atmosphere created (by)[21] this kind of society puts (great)[22] pressure on
14. children to study (as)[23] hard as they can.
15. Although Americans (might)[24] think this overemphasis on studying (damages)[25] children
16. both physically and psychologically,
17. Japanese (children)[26] often beg their parents to (allow)[27] them
18. to attend a neighborhood *juku* (because)[28] their friends attend it.
19. Throughout (history)[29] people all over the world (have)[30] gone to special places
20. where mineral-rich (hot)[31] springs flow from beneath the earth's (surface)[32].
21. Countries with much volcanic activity (such)[33] as Japan have many such hot (springs)[34]
22. and have established over time (many)[35] customs related to taking baths
23. (in)[36] these special waters. But many (other)[37] countries, especially in Europe, also have

24. centuries-old (traditions)[38] associated with visiting springs to (cure)[39] certain types of illnesses.
25. One (of)[40] the oldest such places in (the)[41] world is located in present-day Jordan
26. and Israel. (Actually)[42], it is not a spring, (but)[43] rather a sea, the Dead Sea.
27. The (ancient)[44] Greek philosopher Aristotle wrote about the wonders (of)[45] the Dead Sea
28. 2500 years ago. It is (also)[46] said that the Egyptian
29. Queen Cleopatra used water (from)[47] the Dead Sea to keep her skin (beautiful)[48].
30. The Dead Sea, which has a 33 percent (concentration)[49] of salts and minerals (compared (to)[50]
31. only 3 percent in ocean water), (is)[51] located at the lowest point (on)[52] Earth,
32. 390 meters below sea level. (Because)[53] of this unique location, certain (atmospheric)[54],
33. thermal, chemical and optical characteristics (are)[55] found which occur nowhere else
34. (in)[56] the world. Of course, no (fish)[57] can live in the Dead Sea, but (no)[58] one can
35. drown there either. (The)[59] high concentration of salt allows (a)[60] person to float on the
36. (surface)[61] of the water and read (a)[62] newspaper without getting it wet.

CD Track 07

MET 07 解答：6 単語目ごと

01. Forty years ago, Americans planning a (long)[1] trip overwhelmingly chose to travel
02. (by)[2] car or train, or if (going)[3] overseas, by ship. Air travel (was)[4] still a relatively
03. expensive mode (of)[5] transportation favored by more wealthy Americans.
04. (These)[6] days air travel is an (integral)[7] part of the lives of (the)[8] large
05. majority of travelers in (the)[9] United States. The cost of
06. an air (ticket)[10] has not changed much since 1960, (while)[11] the average

07. American's buying power has (increased)[12] ten times.
08. Even in the (past)[13] ten years, air travel
09. by Americans (has)[14] increased by 37 percent.
10. Unfortunately the (construction)[15] of new airports and the
11. (training)[16] of personnel have not kept (pace)[17] with the
12. demand for more (flights)[18]. These shortfalls, along with the
13. (usual)[19], frequent occurrences of bad weather, (have)[20] resulted in
14. a large number (of)[21] delays in both departures and (arrivals)[22] of airplanes
15. across the country. (In)[23] fact, delays affected 40 percent of (all)[24] domestic
16. flights during the past (year)[25]. These delays have contributed
17. to (increased)[26] frustration among travelers and outbreaks (of)[27] violent
18. behavior during flights, a (new)[28] phenomenon known as "air rage."
19. No one (can)[29] deny that technology is transforming (the)[30] way
20. we live at a (breathtaking)[31] rate. It is hard to (believe)[32] that only
21. a few years (ago)[33] the great majority of people (were)[34] still
22. communicating by letter and (traditional)[35] telephones. Now e-mail
23. and cell phones (are)[36] rapidly replacing the old forms (of)[37] communication.
24. And just around the (corner)[38] are robot vacuum cleaners and (cars)[39] which
25. automatically keep a safe (distance)[40] from the car ahead.
26. All (these)[41] technological advances make our lives
27. (increasingly)[42] more comfortable and convenient.
28. Just (as)[43] the dishwasher, clothes washer and (dryer)[44] and microwave oven
29. made life (easier)[45] and created more leisure time (for)[46] our parents'
30. generation, the technological advances (of)[47] the future will create
31. an (even)[48] more leisurely life for the (future)[49] generation.
32. What worries some people, (however)[50], is that the technological
33. devices (which)[51] are transforming our lives are (at)[52] the same time
34. leading to (less)[53] human interaction. In the future (people)[54]
35. will have to be watchful (to)[55] prevent technology from diminishing
36. our (personal)[56] contacts with our fellow human (beings)[57].

CD Track 08

MET 08 解答：6 単語目ごと

01. The computer and the automobile, (the)¹ mainstays on modern life, share
02. (similar)² pasts. The computer, which has (only)³ recently become a common
03. feature (of)⁴ most people's homes and offices, had (its)⁵ beginnings
04. in the 1830's. At that (time)⁶, the British mathematician, Charles Babbage,
05. developed the mechanical (computer)⁷. In the same way,
06. the (first)⁸ type of automobile was a steam-powered (vehicle)⁹
07. invented in 1769. The gas-powered car was (not)¹⁰ mass-produced until
08. Henry Ford's Model T in 1915, and did not (become)¹¹
09. a common possession for Americans until (several)¹² decades later.
10. Although both the (computer)¹³ and the automobile took a (long)¹⁴ time to
11. become integral parts (of)¹⁵ most people's lives, once they did,
12. (they)¹⁶ revolutionized the whole world. Today (most)¹⁷ people would rather drive
13. their (car)¹⁸ to the office in the (city)¹⁹ than take public transportation, even (though)²⁰
14. the latter may be cheaper, (more)²¹ convenient and safer. The reason (for)²² this is
15. the sense of (freedom)²³, independence and privacy afforded by (car)²⁴ travel.
16. In the same way, (people)²⁵ will now spend a large (amount)²⁶ of money to own
17. a (computer)²⁷ which allows them to communicate (by)²⁸ e-mail instead of by post, and
18. (which)²⁹ allows them to obtain information (from)³⁰ the Internet instead of the (library)³¹.
19. Commercial advertising, especially for television, (lies)³² at the heart of any
20. (business)³³ undertaking these days. The effectiveness (of)³⁴ an advertising
21. campaign for a (product)³⁵ can make or
22. break it. (For)³⁶ this reason, manufacturers' advertising budgets sometimes
23. (exceed)³⁷ their budgets for research and (development)³⁸.
24. The primary aim of a (television)³⁹ advertisement is to catch the
25. audience's (attention)⁴⁰. And, of course, the larger (the)⁴¹ audience the better.
26. Thus, business (leaders)⁴² are keen to gain advertising (time)⁴³ during

27. especially popular television shows, (like)⁴⁴ the Super Bowl, the final professional
28. American football (contest)⁴⁵ of the season. Every January, American (people)⁴⁶ by the tens
29. of millions (arrange)⁴⁷ their schedules far in advance (so)⁴⁸ that
30. they will be sure (to)⁴⁹ be seated comfortably in front
31. (of)⁵⁰ their TV sets on the day (of)⁵¹ the Super Bowl.
32. Knowing this, advertising managers (work)⁵² all year
33. producing their most (creative)⁵³, most attractive and most
34. persuasive (commercials)⁵⁴ to be shown on the (day)⁵⁵ of the Super Bowl.
35. In fact, many (people)⁵⁶ say that they look forward (to)⁵⁷ seeing
36. the TV commercials on that (day)⁵⁸ as much as the football (game)⁵⁹ itself.

CD Track 09

MET 09 解答：6 単語目ごと

01. Life isn't easy for disabled people, (but)¹ it has improved
02. during the (past)² 25 years. Until recently, most disabled
03. (people)³ were kept in hospitals and (other)⁴ such institutions,
04. or else they (stayed)⁵ inside their own homes.
05. But (then)⁶ things changed. Some disabled people,
06. (especially)⁷ those who were not severely
07. (disabled)⁸, thought they should be able
08. (to)⁹ lead a normal life like (other)¹⁰ people.
09. But they needed help. (So)¹¹ around 1970 disabled people formed
10. organizations, (explained)¹² their demands to the public, (and)¹³ put pressure
11. on local institutions, (both)¹⁴ private and public, to help (them)¹⁵.
12. Today we can see the (many)¹⁶ results
13. of this movement: specially (designed)¹⁷ toilets; ramps next to
14. stairs (for)¹⁸ wheelchairs; elevators in subways;
15. loudspeakers (at)¹⁹ crosswalks for the blind;
16. special (areas)²⁰ in concert halls for wheelchairs; (and)²¹ many more.
17. As these conveniences (for)²² disabled people increase, so should
18. (the)²³ understanding and acceptance of the (general)²⁴ public.
19. There is a proverb (in)²⁵ English, "Behind every great man, there (is)²⁶
20. a great woman." In the (context)²⁷ of American presidents, this proverb

21. underlines (the)²⁸ importance of a president's wife
22. for (his)²⁹ success in winning election to (the)³⁰ nation's highest office.
23. A great deal (is)³¹ known and has been written (about)³² the lives of U.S.
24. presidents, including (their)³³ formative years. The mothers of (these)³⁴ men since
25. World War II might deserve more (credit)³⁵ than the wives for molding
26. (their)³⁶ special characters. Almost all presidents' mothers (in)³⁷ the modern era have
27. been strong-willed, (independent)³⁸ women, often with more than (average)³⁹
28. education for their day. They (raised)⁴⁰ their sons with great care (and)⁴¹
29. great love and instilled in (them)⁴² a feeling that they could (do)⁴³
30. anything they put their minds (to)⁴⁴. Invariably they ensure that
31. their (sons)⁴⁵ developed a strong self-image and great self-confidence.
32. (Former)⁴⁶ President Bill Clinton had such a mother, (and)⁴⁷ he also
33. married a woman, Hillary Rodham, (who)⁴⁸ had great intelligence,
34. ambition and self-confidence. (Many)⁴⁹ people predict that someday
35. Hillary Clinton will (become)⁵⁰ the first woman in American history
36. (to)⁵¹ run for the office of (President)⁵² of the United States.

CD Track 10

MET 10 解答：6 単語目ごと

01. The human mouth has three (major)¹ functions. Two of them—eating
02. (and)² breathing—are shared by members (of)³ the animal kingdom.
03. The third (function)⁴—speaking—is one of the (principal)⁵ features which
04. distinguishes human beings (from)⁶ the rest of living creatures.
05. (Although)⁷ primitive man must have had (a)⁸ spoken language,
06. social scientists have (no)⁹ evidence of language as such (until)¹⁰ the
07. appearance of written records (in)¹¹ ancient Mesopotamia and Egypt
08. 5-6000 years ago. Present-day linguists (can)¹² identify over 1500
09. spoken languages, with Mandarin Chinese (being)¹³ spoken by more than three-quarters
10. of (a)¹⁴ billion people. After Mandarin Chinese, English is the (most)¹⁵ widely spoken first
11. language, and (has)¹⁶ become the language of choice (in)¹⁷ international communication.

12. English has not always (been)[18] the international language. Two hundred (years)[19] ago
13. French was the dominant language. (In)[20] ancient times, Aramaic, Greek
14. and Latin were international (languages)[21] at different points in time. (Efforts)[22] have been
15. made throughout history (to)[23] adopt a common universal language (for)[24]
16. all peoples of the world. (The)[25] most successful such effort to (date)[26] was Esperanto which
17. was spoken by (about)[27] 750,000 people at one time in (the)[28] mid-20th century. However,
18. such universal languages (always)[29] fail because of the absence (of)[30] a cultural foundation.
19. Hinduism, the primary (religion)[31] of India, has produced a wealth (of)[32] gods,
20. customs and rituals since (its)[33] origins in prehistory. One of (its)[34] more colorful
21. aspects is the (large)[35] number of wandering beggars called *sadhus*.
22. (Traditionally)[36] a *sadhu* renounces the comforts of (ordinary)[37] life and leads
23. a life (as)[38] a begging nomad. He travels (from)[39] one holy
24. place to another (on)[40] foot, often barefoot with hardly (any)[41] clothes,
25. carrying a begging bowl (and)[42] perhaps a walking stick. In (this)[43] way,
26. he hopes to escape (from)[44] the evils of a materialistic (life)[45].
27. Indian people believe that giving food, (shelter)[46] or
28. money to *sadhus* improves their (chances)[47] of escaping from reincarnation.
29. Reincarnation (is)[48] the belief that one's soul is (repeatedly)[49]
30. reborn in a different body. (For)[50] Hindus, never-ending rebirth is
31. equivalent to the Christian (idea)[51] of hell. Hindus believe that by
32. (performing)[52] many good actions (such as (giving)[53]
33. to *sadhus*), they can enter the Hindu (heaven)[54].
34. Some *sadhus* are truly holy people (with)[55] pure minds and hearts.
35. Others (know)[56] that they can go through (their)[57] whole life without working simply
36. (by)[58] pretending to be a holy (man)[59] and living off the kindness (of)[60] others.

10.3 センター試験版
CD Track 11

MET CT 2017 問題

CDを聞きながら，空いている（　）の中に，英単語を入れて下さい．

01. Now let me tell you (　)¹ story. When we lived in Japan (　)² years ago,
02. my American friend Jane came (　)³ visit us with her Japanese boss,
03. (　)⁴ wanted to meet my husband. (　)⁵ he left, we decided to (　)⁶ the gift
04. that he had (　)⁷. Surprisingly, it was a neatly (　)⁸ live lobster.
05. I started laughing (　)⁹ shouting, "It's alive! It's alive!" But Jane, who'd just (　)¹⁰
06. to the bathroom, thought I (　)¹¹ yelling, "It's a lie! It's a lie!" (　)¹² thought we were
07. having an (　)¹³, so she was afraid to (　)¹⁴ back into the living room.
08. (　)¹⁵ she finally returned, she realized (　)¹⁶ we were not fighting,
09. but (　)¹⁷ at such an unexpected gift.
10. (　)¹⁸ had never cooked a lobster (　)¹⁹, so we didn't know what to (　)²⁰.
11. In those days there was (　)²¹ Internet to get information, so (　)²² went
12. and asked a neighbor. (　)²³, we had put the lobster (　)²⁴ a sink full of water.
13. (　)²⁵ we came home the lobster (　)²⁶ become so lively that
14. we (　)²⁷ longer had the heart to (　)²⁸ it. We managed to get (　)²⁹ back
15. into the box, and (　)³⁰ gave it to the neighbor (　)³¹.
16. So, Reina, what would you do (　)³² we had five million yen (　)³³ improve our school?
17. Hmm. I can (　)³⁴ of so many things, Ichiro. One (　)³⁵ would be
18. to put a (　)³⁶ over the bicycle parking area. Don't (　)³⁷ hate it
19. when it rains (　)³⁸ your bike gets wet?
20. We (　)³⁹ also put some picnic tables (　)⁴⁰ the grassy area over
21. by (　)⁴¹ bike stands. That would give (　)⁴² a place to have lunch
22. (　)⁴³ hang out after school. And (　)⁴⁴ could make the entrance
23. look (　)⁴⁵ lot nicer. What about painting (　)⁴⁶ a bright color

24. and buying (   )⁴⁷ plants and flowers?
25. Well, those (   )⁴⁸ all great ideas, Reina. I especially (   )⁴⁹ putting a roof
26. over the (   )⁵⁰. But to tell the truth, (   )⁵¹ we had that much money (   )⁵² spend,
27. I think it'd be better (   )⁵³ spend it on one big (   )⁵⁴ rather than a lot of
28. (   )⁵⁵ things. Oh, yeah. Good point, Ichiro.
29. (   )⁵⁶ think it'd be better if we (   )⁵⁷ free Wi-Fi everywhere in the school.
30. (   )⁵⁸ access would help us study (   )⁵⁹. We could get a lot (   )⁶⁰ information
31. that would help us (   )⁶¹ our homework, and there are (   )⁶²
32. many educational websites that are (   )⁶³ free.
33. Best of all, we (   )⁶⁴ chat with the students at (   )⁶⁵ sister school in Australia.
34. Don't you (   )⁶⁶, Mayuko?
35. Well, that's a pretty good idea, Ichiro, (   )⁶⁷ the library has Internet access,
36. (   )⁶⁸ most students already have smartphones (   )⁶⁹ tablet PCs. I think it'd be
37. (   )⁷⁰ to buy solar panels instead. (   )⁷¹ electricity could be used
38. all (   )⁷² the school—we could have (   )⁷³ water in the winter
39. and (   )⁷⁴ conditioning in the summer. Oh, (   )⁷⁵ know!
40. We could make a (   )⁷⁶ for the bicycles out of (   )⁷⁷ solar panels.
41. That would kill (   )⁷⁸ birds with one stone!

CD Track 12

MET CT 2016 問題

CD を聞きながら，空いている (   ) の中に，英単語を入れて下さい．

01. In some countries, silver gifts (   )¹ given for 25th wedding anniversaries
02. and (   )² gifts for 50th anniversaries. But in the United Kingdom,
03. (   )³ are also some traditional gifts (   )⁴ to celebrate other anniversaries.
04. Perhaps (   )⁵ are not so familiar with (   )⁶. For example, for third anniversaries,
05. (   )⁷ gifts are usually given. Three (   )⁸ later, gifts containing sugar are
06. (   )⁹. Six years after that, something (   )¹⁰ of silk is the expected (   )¹¹.
07. Some might be surprised to (   )¹² out that diamonds are given (   )¹³ only
08. for engagements, but also (   )¹⁴ 60th anniversaries.

09. Welcome to The Ocean Hotel. Our rooms ( )¹⁵ decorated in traditional French style,
10. but ( )¹⁶ can use the latest technology, ( )¹⁷ example, wireless Internet.
11. Every room ( )¹⁸ a splendid ocean view, so ( )¹⁹ can see the sunset.
12. Our ( )²⁰ has Chinese, Japanese, and Italian restaurants on the ( )²¹ floor
13. and three coffee shops ( )²² the first and second floors,
14. ( )²³ you can enjoy Asian and Western dishes. ( )²⁴ front of the hotel
15. we ( )²⁵ an outdoor swimming pool next ( )²⁶ the beach, and
16. you can ( )²⁷ enjoy an indoor swimming pool ( )²⁸ an exercise room.
17. Palau is a ( )²⁹ in the Pacific. It became an ( )³⁰ republic on October 1, 1994.
18. Palau's flag is ( )³¹ to Japan's because it features a ( )³² circle. However,
19. the circle is ( )³³, and the background is blue. ( )³⁴ is used to represent
20. the ( )³⁵, which the nation depends on ( )³⁶ food. Unlike the Japanese flag,
21. the ( )³⁷ on Palau's flag is a little off-center. ( )³⁸ of the sun,
22. as on ( )³⁹ Japanese flag, the circle represents the ( )⁴⁰, which is traditionally
23. thought to ( )⁴¹ important in the life cycle ( )⁴² customs of the people.
24. Helen Keller, admired ( )⁴³ her work on behalf of ( )⁴⁴ disabilities,
25. visited Japan three times. ( )⁴⁵ was unable to see or ( )⁴⁶, but she was
26. impressed with ( )⁴⁷ kindness of the Japanese people and ( )⁴⁸
27. and appreciation of Japan and its ( )⁴⁹. She first came to Japan in 1937,
28. ( )⁵⁰ she was invited by the Japanese ( )⁵¹ to make
29. a lecture tour ( )⁵² the country. While she was ( )⁵³, she was moved
30. by the ( )⁵⁴ about the faithful Akita dog, Hachiko, and ( )⁵⁵ if she could have
31. such ( )⁵⁶ dog. Ichiro Ogasawara, a police officer in Akita City, ( )⁵⁷ gave her
32. one of his ( )⁵⁸ puppies. She named this dog Kami. ( )⁵⁹ took Kami home with her,
33. which ( )⁶⁰ Kami the first Akita dog to ( )⁶¹ to the United States. In a letter
34. to ( )⁶² friend, she called Kami an "angel ( )⁶³ fur" and said that
35. he ( )⁶⁴ especially gentle and devoted. She ( )⁶⁵ this dog so much
36. that ( )⁶⁶ asked for another Akita dog, which ( )⁶⁷ sent to her in 1939.

37. This (   )⁶⁸ was Kami's brother, and she called (   )⁶⁹ Go-Go.
38. Helen Keller's dogs received a lot of (   )⁷⁰ in the United States,
39. which helped to introduce Akita (   )⁷¹ as popular pets for Americans.

CD Track 13

MET CT 2015 問題

CD を聞きながら，空いている (   ) の中に，英単語を入れて下さい．

01. If you're going to Machu Picchu in highland Peru, (   )¹ should consider visiting Cuzco,
02. at 3,400 meters (   )² sea level. You will enjoy (   )³ through the Plaza de Armas
03. and visiting (   )⁴ Temple of the Sun. You can also look at Cuzco's (   )⁵ museums
04. and beautiful houses as (   )⁶ as its magnificent churches. Remember, (   )⁷, that
05. these churches close for (   )⁸ few hours around noon. In (   )⁹, you can take advantage of
06. (   )¹⁰ hotels and restaurants, and at (   )¹¹ same time, see Cuzco's fascinating history
07. (   )¹² in its architecture, language, and (   )¹³ treasures.
08. When you start living (   )¹⁴, you might find it difficult (   )¹⁵ manage your money.
09. Here are (   )¹⁶ tips that you may find (   )¹⁷. One hint is first to (   )¹⁸
10. a detailed budget, or plan, (   )¹⁹ how much money you have (   )²⁰ what you are going to
11. (   )²¹ it on each month. Then, (   )²² at your budget and decide (   )²³
12. you can buy fewer items. (   )²⁴, use less electricity, water, or (   )²⁵ utilities
13. by turning off lights, (   )²⁶ example. Finally, before shopping, make (   )²⁷ list of
14. what you need (   )²⁸ compare prices on those items (   )²⁹ different shops.
15. Have you ever (   )³⁰ the phrase "It's all Greek to me"? (   )³¹ use it when we don't
16. understand (   )³² foreign language or a difficult (   )³³. If someone tries to

17. explain (   )³⁴ theory from physics or mathematics (   )³⁵ we cannot comprehend,
18. we could (   )³⁶, "It's all Greek to me." This phrase (   )³⁷ in William Shakespeare's
19. play *Julius Caesar*, where one Roman tells (   )³⁸ that he couldn't understand somebody
20. because (   )³⁹ spoke Greek. Although this phrase had (   )⁴⁰ used earlier by different
21. writers, Shakespeare's (   )⁴¹ of the phrase helped to (   )⁴² it popular,
22. and it continues (   )⁴³ be used even today.
23. Americans have (   )⁴⁴ wanted to live apart from (   )⁴⁵ parents, as personal
24. independence is (   )⁴⁶ thought to be very important. (   )⁴⁷, in most cases, the elderly
25. (   )⁴⁸ in their own homes, while (   )⁴⁹ grown children move away and
26. (   )⁵⁰ elsewhere. However, some elderly people (   )⁵¹ their grown-up children have
27. decided (   )⁵² combine households, and this trend (   )⁵³ been increasing in recent years.
28. (   )⁵⁴ certainly are benefits to living (   )⁵⁵ a multi-generational family
29. in the (   )⁵⁶ house. Grandparents take care of (   )⁵⁷ children while the parents go
30. (   )⁵⁸ work. Young children learn about (   )⁵⁹ family history, cooking, and household
31. (   )⁶⁰ skills from their grandparents. Senior (   )⁶¹ also get a lot
32. out (   )⁶² spending time with their grandchildren. (   )⁶³ stay in good health, hiking
33. (   )⁶⁴ playing sports with the grandchildren. (   )⁶⁵ grandchildren can teach their
34. grandparents (   )⁶⁶ to use computers and keep (   )⁶⁷ with the latest technology.
35. Parents (   )⁶⁸ teach their children proper manners (   )⁶⁹ older people through
36. their own (   )⁷⁰ toward their parents. Children learn (   )⁷¹ seeing their parents
37. interact with (   )⁷² grandparents. Parents can get the (   )⁷³ of the children
38. in watching (   )⁷⁴ for the safety of the (   )⁷⁵, thus sharing the burden
39. if (   )⁷⁶ state of their health becomes (   )⁷⁷ problem.

CD Track 14

MET CT 2014 問題

CD を聞きながら，空いている（　　）の中に，英単語を入れて下さい．

01. Angora rabbits are soft and lovable (　　)[1]. There are different kinds in (　　)[2] countries,
02. but Angoras originated in Ankara, Turkey, before (　　)[3] around the world.
03. One place (　　)[4] became popular was France. They were (　　)[5] by the French royal family
04. and (　　)[6] elites in the mid-18th century. Soon, Angoras (　　)[7] popular outside France
05. and could be (　　)[8] throughout Europe by the end of (　　)[9] century. Later, people in
06. the United States started (　　)[10] them as household pets in (　　)[11] early 1900s.
07. Wherever you find them, (　　)[12] long-haired rabbits live five to (　　)[13] years
08. when kept indoors and (　　)[14] for properly.
09. To make a (　　)[15] kimchi meat sauce, put some finely-chopped (　　)[16] into a pan
10. with two (　　)[17] of olive oil. Turn the (　　)[18] on, and when you smell (　　)[19]
11. garlic cooking, add one chopped (　　)[20] and cook for about two (　　)[21]. After adding
12. 500 grams of ground (　　)[22], cook until light brown, then (　　)[23] one can of
13. chopped tomatoes (　　)[24] with about three tablespoons of (　　)[25].
14. Before turning the heat down (　　)[26] low and cooking everything
15. for (　　)[27] thirty minutes, don't forget to add (　　)[28] tablespoons
16. of kimchi base. This sauce (　　)[29] great on either spaghetti or (　　)[30]!
17. Growing food locally in American cities (　　)[31] been getting more popular recently.
18. (　　)[32] fact, the vegetables you buy (　　)[33] the supermarket may be
19. grown (　　)[34] down the street. Shoppers may (　　)[35] surprised,
20. but actually urban farming (　　)[36] deep roots, especially in the northeastern US.
21. Before (　　)[37] had good highways and air (　　)[38], fruits and vegetables

第 10 章　MET：実際の問題と解答　　　207

22. were often (　　)³⁹ in city greenhouses during the (　　)⁴⁰ instead of being shipped
23. in (　　)⁴¹ faraway states or other countries. (　　)⁴² it reduces transportation costs
24. and (　　)⁴³ people with fresh food more (　　)⁴⁴, urban farming is
25. making a (　　)⁴⁵.
26. There are many kinds of (　　)⁴⁶ and reasons why people build (　　)⁴⁷.
27. People enjoy spending time and (　　)⁴⁸ gathering, organizing, and displaying
28. almost (　　)⁴⁹. A serious collector can even (　　)⁵⁰ a career as a respected (　　)⁵¹.
29. Some people love certain musicians, (　　)⁵², or TV programs so much that (　　)⁵³ must
30. have any items associated (　　)⁵⁴ them. Collectors meet other fans, (　　)⁵⁵ information
31. online, and compete to (　　)⁵⁶ who has the biggest and (　　)⁵⁷ collection. Other people
32. may start (　　)⁵⁸ collection by accident. For example, (　　)⁵⁹ a friend gives you
33. a (　　)⁶⁰ whale souvenir and you keep (　　)⁶¹ on your desk. Then, your (　　)⁶²
34. notices it and gives you (　　)⁶³ umbrella with a whale design. (　　)⁶⁴ collection continues
35. to grow by (　　)⁶⁵ as others give you similar (　　)⁶⁶. It may take over your (　　)⁶⁷
36. if you aren't careful! Collecting may (　　)⁶⁸ have a deeper meaning. Some (　　)⁶⁹
37. believe it begins with childhood (　　)⁷⁰ needs. They say we all (　　)⁷¹
38. uncertainty as children or wanted (　　)⁷² we could not have, so (　　)⁷³ may give us
39. a greater (　　)⁷⁴ of control over our lives. (　　)⁷⁵ the motivation may be,
40. collecting (　　)⁷⁶ a satisfying and enjoyable hobby (　　)⁷⁷ many people.

CD Track 15

MET CT 2013 問題

CD を聞きながら，空いている (　　) の中に，英単語を入れて下さい．

01. Towering skyscrapers are a symbol ( )^1 modern society. In the late 1800s,
02. ( )^2 technological developments made very tall ( )^3 possible. One development
03. was steel ( )^4 technology. Before that, architects were ( )^5 to create thicker
04. stone walls ( )^6 support taller buildings. These walls ( )^7 extremely heavy and
05. allowed less ( )^8 for windows and light. After ( )^9 production of steel was introduced,
06. ( )^{10} began to use steel frames ( )^{11} support a building's weight.
07. Steel ( )^{12} much lighter and stronger than ( )^{13}, while taking up
08. much less ( )^{14}. At the same time, elevator ( )^{15} and fire-resistant
09. building materials also ( )^{16} make skyscrapers possible.
10. Ireland is a ( )^{17} place to visit all through ( )^{18} year. The peak months of
11. ( )^{19} tourist season are July and August, but the ( )^{20} in May, June, and September
12. is usually good ( )^{21} well, and hotels are not ( )^{22}.
13. Flowers are most beautiful in April ( )^{23} May. In October, many art festivals are ( )^{24}.
14. Winter has its own appeal. ( )^{25} can have fantastic places all ( )^{26} yourself,
15. like the beach at Roses Point ( )^{27} the town of Sligo. Although it ( )^{28} dark early and
16. some museums ( )^{29} attractions are closed, as are ( )^{30} hotels,
17. this quiet season is ( )^{31} relaxing for some visitors.
18. You ( )^{32} reached ISSC, the International Student Support ( )^{33}.
19. Our business hours are Monday through Friday, 8 am ( )^{34} 6 pm. Stay on the line
20. for ( )^{35} help messages. Press one for dining ( )^{36} and assistance for students
21. with ( )^{37} dietary needs; press two for dormitory ( )^{38} apartment rentals; press three for
22. Internet ( )^{39} telephone connections; press four for library ( )^{40} bookstore locations.
23. Students with questions ( )^{41} part-time work on campus should ( )^{42} to
24. make an appointment to ( )^{43} our staff at the center.

25. (　　)⁴⁴ the case of a medical (　　)⁴⁵ or illness,
26. dial 911 or go (　　)⁴⁶ to the clinic. Thank you (　　)⁴⁷ calling.
27. What can a colorful, (　　)⁴⁸ shirt tell you about a (　　)⁴⁹?
28. If it's an aloha shirt from Hawaii, (　　)⁵⁰ a bit. Alohas show island life (　　)⁵¹
29. the same way that films, (　　)⁵², and paintings do. They are (　　)⁵³ diverse as
30. the islands they (　　)⁵⁴ from. These shirts are said to (　　)⁵⁵ begun as simple clothing
31. worn (　　)⁵⁶ plantation workers from the Philippines. Then, in (　　)⁵⁷ 1930s,
32. a local Chinese merchant made some (　　)⁵⁸ leftover Japanese kimono cloth.
33. Eventually, tropical Polynesian (　　)⁵⁹ were added and aloha shirts were (　　)⁶⁰.
34. They represent the mix of (　　)⁶¹ in Hawaii. Although some people thought Hawaiian
35. (　　)⁶² were cheap-looking, alohas became very popular. (　　)⁶³ the 1950s, air travel
36. from the (　　)⁶⁴ became cheaper, the standard of (　　)⁶⁵ in America was improving,
37. and people (　　)⁶⁶ clothes as bright and flashy (　　)⁶⁷ their hopes for the future.
38. (　　)⁶⁸ stars and presidents alike put (　　)⁶⁹ alohas and a trend took off.
39. (　　)⁷⁰ Hawaii, the aloha symbolized fun times, but (　　)⁷¹ on the islands,
40. aloha shirts were (　　)⁷² in place of a suit (　　)⁷³ tie.
41. Hawaiians take pride in their culture, (　　)⁷⁴ aloha shirts. Unfortunately,
42. not many of (　　)⁷⁵ earliest alohas have survived; these can (　　)⁷⁶ for thousands of
43. dollars. Whether (　　)⁷⁷ or high-priced, these comfortable shirts (　　)⁷⁸ the world
44. a snapshot of Hawaiian (　　)⁷⁹.

CD Track 16

MET CT 2012 問題

CDを聞きながら，空いている（　　）の中に，英単語を入れて下さい．

01. Moving to a new home ( )¹ your pet can be difficult. ( )² are very
02. sensitive animals, and ( )³ is quite an upsetting experience ( )⁴ them.
03. When you arrive at ( )⁵ new home, it may be ( )⁶ good idea to put your ( )⁷
04. in a quiet room, if ( )⁸. Leave him in peace with ( )⁹ old bed, his litter box,
05. and some food until everything calms ( )¹⁰. After that, let him come ( )¹¹
06. and join you only if ( )¹² wants to. He should also ( )¹³ indoors
07. until he becomes familiar ( )¹⁴ his new home and environment.

08. ( )¹⁵ to Greenland, the largest island in ( )¹⁶ world. You are now
09. in Nuuk, ( )¹⁷ capital city located on the ( )¹⁸ coast
10. where there are small ( )¹⁹, hotels, and villages.
11. In contrast, ( )²⁰ the eastern coast, which is ( )²¹ least accessible area,
12. we can ( )²² some of the finest, breathtaking Arctic ( )²³.
13. Travelers to the eastern shore ( )²⁴ describe the view as spectacular
14. ( )²⁵ magnificent. However, the trip is ( )²⁶ possible for a few weeks ( )²⁷ year
15. when the frozen ocean ( )²⁸ enough to allow expedition ships ( )²⁹.

16. Attention, please. I have a ( )³⁰ from your history teacher.
17. Because ( )³¹ a family emergency, today's class is ( )³², and the makeup class
18. will ( )³³ held this coming Saturday. The ( )³⁴ is scheduled for second period
19. ( )³⁵ usual, but in a different ( )³⁶, Room 305 on the third floor.
20. At that ( )³⁷, your teacher will collect the ( )³⁸ you were supposed to
21. submit ( )³⁹. The midterm examination will be ( )⁴⁰.
22. The main entrance to the ( )⁴¹ is closed on Saturdays,
23. so ( )⁴² should enter through the side ( )⁴³. If you have questions
24. or ( )⁴⁴ more information, please email your ( )⁴⁵.

25. Nursery rhymes are simple poems ( )⁴⁶ exist in many cultures.
26. Through ( )⁴⁷ poems, children have fun singing, ( )⁴⁸ games,
27. and learning basic language ( )⁴⁹ counting skills. What is remarkable ( )⁵⁰
28. these poems is that they ( )⁵¹ often passed down orally from one ( )⁵²
29. to another in the home. ( )⁵³ nursery rhymes, Mother Goose rhymes may be

第10章　MET：実際の問題と解答　　　　　　　　　　211

30. (　　)⁵⁴ best known. But, was there (　　)⁵⁵ a person named Mother Goose?
31. We are (　　)⁵⁶ sure. There are several interesting (　　)⁵⁷ about the origin
32. of Mother Goose. Some (　　)⁵⁸ suggest that it was the French (　　)⁵⁹,
33. Charles Perrault, who said in the 1600s that (　　)⁶⁰ poems were told by
34. an (　　)⁶¹ woman who kept geese. Others (　　)⁶² that the English author,
35. John Newbury, first used (　　)⁶³ name in a book he (　　)⁶⁴ in 1765.
36. Still others insist that Mother Goose (　　)⁶⁵ Elizabeth Goose,
37. who lived in Boston in the 18th (　　)⁶⁶ and entertained her grandchildren
38. by (　　)⁶⁷ nursery rhymes. Regardless of how (　　)⁶⁸ term originated,
39. Mother Goose rhymes are the (　　)⁶⁹ familiar children's poems
40. and are enjoyed (　　)⁷⁰. Teachers of English often use them
41. (　　)⁷¹ introduce the natural sounds and (　　)⁷² of the language in a
    (　　)⁷³ way.
42. Today, many works of (　　)⁷⁴, popular songs,
43. and movies also (　　)⁷⁵ reference to Mother Goose rhymes.

CD Track 17

MET CT 2011 問題

CD を聞きながら，空いている (　　) の中に，英単語を入れて下さい．

01. Our airline welcomes children. More (　　)¹ 45,000 unaccompanied children fly with us
02. (　　)² year. Whether it's a short (　　)³ or a long journey, your (　　)⁴ will enjoy
03. a safe and (　　)⁵ trip. Here's some important information.
04. (　　)⁶ aged 5 and above may travel (　　)⁷ on flights.
05. Children under 5 must (　　)⁸ accompanied by someone aged 17 or (　　)⁹.
06. When your child is travelling (　　)¹⁰, please call our reservations desk.
07. (　　)¹¹ will give you more details (　　)¹² services for young passengers.
08. Tonight's (　　)¹³ on "Pets in the News" (　　)¹⁴ about a cat
09. that traveled (　　)¹⁵ around the world with a (　　)¹⁶ of cotton from Egypt.
10. When the (　　)¹⁷ arrived in Seattle, a worker found (　　)¹⁸ cat
11. that had been trapped (　　)¹⁹ the containers for nearly a (　　)²⁰.
12. The cat was taken to (　　)²¹ animal shelter where her physical (　　)²² was checked.

13. People were amazed ( )²³ cat survived so long. Interestingly, ( )²⁴ ship,
14. which had previously had ( )²⁵ rat problem, was now free ( )²⁶ rats.
15. As a professional photographer ( )²⁷ would like to give you ( )²⁸ suggestions
16. for successful landscape photography. ( )²⁹ winter, for example, when the ( )³⁰
17. are short, you need to ( )³¹ where you're going and what ( )³² want to photograph.
18. You can ( )³³ familiar with the area you're ( )³⁴ to visit by
19. reading guidebooks ( )³⁵ studying maps. Then, you'll know ( )³⁶
20. where the most attractive locations ( )³⁷, rather than leaving it to ( )³⁸.
21. At the location, you may ( )³⁹ to get off the main ( )⁴⁰,
22. so you should be careful. ( )⁴¹ take a good photo, it ( )⁴² be necessary to be
23. in ( )⁴³ conditions which might be dangerous.
24. ( )⁴⁴ of the world's best-loved symphonies ( )⁴⁵ known by
25. popular nicknames given ( )⁴⁶ the general public or music ( )⁴⁷
26. rather than by their composers. ( )⁴⁸ number of Haydn's symphonies
27. have nicknames ( )⁴⁹ as the *Surprise Symphony*, the *Military Symphony* and the
28. *Clock Symphony*. Another example of ( )⁵⁰ type is the *Farewell Symphony*, in which
29. the ( )⁵¹ leave the stage one by one as ( )⁵² finish playing.
30. Eventually, the two violinists ( )⁵³ are left put down their ( )⁵⁴
31. and walk away from the ( )⁵⁵ in silence. This ends the ( )⁵⁶.
32. The story behind this piece ( )⁵⁷ that the prince, for whom Haydn ( )⁵⁸,
33. had taken all of the ( )⁵⁹ to his second palace in ( )⁶⁰ countryside
34. where he liked to ( )⁶¹ hunting. The musicians found the ( )⁶² and
35. working conditions at this ( )⁶³ to be very unpleasant. Moreover,
36. ( )⁶⁴ missed their families and the ( )⁶⁵ comforts of home.
37. When the *Farewell Symphony* was ( )⁶⁶ performed at the country palace,
38. ( )⁶⁷ prince understood the message of Haydn's ( )⁶⁸ at once.
39. The next day ( )⁶⁹ ordered that his entire household ( )⁷⁰ to the city
40. so they ( )⁷¹ be with their families in ( )⁷² for Christmas.

CD Track 18

MET CT 2010 問題

CDを聞きながら，空いている（　）の中に，英単語を入れて下さい．

01. When I first came to Japan, (　)¹ was surprised when people asked
02. (　)² I was annoyed by the (　)³ of insects such as cicadas.
03. (　)⁴ had heard many western people couldn't (　)⁵ such sounds.
04. Actually, the sound (　)⁶ cicadas—which are called *semi* in Japanese—
05. makes (　)⁷ feel at home. When I (　)⁸ growing up, the cicadas would
06. (　)⁹ in a tree just outside (　)¹⁰ bedroom window all summer long.
07. (　)¹¹ would lie on my bed, (　)¹² to their peaceful song.
08. When (　)¹³ heard the cicadas during my first (　)¹⁴ in Japan,
09. it brought back happy (　)¹⁵ memories.
10. Hello, Takashi? This is Rose. I'm in Kyoto now. (　)¹⁶ enjoyed staying
11. with you and (　)¹⁷ family last week. Sorry to (　)¹⁸ you,
12. but I've got a problem. (　)¹⁹ can't find my gloves. Have you (　)²⁰ them?
13. Maybe I left them (　)²¹ the table in the bedroom, (　)²² I'm not sure.
14. They're green and match (　)²³ coat. If you have them, (　)²⁴ you please
15. call me here? (　)²⁵ number is ... oh, I hardly stay (　)²⁶ my hotel room,
16. so I'll contact (　)²⁷ again tomorrow. Thanks. Talk to (　)²⁸ later.
17. Welcome to Marine Park. Before you (　)²⁹ your marine adventure,
18. we have (　)³⁰ few announcements to make. As (　)³¹, from 12:30,
19. you can see our (　)³² popular sea animal show with (　)³³ jumping
20. through hoops and playing (　)³⁴. We are sorry that Penguin Village is
21. (　)³⁵ today, but starting at 3:00, in (　)³⁶ to our usual attractions,
22. you (　)³⁷ see your favorite animation characters (　)³⁸ and dance in the
23. plaza (　)³⁹ front of the waterfall. You (　)⁴⁰ get there easily
24. if you (　)⁴¹ the miniature train from the (　)⁴² center.
25. Don't miss this exciting event!
26. (　)⁴³ the head of the International Relations Department I (　)⁴⁴ pleased to
27. announce our new (　)⁴⁵ journal, *The Global Village*. After hosting an
28. international (　)⁴⁶ on global issues, the department (　)⁴⁷

29. a blog to stay in (   )⁴⁸ and communicate about important issues
30. (   )⁴⁹ as the energy crisis and (   )⁵⁰ rights. Soon our blog started
31. (   )⁵¹ attract exciting ideas and articles (   )⁵² journalists, scholars and
32. even students (   )⁵³ had heard about us. In (   )⁵⁴, some of the best
33. responses (   )⁵⁵ our blog were from nonacademics and (   )⁵⁶
34. who acknowledged the seriousness of (   )⁵⁷ issues. Therefore, when
35. we decided (   )⁵⁸ form the editorial group, students (   )⁵⁹ also included.
36. A professor in (   )⁶⁰ department was chosen as the (   )⁶¹ editor,
37. but the assistant editor (   )⁶² a student with previous experience (   )⁶³
38. an online journal. *The Global Village* will be (   )⁶⁴ bridge between journalists,
39. scholars and (   )⁶⁵ who share a common interest (   )⁶⁶ global issues.
40. Our eventual objective (   )⁶⁷ to make world leaders aware (   )⁶⁸ our
41. concerns, especially those of (   )⁶⁹ people. They're the ones who
42. will (   )⁷⁰ the earth. We would like (   )⁷¹ leaders to realize this.
43. Thank (   )⁷² for your time.

CD Track 19

MET CT 2009 問題

CD を聞きながら，空いている（　）の中に，英単語を入れて下さい．

01. Gooooood morning! This is Pop Music Top Twenty!
02. Have we (   )¹ a surprise for you: a (   )² guest right here in our (   )³!
03. Last week, she broke the (   )⁴ to become the first singer (   )⁵
04. another country to stay at (   )⁶ top of the charts for seventeen (   )⁷ in a row.
05. Plus, she's only two (   )⁸ away from the all-time record set
06. (   )⁹ the rock band the A.B. Brothers seven years (   )¹⁰. By now you should know
07. (   )¹¹ our guest is. Yes, it's the one (   )¹² only Maria M. from Italy!
08. Waverly Hills welcomes you to (   )¹³ spacious grounds and facilities
09. right (   )¹⁴ the middle of the Smokey Mountains. The (   )¹⁵ farmhouse
10. has been completely modernized (   )¹⁶ tastefully decorated rooms.
11. There's plenty to (   )¹⁷ in the area. You can (   )¹⁸ swimming in the summer,

第 10 章　MET：実際の問題と解答　　　　　　　　　　　　　　　　　　215

12. skiing (　)¹⁹ the winter, or a run (　)²⁰ the woods. You can work (　)²¹
13. a good appetite to enjoy country-style (　)²² prepared in
14. our own kitchen with (　)²³ organically-grown vegetables.
15. Between meals you can (　)²⁴ us for a glass of (　)²⁵ milk and
16. homemade cookies. We're often (　)²⁶ booked, so make your reservations (　)²⁷.
17. Attention please. It is now 5:30, (　)²⁸ the museum will close in 30 (　)²⁹.
18. When you have finished looking (　)³⁰ the exhibits in the room (　)³¹ are in,
19. please make your (　)³² to the exit. We hope (　)³³ have enjoyed the exhibition.
20. For (　)³⁴ information, the museum is open (　)³⁵ day including holidays.
21. Opening hours (　)³⁶ from 10 a.m. to 6 p.m. Monday through Thursday.
22. (　)³⁷ Friday to Sunday, the museum (　)³⁸ open from noon to 9 p.m.
23. The (　)³⁹ exhibition on Leonardo da Vinci will start on (　)⁴⁰ 10th.
24. We hope you will visit (　)⁴¹ again soon.
25. The other day, (　)⁴² friend of mine came back (　)⁴³ Hawaii and gave me
26. some live Hawaiian Red Shrimp. They're (　)⁴⁴ thin and tiny, less than
27. one (　)⁴⁵ long, but if you look (　)⁴⁶, you'll see that they're shaped like
28. any (　)⁴⁷ shrimp. They live in pools (　)⁴⁸ "brackish water," which is slightly
29. salty (　)⁴⁹ found along the shore where (　)⁵⁰ water from the land and
30. (　)⁵¹ water mix. I was given (　)⁵² twenty of them as a souvenir, (　)⁵³ a small,
31. clear plastic bottle, (　)⁵⁴ kind that mineral water comes (　)⁵⁵. The shrimp
32. were playing around (　)⁵⁶ the bottle. I planned to (　)⁵⁷ and find a nice glass
33. (　)⁵⁸ on the weekend so my (　)⁵⁹ pets could swim in it (　)⁶⁰ I could enjoy
34. watching them (　)⁶¹ around. I left the bottle (　)⁶² the kitchen table and
35. went (　)⁶³ bed. The next morning when (　)⁶⁴ woke up, I suddenly remembered
36. (　)⁶⁵ my mother makes coffee every (　)⁶⁶ using mineral water. I ran
37. (　)⁶⁷ the kitchen, and there she (　)⁶⁸, holding my bottle in her (　)⁶⁹.
38. I was about to say "(　)⁷⁰!" when she said, "Ugh, something's moving
39. in (　)⁷¹ water!" So I told her (　)⁷² story and prevented a disaster (　)⁷³ in time.

CD Track 20

MET CT 2008 問題

CDを聞きながら，空いている（　　）の中に，英単語を入れて下さい．

01. Thank you for calling the Southeast Coast Weather Center. Here's (　　)[1]
02. weekend beach report. Saturday morning, (　　)[2] weather is expected
03. with partly (　　)[3] skies and mild winds with (　　)[4] in the lower 30s.
04. In the (　　)[5], clouds will increase and occasional (　　)[6] are expected.
05. The forecast for (　　)[7] is light rain continuing until (　　)[8], gradually becoming
06. clear and sunny. (　　)[9], winds will increase and high (　　)[10] are likely,
07. so beach-goers are advised (　　)[11] refrain from swimming throughout the (　　)[12].
08. Good morning, everybody. Welcome to Central City's (　　)[13] community
09. cleanup day. Today we'll pick (　　)[14] litter along a one-kilometer section of (　　)[15] river.
10. Pick up a bag (　　)[16] a pair of gloves before (　　)[17] get started. At 10:30 we'll take
11. a (　　)[18] for cold drinks and snacks. (　　)[19] we finish around noon, stop (　　)[20] the
12. Community Center to receive a free (　　)[21] for a movie of your (　　)[22] at any of
13. our local (　　)[23]. This is our way of (　　)[24] thank you for volunteering.
14. OK, Pat. Here's the (　　)[25] for your cold. There are two (　　)[26].
15. These yellow tablets are for (　　)[27] sore throat. Take two of them three (　　)[28] a day,
16. after each meal. (　　)[29] one of these green pills after (　　)[30] only
17. when you have a (　　)[31] high fever. They'll bring your temperature
18. (　　)[32] to normal. They're strong, so take (　　)[33] more than three a day.
19. In 1995 (　　)[34] special prize for female novelists, (　　)[35] the Orange Prize for Fiction,
20. was established in Britain. The (　　)[36] of giving this prize was (　　)[37] encourage
21. women writers and attract (　　)[38] attention to their works. Recently, (　　)[39] order to

22. find out if people's ( )⁴⁰ habits had changed since the Orange Prize ( )⁴¹ started,
23. researchers asked a group ( )⁴² 100 British professors and writers about
24. the ( )⁴³ they read. This group included ( )⁴⁴ men and women. All of ( )⁴⁵
25. 100 people said they supported the Orange Prize ( )⁴⁶ that they never chose
26. or ( )⁴⁷ a book because of the author's ( )⁴⁸. Nevertheless, it was found that
27. ( )⁴⁹ men mainly read works by ( )⁵⁰ men. When the researchers asked,
28. "( )⁵¹ novels by women writers have ( )⁵² read recently?" a majority of
29. ( )⁵³ men found it hard to ( )⁵⁴ or could not answer. However, ( )⁵⁵ asked
30. the same question, many ( )⁵⁶ the women were able to ( )⁵⁷ several book titles.
31. The researchers ( )⁵⁸ that although men seem to ( )⁵⁹ the Orange Prize,
32. it appears that they ( )⁶⁰ to read novels written by ( )⁶¹.

CD Track 11

MET CT 2017 解答

01. Now let me tell you (a)¹ story. When we lived in Japan (many)² years ago,
02. my American friend Jane came (to)³ visit us with her Japanese boss,
03. (who)⁴ wanted to meet my husband. (After)⁵ he left, we decided to (open)⁶ the gift
04. that he had (brought)⁷. Surprisingly, it was a neatly (packed)⁸ live lobster.
05. I started laughing (and)⁹ shouting, "It's alive! It's alive!" But Jane, who'd just (gone)¹⁰
06. to the bathroom, thought I (was)¹¹ yelling, "It's a lie! It's a lie!" (She)¹²
07. thought we were having an (argument)¹³, so she was afraid to (come)¹⁴ back into the living room.
08. (When)¹⁵ she finally returned, she realized (that)¹⁶ we were not fighting,
09. but (laughing)¹⁷ at such an unexpected gift.

10. (We)[18] had never cooked a lobster (before)[19], so we didn't know what to (do)[20].
11. In those days there was (no)[21] Internet to get information, so (we)[22] went
12. and asked a neighbor. (Meanwhile)[23], we had put the lobster (in)[24] a sink full of water.
13. (When)[25] we came home the lobster (had)[26] become so lively that
14. we (no)[27] longer had the heart to (cook)[28] it. We managed to get (it)[29] back
15. into the box, and (we)[30] gave it to the neighbor (instead)[31].
16. So, Reina, what would you do (if)[32] we had five million yen (to)[33] improve our school?
17. Hmm. I can (think)[34] of so many things, Ichiro. One (idea)[35] would be
18. to put a (roof)[36] over the bicycle parking area. Don't (you)[37] hate it
19. when it rains (and)[38] your bike gets wet?
20. We (could)[39] also put some picnic tables (on)[40] the grassy area over
21. by (the)[41] bike stands. That would give (students)[42] a place to have lunch
22. (or)[43] hang out after school. And (we)[44] could make the entrance
23. look (a)[45] lot nicer. What about painting (it)[46] a bright color
24. and buying (some)[47] plants and flowers?
25. Well, those (are)[48] all great ideas, Reina. I especially (like)[49] putting a roof
26. over the (bicycles)[50]. But to tell the truth, (if)[51] we had that much money (to)[52] spend,
27. I think it'd be better (to)[53] spend it on one big (thing)[54] rather than a lot of
28. (little)[55] things. Oh, yeah. Good point, Ichiro.
29. (I)[56] think it'd be better if we (had)[57] free Wi-Fi everywhere in the school.
30. (Internet)[58] access would help us study (more)[59]. We could get a lot (of)[60] information
31. that would help us (with)[61] our homework, and there are (so)[62]
32. many educational websites that are (usually)[63] free.
33. Best of all, we (could)[64] chat with the students at (our)[65] sister school in Australia.
34. Don't you (agree)[66], Mayuko?
35. Well, that's a pretty good idea, Ichiro, (but)[67] the library has Internet access,
36. (and)[68] most students already have smartphones (or)[69] tablet PCs. I think it'd be
37. (better)[70] to buy solar panels instead. (That)[71] electricity could be used
38. all (over)[72] the school—we could have (hot)[73] water in the winter

39. and (air)⁷⁴ conditioning in the summer. Oh, (I)⁷⁵ know!
40. We could make a (roof)⁷⁶ for the bicycles out of (the)⁷⁷ solar panels.
41. That would kill (two)⁷⁸ birds with one stone!

CD Track 12

MET CT 2016 解答

01. In some countries, silver gifts (are)¹ given for 25th wedding anniversaries
02. and (gold)² gifts for 50th anniversaries. But in the United Kingdom,
03. (there)³ are also some traditional gifts (given)⁴ to celebrate other anniversaries.
04. Perhaps (people)⁵ are not so familiar with (them)⁶. For example, for third anniversaries,
05. (leather)⁷ gifts are usually given. Three (years)⁸ later, gifts containing sugar are
06. (appropriate)⁹. Six years after that, something (made)¹⁰ of silk is the expected (gift)¹¹.
07. Some might be surprised to (find)¹² out that diamonds are given (not)¹³ only
08. for engagements, but also (for)¹⁴ 60th anniversaries.
09. Welcome to The Ocean Hotel. Our rooms (are)¹⁵ decorated in traditional French style,
10. but (you)¹⁶ can use the latest technology, (for)¹⁷ example, wireless Internet.
11. Every room (offers)¹⁸ a splendid ocean view, so (you)¹⁹ can see the sunset.
12. Our (hotel)²⁰ has Chinese, Japanese, and Italian restaurants on the (top)²¹ floor
13. and three coffee shops (on)²² the first and second floors,
14. (so)²³ you can enjoy Asian and Western dishes. (In)²⁴ front of the hotel
15. we (have)²⁵ an outdoor swimming pool next (to)²⁶ the beach, and
16. you can (also)²⁷ enjoy an indoor swimming pool (and)²⁸ an exercise room.
17. Palau is a (country)²⁹ in the Pacific. It became an (independent)³⁰ republic on October 1, 1994.
18. Palau's flag is (similar)³¹ to Japan's because it features a (single)³² circle. However,
19. the circle is (yellow)³³, and the background is blue. (Blue)³⁴ is used to represent

20. the (ocean)³⁵, which the nation depends on (for)³⁶ food. Unlike the Japanese flag,
21. the (circle)³⁷ on Palau's flag is a little off-center. (Instead)³⁸ of the sun,
22. as on (the)³⁹ Japanese flag, the circle represents the (moon)⁴⁰, which is traditionally
23. thought to (be)⁴¹ important in the life cycle (and)⁴² customs of the people.
24. Helen Keller, admired (for)⁴³ her work on behalf of (people)⁴⁴ with disabilities,
25. visited Japan three times. (She)⁴⁵ was unable to see or (hear)⁴⁶, but she was
26. impressed with (the)⁴⁷ kindness of the Japanese people and (developed)⁴⁸
27. and appreciation of Japan and its (culture)⁴⁹. She first came to Japan in 1937,
28. (when)⁵⁰ she was invited by the Japanese (government)⁵¹ to make
29. a lecture tour (throughout)⁵² the country. While she was (here)⁵³, she was moved
30. by the (story)⁵⁴ about the faithful Akita dog, Hachiko, and (wondered)⁵⁵ if she could have
31. such (a)⁵⁶ dog. Ichiro Ogasawara, a police officer in Akita City, (kindly)⁵⁷ gave her
32. one of his (own)⁵⁸ puppies. She named this dog Kami. (She)⁵⁹ took Kami home with her,
33. which (made)⁶⁰ Kami the first Akita dog to (go)⁶¹ to the United States. In a letter
34. to (a)⁶² friend, she called Kami an "angel (in)⁶³ fur" and said that
35. he (was)⁶⁴ especially gentle and devoted. She (loved)⁶⁵ this dog so much
36. that (she)⁶⁶ asked for another Akita dog, which (was)⁶⁷ sent to her in 1939.
37. This (dog)⁶⁸ was Kami's brother, and she called (him)⁶⁹ Go-Go.
38. Helen Keller's dogs received a lot of (attention)⁷⁰ in the United States,
39. which helped to introduce Akita (dogs)⁷¹ as popular pets for Americans.

CD Track 13

MET CT 2015 解答

01. If you're going to Machu Picchu in highland Peru, (you)¹ should consider visiting Cuzco,
02. at 3,400 meters (above)² sea level. You will enjoy (walking)³ through the Plaza de Armas

第 10 章　MET：実際の問題と解答　　　　　　　　　　　　　　　　　　221

03. and visiting (the)⁴ Temple of the Sun. You can also look at Cuzco's (interesting)⁵ museums
04. and beautiful houses as (well)⁶ as its magnificent churches. Remember, (however)⁷, that
05. these churches close for (a)⁸ few hours around noon. In (addition)⁹, you can take advantage of
06. (modern)¹⁰ hotels and restaurants, and at (the)¹¹ same time, see Cuzco's fascinating history
07. (preserved)¹² in its architecture, language, and (ancient)¹³ treasures.
08. When you start living (alone)¹⁴, you might find it difficult (to)¹⁵ manage your money.
09. Here are (some)¹⁶ tips that you may find (helpful)¹⁷. One hint is first to (make)¹⁸
10. a detailed budget, or plan, (of)¹⁹ how much money you have (and)²⁰ what you are going to
11. (spend)²¹ it on each month. Then, (look)²² at your budget and decide (if)²³
12. you can buy fewer items. (Also)²⁴, use less electricity, water, or (other)²⁵ utilities
13. by turning off lights, (for)²⁶ example. Finally, before shopping, make (a)²⁷ list of
14. what you need (and)²⁸ compare prices on those items (from)²⁹ different shops.
15. Have you ever (heard)³⁰ the phrase "It's all Greek to me"? (We)³¹ use it when we don't
16. understand (a)³² foreign language or a difficult (concept)³³. If someone tries to
17. explain (a)³⁴ theory from physics or mathematics (that)³⁵ we cannot comprehend,
18. we could (say)³⁶, "It's all Greek to me." This phrase (appears)³⁷ in William Shakespeare's
19. play *Julius Caesar*, where one Roman tells (another)³⁸ that he couldn't understand somebody
20. because (he)³⁹ spoke Greek. Although this phrase had (been)⁴⁰ used earlier by different
21. writers, Shakespeare's (use)⁴¹ of the phrase helped to (make)⁴² it popular,
22. and it continues (to)⁴³ be used even today.

23. Americans have (traditionally)⁴⁴ wanted to live apart from (their)⁴⁵ parents, as personal
24. independence is (often)⁴⁶ thought to be very important. (Therefore)⁴⁷, in most cases, the elderly
25. (live)⁴⁸ in their own homes, while (their)⁴⁹ grown children move away and
26. (live)⁵⁰ elsewhere. However, some elderly people (and)⁵¹ their grown-up children have
27. decided (to)⁵² combine households, and this trend (has)⁵³ been increasing in recent years.
28. (There)⁵⁴ certainly are benefits to living (as)⁵⁵ a multi-generational family
29. in the (same)⁵⁶ house. Grandparents take care of (young)⁵⁷ children while the parents go
30. (to)⁵⁸ work. Young children learn about (their)⁵⁹ family history, cooking, and household
31. (repair)⁶⁰ skills from their grandparents. Senior (citizens)⁶¹ also get a lot
32. out (of)⁶² spending time with their grandchildren. (Grandparents)⁶³ stay in good health,
33. hiking (and)⁶⁴ playing sports with the grandchildren. (The)⁶⁵ grandchildren can teach their
34. grandparents (how)⁶⁶ to use computers and keep (up)⁶⁷ with the latest technology.
35. Parents (can)⁶⁸ teach their children proper manners (toward)⁶⁹ older people through
36. their own (behavior)⁷⁰ toward their parents. Children learn (from)⁷¹ seeing their parents
37. interact with (the)⁷² grandparents. Parents can get the (help)⁷³ of the children
38. in watching (out)⁷⁴ for the safety of the (grandparents)⁷⁵, thus sharing the burden
39. if (the)⁷⁶ state of their health becomes (a)⁷⁷ problem.

CD Track 14

MET CT 2014 解答

01. Angora rabbits are soft and lovable (pets)¹. There are different kinds in (different)² countries,

第 10 章　MET：実際の問題と解答　　　　　　　　　　　　　　　　　223

02. but Angoras originated in Ankara, Turkey, before (spreading)³ around the world.
03. One place (they)⁴ became popular was France. They were (kept)⁵ by the French royal family
04. and (other)⁶ elites in the mid-18th century. Soon, Angoras (became)⁷ popular outside France
05. and could be (found)⁸ throughout Europe by the end of (the)⁹ century. Later, people in
06. the United States started (keeping)¹⁰ them as household pets in (the)¹¹ early 1900s.
07. Wherever you find them, (these)¹² long-haired rabbits live five to (seven)¹³ years
08. when kept indoors and (cared)¹⁴ for properly.
09. To make a (simple)¹⁵ kimchi meat sauce, put some finely-chopped (garlic)¹⁶ into a pan
10. with two (tablespoons)¹⁷ of olive oil. Turn the (heat)¹⁸ on, and when you smell (the)¹⁹
11. garlic cooking, add one chopped (onion)²⁰ and cook for about two (minutes)²¹. After adding
12. 500 grams of ground (beef)²², cook until light brown, then (add)²³ one can of
13. chopped tomatoes (together)²⁴ with about three tablespoons of (ketchup)²⁵.
14. Before turning the heat down (to)²⁶ low and cooking everything
15. for (about)²⁷ thirty minutes, don't forget to add (three)²⁸ tablespoons
16. of kimchi base. This sauce (is)²⁹ great on either spaghetti or (rice)³⁰!
17. Growing food locally in American cities (has)³¹ been getting more popular recently.
18. (In)³² fact, the vegetables you buy (in)³³ the supermarket may be
19. grown (just)³⁴ down the street. Shoppers may (be)³⁵ surprised,
20. but actually urban farming (has)³⁶ deep roots, especially in the northeastern US.
21. Before (we)³⁷ had good highways and air (transport)³⁸, fruits and vegetables
22. were often (grown)³⁹ in city greenhouses during the (winter)⁴⁰, instead of being shipped
23. in (from)⁴¹ faraway states or other countries. (Because)⁴² it reduces transportation costs
24. and (provides)⁴³ people with fresh food more (quickly)⁴⁴, urban farming is

25. making a (comeback)⁴⁵.
26. There are many kinds of (collections)⁴⁶ and reasons why people build (them)⁴⁷.
27. People enjoy spending time and (money)⁴⁸ gathering, organizing, and displaying
28. almost (anything)⁴⁹. A serious collector can even (have)⁵⁰ a career as a respected (expert)⁵¹.
29. Some people love certain musicians, (movies)⁵², or TV programs so much that (they)⁵³ must
30. have any items associated (with)⁵⁴ them. Collectors meet other fans, (trade)⁵⁵ information
31. online, and compete to (see)⁵⁶ who has the biggest and (best)⁵⁷ collection. Other people
32. may start (a)⁵⁸ collection by accident. For example, (suppose)⁵⁹ a friend gives you
33. a (toy)⁶⁰ whale souvenir and you keep (it)⁶¹ on your desk. Then, your (mother)⁶²
34. notices it and gives you (an)⁶³ umbrella with a whale design. (Your)⁶⁴ collection continues
35. to grow by (itself)⁶⁵ as others give you similar (gifts)⁶⁶. It may take over your (home)⁶⁷
36. if you aren't careful! Collecting may (also)⁶⁸ have a deeper meaning. Some (researchers)⁶⁹
37. believe it begins with childhood (psychological)⁷⁰ needs. They say we all (experienced)⁷¹
38. uncertainty as children or wanted (things)⁷² we could not have, so (collecting)⁷³ may give us
39. a greater (sense)⁷⁴ of control over our lives. (Whatever)⁷⁵ the motivation may be,
40. collecting (is)⁷⁶ a satisfying and enjoyable hobby (for)⁷⁷ many people.

CD Track 15

MET CT 2013 解答

01. Towering skyscrapers are a symbol (of)¹ modern society. In the late 1800s,

02. (new)² technological developments made very tall (buildings)³ possible. One development
03. was steel (building)⁴ technology. Before that, architects were (required)⁵ to create thicker
04. stone walls (to)⁶ support taller buildings. These walls (were)⁷ extremely heavy and
05. allowed less (room)⁸ for windows and light. After (mass)⁹ production of steel was introduced,
06. (architects)¹⁰ began to use steel frames (to)¹¹ support a building's weight.
07. Steel (was)¹² much lighter and stronger than (stone)¹³, while taking up much less (space)¹⁴.
08. At the same time, elevator (technology)¹⁵ and fire-resistant building materials
09. also (helped)¹⁶ make skyscrapers possible.
10. Ireland is a (nice)¹⁷ place to visit all through (the)¹⁸ year. The peak months of
11. (the)¹⁹ tourist season are July and August, but the (weather)²⁰ in May, June, and September
12. is usually good (as)²¹ well, and hotels are not (busy)²².
13. Flowers are most beautiful in April (and)²³ May. In October, many art festivals are (held)²⁴.
14. Winter has its own appeal. (You)²⁵ can have fantastic places all (to)²⁶ yourself,
15. like the beach at Roses Point (near)²⁷ the town of Sligo. Although it (gets)²⁸ dark early and
16. some museums (and)²⁹ attractions are closed, as are (many)³⁰ hotels,
17. this quiet season is (most)³¹ relaxing for some visitors.
18. You (have)³² reached ISSC, the International Student Support (Center)³³.
19. Our business hours are Monday through Friday, 8 am (to)³⁴ 6 pm. Stay on the line
20. for (recorded)³⁵ help messages. Press one for dining (services)³⁶ and assistance for students
21. with (special)³⁷ dietary needs; press two for dormitory (or)³⁸ apartment rentals; press three for
22. Internet (and)³⁹ telephone connections; press four for library (and)⁴⁰ bookstore locations.
23. Students with questions (about)⁴¹ part-time work on campus should (call)⁴² to
24. make an appointment to (see)⁴³ our staff at the center.

25. (In)⁴⁴ the case of a medical (emergency)⁴⁵ or illness,
26. dial 911 or go (directly)⁴⁶ to the clinic. Thank you (for)⁴⁷ calling.
27. What can a colorful, (casual)⁴⁸ shirt tell you about a (culture)⁴⁹?
28. If it's an aloha shirt from Hawaii, (quite)⁵⁰ a bit. Alohas show island life (in)⁵¹
29. the same way that films, (maps)⁵², and paintings do. They are (as)⁵³ diverse as
30. the islands they (come)⁵⁴ from. These shirts are said to (have)⁵⁵ begun as simple clothing
31. worn (by)⁵⁶ plantation workers from the Philippines. Then, in (the)⁵⁷ 1930s,
32. a local Chinese merchant made some (with)⁵⁸ leftover Japanese kimono cloth.
33. Eventually, tropical Polynesian (images)⁵⁹ were added and aloha shirts were (born)⁶⁰.
34. They represent the mix of (peoples)⁶¹ in Hawaii. Although some people thought Hawaiian
35. (shirts)⁶² were cheap-looking, alohas became very popular. (In)⁶³ the 1950s, air travel
36. from the (mainland)⁶⁴ became cheaper, the standard of (living)⁶⁵ in America was improving,
37. and people (wanted)⁶⁶ clothes as bright and flashy (as)⁶⁷ their hopes for the future.
38. (Pop)⁶⁸ stars and presidents alike put (on)⁶⁹ alohas and a trend took off.
39. (Outside)⁷⁰ Hawaii, the aloha symbolized fun times, but (back)⁷¹ on the islands,
40. aloha shirts were (acceptable)⁷² in place of a suit (and)⁷³ tie.
41. Hawaiians take pride in their culture, (especially)⁷⁴ aloha shirts. Unfortunately,
42. not many of (the)⁷⁵ earliest alohas have survived; these can (sell)⁷⁶ for thousands of
43. dollars. Whether (inexpensive)⁷⁷ or high-priced, these comfortable shirts (show)⁷⁸ the world
44. a snapshot of Hawaiian (life)⁷⁹.

CD Track 16

MET CT 2012 解答

01. Moving to a new home (with)[1] your pet can be difficult. (Cats)[2] are very
02. sensitive animals, and (moving)[3] is quite an upsetting experience (for)[4] them.
03. When you arrive at (your)[5] new home, it may be (a)[6] good idea to put your (cat)[7]
04. in a quiet room, if (possible)[8]. Leave him in peace with (his)[9] old bed, his litter box,
05. and some food until everything calms (down)[10]. After that, let him come (out)[11]
06. and join you only if (he)[12] wants to. He should also (stay)[13] indoors
07. until he becomes familiar (with)[14] his new home and environment.
08. (Welcome)[15] to Greenland, the largest island in (the)[16] world. You are now
09. in Nuuk, (the)[17] capital city located on the (southwestern)[18] coast
10. where there are small (airports)[19], hotels, and villages.
11. In contrast, (along)[20] the eastern coast, which is (the)[21] least accessible area,
12. we can (see)[22] some of the finest, breathtaking Arctic (scenery)[23].
13. Travelers to the eastern shore (always)[24] describe the view as spectacular
14. (and)[25] magnificent. However, the trip is (only)[26] possible for a few weeks (a)[27] year
15. when the frozen ocean (melts)[28] enough to allow expedition ships (through)[29].
16. Attention, please. I have a (message)[30] from your history teacher.
17. Because (of)[31] a family emergency, today's class is (canceled)[32], and the makeup class
18. will (be)[33] held this coming Saturday. The (class)[34] is scheduled for second period
19. (as)[35] usual, but in a different (classroom)[36], Room 305 on the third floor.
20. At that (time)[37], your teacher will collect the (assignment)[38] you were supposed to
21. submit (today)[39]. The midterm examination will be (postponed)[40].
22. The main entrance to the (building)[41] is closed on Saturdays,
23. so (you)[42] should enter through the side (door)[43]. If you have questions
24. or (need)[44] more information, please email your (teacher)[45].
25. Nursery rhymes are simple poems (which)[46] exist in many cultures.

26. Through (these)⁴⁷ poems, children have fun singing, (playing)⁴⁸ games,
27. and learning basic language (and)⁴⁹ counting skills. What is remarkable (about)⁵⁰
28. these poems is that they (are)⁵¹ often passed down orally from one (generation)⁵²
29. to another in the home. (Among)⁵³ nursery rhymes, Mother Goose rhymes may be
30. (the)⁵⁴ best known. But, was there (really)⁵⁵ a person named Mother Goose?
31. We are (not)⁵⁶ sure. There are several interesting (theories)⁵⁷ about the origin
32. of Mother Goose. Some (scholars)⁵⁸ suggest that it was the French (author)⁵⁹,
33. Charles Perrault, who said in the 1600s that (the)⁶⁰ poems were told by
34. an (old)⁶¹ woman who kept geese. Others (say)⁶² that the English author,
35. John Newbury, first used (the)⁶³ name in a book he (published)⁶⁴ in 1765.
36. Still others insist that Mother Goose (was)⁶⁵ Elizabeth Goose,
37. who lived in Boston in the 18th (century)⁶⁶ and entertained her grandchildren
38. by (singing)⁶⁷ nursery rhymes. Regardless of how (the)⁶⁸ term originated,
39. Mother Goose rhymes are the (most)⁶⁹ familiar children's poems
40. and are enjoyed (worldwide)⁷⁰. Teachers of English often use them
41. (to)⁷¹ introduce the natural sounds and (rhythms)⁷² of the language in a (fun)⁷³ way.
42. Today, many works of (literature)⁷⁴, popular songs,
43. and movies also (make)⁷⁵ reference to Mother Goose rhymes.

CD Track 17

MET CT 2011 解答

01. Our airline welcomes children. More (than)¹ 45,000 unaccompanied children fly with us
02. (each)² year. Whether it's a short (flight)³ or a long journey, your (child)⁴ will enjoy
03. a safe and (comfortable)⁵ trip. Here's some important information.
04. (Children)⁶ aged 5 and above may travel (alone)⁷ on flights.
05. Children under 5 must (be)⁸ accompanied by someone aged 17 or (older)⁹.

06. When your child is travelling (alone)[10], please call our reservations desk.
07. (We)[11] will give you more details (about)[12] services for young passengers.
08. Tonight's (story)[13] on "Pets in the News" (is)[14] about a cat
09. that traveled (halfway)[15] around the world with a (shipment)[16] of cotton from Egypt.
10. When the (ship)[17] arrived in Seattle, a worker found (a)[18] cat
11. that had been trapped (among)[19] the containers for nearly a (month)[20].
12. The cat was taken to (an)[21] animal shelter where her physical (condition)[22] was checked.
13. People were amazed (the)[23] cat survived so long. Interestingly, (the)[24] ship,
14. which had previously had (a)[25] rat problem, was now free (of)[26] rats.
15. As a professional photographer (I)[27] would like to give you (some)[28] suggestions
16. for successful landscape photography. (In)[29] winter, for example, when the (days)[30]
17. are short, you need to (know)[31] where you're going and what (you)[32] want to photograph.
18. You can (get)[33] familiar with the area you're (planning)[34] to visit by
19. reading guidebooks (and)[35] studying maps. Then, you'll know (beforehand)[36]
20. where the most attractive locations (are)[37], rather than leaving it to (chance)[38].
21. At the location, you may (need)[39] to get off the main (path)[40],
22. so you should be careful. (To)[41] take a good photo, it (may)[42] be necessary to be
23. in (freezing)[43] conditions which might be dangerous.
24. (Many)[44] of the world's best-loved symphonies (are)[45] known by
25. popular nicknames given (by)[46] the general public or music (publishers)[47]
26. rather than by their composers. (A)[48] number of Haydn's symphonies
27. have nicknames (such)[49] as the *Surprise Symphony*, the *Military Symphony* and the
28. *Clock Symphony*. Another example of (this)[50] type is the *Farewell Symphony*, in which
29. the (musicians)[51] leave the stage one by one as (they)[52] finish playing.
30. Eventually, the two violinists (who)[53] are left put down their (instruments)[54]
31. and walk away from the (stage)[55] in silence. This ends the (performance)[56].

32. The story behind this piece (is)⁵⁷ that the prince, for whom Haydn (worked)⁵⁸,
33. had taken all of the (musicians)⁵⁹ to his second palace in (the)⁶⁰ countryside
34. where he liked to (go)⁶¹ hunting. The musicians found the (weather)⁶² and
35. working conditions at this (place)⁶³ to be very unpleasant. Moreover,
36. (they)⁶⁴ missed their families and the (simple)⁶⁵ comforts of home.
37. When the *Farewell Symphony* was (first)⁶⁶ performed at the country palace,
38. (the)⁶⁷ prince understood the message of Haydn's (music)⁶⁸ at once.
39. The next day (he)⁶⁹ ordered that his entire household (return)⁷⁰ to the city
40. so they (could)⁷¹ be with their families in (time)⁷² for Christmas.

CD Track 18

MET CT 2010 解答

01. When I first came to Japan, (I)¹ was surprised when people asked
02. (if)² I was annoyed by the (sounds)³ of insects such as cicadas.
03. (They)⁴ had heard many western people couldn't (stand)⁵ such sounds.
04. Actually, the sound (of)⁶ cicadas—which are called *semi* in Japanese—
05. makes (me)⁷ feel at home. When I (was)⁸ growing up, the cicadas would
06. (sing)⁹ in a tree just outside (my)¹⁰ bedroom window all summer long.
07. (I)¹¹ would lie on my bed, (listening)¹² to their peaceful song.
08. When (I)¹³ heard the cicadas during my first (summer)¹⁴ in Japan,
09. it brought back happy (childhood)¹⁵ memories.

10. Hello, Takashi? This is Rose. I'm in Kyoto now. (I)¹⁶ enjoyed staying
11. with you and (your)¹⁷ family last week. Sorry to (bother)¹⁸ you,
12. but I've got a problem. (I)¹⁹ can't find my gloves. Have you (seen)²⁰ them?
13. Maybe I left them (on)²¹ the table in the bedroom, (but)²² I'm not sure.
14. They're green and match (my)²³ coat. If you have them, (can)²⁴ you please
15. call me here? (The)²⁵ number is ... oh, I hardly stay (in)²⁶ my hotel room,
16. so I'll contact (you)²⁷ again tomorrow. Thanks. Talk to (you)²⁸ later.

17. Welcome to Marine Park. Before you (begin)²⁹ your marine adventure,
18. we have (a)³⁰ few announcements to make. As (always)³¹, from 12:30,
19. you can see our (very)³² popular sea animal show with (dolphins)³³ jumping
20. through hoops and playing (basketball)³⁴. We are sorry that Penguin Village is
21. (closed)³⁵ today, but starting at 3:00, in (addition)³⁶ to our usual attractions,

32. were playing around (in)⁵⁶ the bottle. I planned to (go)⁵⁷ and find a nice glass
33. (fishbowl)⁵⁸ on the weekend so my (new)⁵⁹ pets could swim in it (and)⁶⁰ I could enjoy
34. watching them (swim)⁶¹ around. I left the bottle (on)⁶² the kitchen table and
35. went (to)⁶³ bed. The next morning when (I)⁶⁴ woke up, I suddenly remembered
36. (that)⁶⁵ my mother makes coffee every (morning)⁶⁶ using mineral water. I ran
37. (to)⁶⁷ the kitchen, and there she (was)⁶⁸, holding my bottle in her (hand)⁶⁹.
38. I was about to say "(Stop)⁷⁰!" when she said, "Ugh, something's moving
39. in (this)⁷¹ water!" So I told her (the)⁷² story and prevented a disaster (just)⁷³ in time.

CD Track 20

MET CT 2008 解答

01. Thank you for calling the Southeast Coast Weather Center. Here's (the)¹
02. weekend beach report. Saturday morning, (good)² weather is expected
03. with partly (cloudy)³ skies and mild winds with (temperatures)⁴ in the lower 30s.
04. In the (afternoon)⁵, clouds will increase and occasional (showers)⁶ are expected.
05. The forecast for (Sunday)⁷ is light rain continuing until (noon)⁸, gradually becoming
06. clear and sunny. (However)⁹, winds will increase and high (waves)¹⁰ are likely,
07. so beach-goers are advised (to)¹¹ refrain from swimming throughout the (afternoon)¹².
08. Good morning, everybody. Welcome to Central City's (annual)¹³ community
09. cleanup day. Today we'll pick (up)¹⁴ litter along a one-kilometer section of (the)¹⁵ river.
10. Pick up a bag (and)¹⁶ a pair of gloves before (you)¹⁷ get started. At 10:30 we'll take
11. a (break)¹⁸ for cold drinks and snacks. (After)¹⁹ we finish around noon, stop (by)²⁰ the

12. Community Center to receive a free (ticket)²¹ for a movie of your (choice)²² at any of
13. our local (theaters)²³. This is our way of (saying)²⁴ thank you for volunteering.
14. OK, Pat. Here's the (medicine)²⁵ for your cold. There are two (kinds)²⁶.
15. These yellow tablets are for (your)²⁷ sore throat. Take two of them three (times)²⁸ a day,
16. after each meal. (Take)²⁹ one of these green pills after (meals)³⁰ only
17. when you have a (very)³¹ high fever. They'll bring your temperature
18. (down)³² to normal. They're strong, so take (no)³³ more than three a day.
19. In 1995 (a)³⁴ special prize for female novelists, (called)³⁵ the Orange Prize for Fiction,
20. was established in Britain. The (point)³⁶ of giving this prize was (to)³⁷ encourage
21. women writers and attract (more)³⁸ attention to their works. Recently, (in)³⁹ order to
22. find out if people's (reading)⁴⁰ habits had changed since the Orange Prize (was)⁴¹ started,
23. researchers asked a group (of)⁴² 100 British professors and writers about
24. the (novels)⁴³ they read. This group included (both)⁴⁴ men and women. All of (these)⁴⁵
25. 100 people said they supported the Orange Prize (and)⁴⁶ that they never chose
26. or (avoided)⁴⁷ a book because of the author's (sex)⁴⁸. Nevertheless, it was found that
27. (the)⁴⁹ men mainly read works by (other)⁵⁰ men. When the researchers asked,
28. "(What)⁵¹ novels by women writers have (you)⁵² read recently?" a majority of
29. (the)⁵³ men found it hard to (recall)⁵⁴ or could not answer. However, (when)⁵⁵ asked
30. the same question, many (of)⁵⁶ the women were able to (name)⁵⁷ several book titles.
31. The researchers (concluded)⁵⁸ that although men seem to (support)⁵⁹ the Orange Prize,
32. it appears that they (choose)⁶⁰ to read novels written by (men)⁶¹.

参考文献

Bai, Chun-Hua (2007) *The Minimal English Test in China*, Master's thesis, Gifu University.
Chomsky, Noam (1981) *Lectures on Government and Binding: The Pisa Lectures*, Foris, Dordrecht.
College English Test (http://www.cet.edu.cn/index.php)
大学入試センター (http://www.dnc.ac.jp/)
Dawson, Catherine (2001) *English*, Oxford University Press, Oxford/江蘇訳林出版社, 南京.
Educational Testing Service (ETS) (https://www.ets.org/)
フォード丹羽順子・小林典子・山元啓史 (1994)「日本語能力簡易試験 (SPOT) における音声テープの役割に関する研究」『日本語教育方法研究会誌』1号3巻, 18-19.
フォード丹羽順子・小林 典子・山元啓史 (1995)「日本語能力簡易試験 SPOT は何を測定しているか——音声テープ要因の分析——」『日本語教育』86号, 93-102.
Goto, Kenichi, Hideki Maki and Chise Kasai (2010) "The Minimal English Test: A New Method to Measure English as a Second Language Proficiency," *Evaluation & Research in Education* 23.2, 91-104.
Gould, Dinah, Daniel Kelly, Len Goldstone and John Gammon (2001) "Examining the Validity of Pressure Ulcer Risk Assessment Scales: Developing and Using Illustrated Patient Simulations to Collect the Data," *Journal of Clinical Nursing* 10, 697-706.
Hasebe, Megumi, Hideki Maki, Chise Kasai, Hirotaka Imamaki, Akane Ishikawa and Yumi Kimura (2008) "The junior Minimal English Test (jMET)," *The 33rd Annual Conference of the Applied Linguistics Association of Australia*, University of Sydney, July 4, 2008.
Hasebe, Megumi, Juri Yoshimura, Hideki Maki and Hiromasa Hamatani (2010) "The junior Minimal English Test (jMET) for the 8th and 9th Graders," *Proceedings of the Second Annual Asian Conference on Education 2010 Conference*, 1253-1264.
Hasebe, Megumi, Hideki Maki, Toshiro Umezawa, Asako No, and Shogo Tokugawa (2012a) "On the *That*-Trace Effect by Japanese ESL Learners: A VAS-Based Analysis," *Proceedings of the 40th Western Conference on Linguistics Volume 21*, ed. by Christina Galeano, Emrah Gorgulu, and Irina Presnyakova, 106-114, Department of Linguistics, California State University, Fresno.

Hasebe, Megumi, Hideki Maki and Toshiro Umezawa (2012b) "Two Types of Asymmetries in Acquisition of the Wh-Interrogative Construction by Japanese ESL Learners," *The Japan Association of Language and Culture* 38, 3-14.

Hasebe, Megumi and Hideki Maki (2014) "Acquisition of the Wh-Interrogative Construction by Japanese Junior High School EFL Learners," *Selected Proceedings of the 2012 Second Language Research Forum: Building Bridges Between Disciplines*, ed. by Ryan T. Miller, Katherine I. Martin, Chelsea M. Eddington, Ashlie Henery, Nausica Marcos Miguel, Alison M. Tseng, Alba Tuninetti and Daniel Walter, 76-88, Cascadilla, Somerville, MA.

Hasebe, Megumi, Hideki Maki, Toshiro Umezawa, Ling-Yun Fan, Yong-Xin Gao and Jessica Dunton (2015) "The Acquisition of *Wh*-Interrogatives and Relative Clauses by Japanese EFL Learners," *Proceedings of the Chubu English Language Education Society* 44, 9-16.

石黒昭博 (2000) *All-Round Level B*, 美誠社, 京都.

Kanno, Kazue (1996) "The Status of a Nonparameterized Principle in the L2 Initial State," *Language Acquisition* 5, 317-332.

Kasai, Chise, Hideki Maki and Fumikazu Niinuma (2005) "The Minimal English Test: A Strong Correlation with the Paul Nation Vocabulary Test: A Preliminary Study," *Bulletin of the Faculty of Regional Studies, Gifu University* 17, 45-52.

笠島準一・浅野博・下村勇三郎・牧野勤・池田正雄・ほか49名 (2006a) *New Horizon English Course 1*, 東京書籍, 東京.

笠島準一・浅野博・下村勇三郎・牧野勤・池田正雄・ほか49名 (2006b) *New Horizon English Course 2*, 東京書籍, 東京.

笠島準一・浅野博・下村勇三郎・牧野勤・池田正雄・ほか49名 (2006c) *New Horizon English Course 3*, 東京書籍, 東京.

Kawana, Norihito and Stuart Walker (2002) *This is Media.com*, 成美堂, 東京.

Kent, Joanne Claire (2003) *Advance with English*, Oxford University Press, Oxford/江蘇訳林出版社, 南京.

小林典子・フォード順子 (1992)「文法項目の音声聴取に関する実証的研究」『日本語教育』78号, 167-177.

小林典子・丹羽順子・山元啓史 (1994)「日本語能力簡易試験としての「聞きテスト」:解答形式の漢字要因に関する分析」『筑波大学留学生教育センター日本語教育論集』9号, 149-158.

小林典子・フォード丹羽順子・山元啓史 (1995)「日本語能力簡易試験 (SPOT) の得点分布傾向:中上級向けテストと初級向けテスト」『筑波大学留学生センター日本語教育論集』10号, 107-119.

小林典子・フォード丹羽順子・山元啓史 (1996)「日本語能力の新しい測定法『SPOT』」『世界の日本語教育』6号, 201-236.

Lasnik, Howard and Mamoru Saito (1984) "On the Nature of Proper Government," *Linguistic Inquiry* 15, 235-289.
Lasnik, Howard and Mamoru Saito (1992) *Move α: Conditions on Its Application and Output*, MIT Press, Cambridge, MA.
Lee, Sun-Young (2008) "Argument-Adjunct Asymmetry in the Acquisition of Inversion in Wh-Questions by Korean Learners of English," *Language Learning* 58, 625-663.
李荫華・王徳明・夏国佐・余建中・ほか5名 (2013) *New College English Integrated Course 1*, 上海外語教育出版社, 上海.
Ma, Wen (in progress) Develoment of Versions of the Minimal English Test to Measure English Proficiency of Chinese Learners of English as a Second Language, Master's thesis, Gifu University.
Maki, Hideki (2003) "The Minimal English Test: MET 1-MET 10," ms., Gifu University.
Maki, Hideki (2010) "Introduction to the Minimal English Test,"『言語教育研究第3号』盛岡大学言語教育研究委員会 (編), 15-26, 青山社, 神奈川.
牧秀樹 (2015)「The Minimal English Test (最小英語テスト) の有用性」『日本の英語教育の今, そして, これから』長谷川信子 (編), 300-316, 開拓社, 東京.
Maki, Hideki and Fumikazu Niinuma (2005) "The Minimal English Test: From Proficiency Measurement to Proficiency Improvement," *Bulletin of the Faculty of Regional Studies, Gifu University* 16, 7-12.
Maki, Hideki, Jessica Dunton and Carlyn Obringer (1999) "What Grade Would I Be in If I Were Japanese?" paper presented at *The 14th Annual Conference of the Association of Teachers of Japanese*.
牧秀樹・和佐田裕昭・橋本永貢子 (2003)「最小英語テスト (MET):初期研究」『英語教育』53.10, 47-50.
Maki, Hideki, Takane Ito, Yoichi Miyamoto, Satoshi Oku, Asako Uchibori and Yukiko Ueda (2004) "The Minimal English Test: Its Correlation with the College Entrance Examination (English Part) 2003," *Bulletin of the Faculty of Regional Studies, Gifu University* 15, 39-46.
Maki, Hideki, Alexandra von Fragstein, Tamami Morishima, Ryoko Tsuruta, Takane Ito, Yoichi Miyamoto, Satoshi Oku, Asako Uchibori, Masahiko Date and Kenjiro Tagawa (2005a) "The Minimal English Test: Its Correlation with the College Entrance Examination (English Part) 2004," *Bulletin of the Faculty of Regional Studies, Gifu University* 17, 53-57.
Maki, Hideki, Chise Kasai, Kenichi Goto, Yuka Morita, Yoko Yumoto, Masao Ochi, Satoshi Oku and Masahiko Date (2006a) "The Minimal English Test: Its Correlation with the College Entrance Examination (English Part) 2005," *Bulletin of the*

Faculty of Regional Studies, Gifu University 19, 33-37.

Maki, Hideki, Chise Kasai, Kenichi Goto, Myung-Hwan Lee, Hee-Won Lee and Dae-Jin Kim (2006b) "The Minimal English Test in Korea: Its Correlation with the College Scholastic Achievement Test (English Part) 2005," Proceedings of *the 2006 KALS-KASELL International Conference on English and Linguistics*, 201-213.

Maki, Hideki, Chise Kasai, Kenichi Goto, Takane Ito, Yoichi Miyamoto and Satoshi Oku (2007a) "The Minimal English Test: Its Correlation with the College Entrance Examination (English Part) 2006," *Bulletin of the Faculty of Regional Studies, Gifu University* 21, 127-134.

Maki, Hideki, Yuka Morita, Kenyu Ichihara, Shinya Furukawa, Chise Kasai and Kenichi Goto (2007b) "The Minimal English Test in High School: The Case of Kamo High School," *Bulletin of the Faculty of Regional Studies, Gifu University* 20, 107-111.

Maki, Hideki, Chise Kasai, Kenichi Goto, Akina Okada, Kazushige Takahashi, Megumi Hasebe, Hirotaka Imamaki, Akane Ishikawa, Takane Ito, Satoshi Oku, Yoko Yumoto, Yoichi Miyamoto, Masao Ochi, Michiyo Hamasaki, Yukiko Ueda, Kosuke Nagasue, Hironobu Kasai and Jessica Dunton (2008a) "The Minimal English Test: Its Correlation with the University Entrance Examination (English Part) 2007," *Bulletin of the Faculty of Regional Studies, Gifu University* 23, 79-86.

Maki, Hideki, Yuka Morita, Kenyu Ichihara, Shinya Furukawa, Kenichi Goto, Chise Kasai and Jessica Dunton (2008b) "The Minimal English Test (MET) in High School: Correlation Between the Scores on the MET and the Scores on the Global Test of English Communication for Students (GTEC)," *Bulletin of the Faculty of Regional Studies, Gifu University* 23, 87-94.

Maki, Hideki, Chise Kasai, Kenichi Goto, Megumi Hasebe, Satoshi Oku, Yoichi Miyamoto, Michiyo Hamasaki, Yukiko Ueda, Kosuke Nagasue, Hironobu Kasai and Jessica Dunton (2009a) "The Minimal English Test: Its Correlation with the University Entrance Examination (English Part) 2008," *Bulletin of the Faculty of Regional Studies, Gifu University* 24, 53-60.

Maki, Hideki, Chise Kasai, Kenichi Goto, Megumi Hasebe, Akane Ishikawa, Juri Yoshimura, Asuka Kuroshita, Toshiro Umezawa, Satoshi Oku, Yoichi Miyamoto, Michiyo Hamasaki, Yukiko Ueda, Kosuke Nagasue, Hironobu Kasai and Jessica Dunton (2009b) "The Minimal English Test: A Version with Words with 5 Letters or Fewer," *Bulletin of the Faculty of Regional Studies, Gifu University* 25, 69-81.

Maki, Hideki, Sarenqimuge, Juri Yoshimura, Yuki Makino, Megumi Hasebe, Kenichi Goto, Chise Kasai, Toshiro Umezawa, Takane Ito, Yoko Yumoto, Satoshi Oku,

Michiyo Hamasaki, Yukiko Ueda, Kosuke Nagasue, Hironobu Kasai, Takashi Munakata and Jessica Dunton (2010a) "The Minimal English Test: Its Correlation with the University Entrance Examination (English Part) 2009," *Bulletin of the Faculty of Regional Studies, Gifu University* 26, 35-42.

Maki, Hideki, Sarenqimuge, Juri Yoshimura, Yuki Makino, Megumi Hasebe, Kenichi Goto, Takane Ito, Yoko Yumoto, Saotshi Oku, Michiyo Hamasaki, Yukiko Ueda, Kosuke Nagasue, Hironobu Kasai, Takashi Munakata and Jessica Dunton (2010b) "The Minimal English Test: A Revised Version," *KOTESOL Proceedings 2009*, 225-232.

Maki, Hideki, Megumi Hasebe, and Toshiro Umezawa (2010c) "A Study of Correlation Between the Scores on the Minimal English Test (MET) and the Scores on the Test of English for International Communication (TOEIC)," *Bulletin of the Faculty of Regional Studies, Gifu University* 27, 53-63.

Maki, Hideki, Hiromasa Hamatani, Megumi Hasebe, Chise Kasai, Kenichi Goto and Jessica Dunton (2010d) "The junior Minimal English Test (jMET): The *New Horizon* Version," *Bulletin of the Faculty of Regional Studies, Gifu University* 27, 47-52.

Maki, Hideki, Shogo Tokugawa, Mizuki Sugiyama, Megumi Hasebe, Juri Yoshimura, Chise Kasai, Toshiro Umezawa, Yoko Yumoto, Michiyo Hamasaki, Yukiko Ueda, Kosuke Nagasue, Hironobu Kasai, Takashi Munakata and Jessica Dunton (2011a) "The Minimal English Test: Its Correlation with the University Entrance Examination (English Part) 2010," *Bulletin of the Faculty of Regional Studies, Gifu University* 28, 51-58.

Maki, Hideki, Megumi Hasebe and Jessica Dunton (2011b) "The Minimal English Test: The "Practice Makes Perfect" Effect," *Bulletin of the Faculty of Regional Studies, Gifu University* 29, 43-51.

Maki, Hideki, Shogo Tokugawa, Megumi Kato, Megumi Hasebe, Chise Kasai, Toshiro Umezawa, Takashi Munakata and Jessica Dunton (2012a) "The Minimal English Test: Its Correlation with the University Entrance Examination (English Part) 2011," *Bulletin of the Faculty of Regional Studies, Gifu University* 30, 47-54.

Maki, Hideki, Shogo Tokugawa, Megumi Kato, Megumi Hasebe, Chise Kasai, Toshiro Umezawa, Takashi Munakata and Jessica Dunton (2012b) "The MET 8: Its Correlation with the University Entrance Examination (English Part) 2011," *Bulletin of the Faculty of Regional Studies, Gifu University* 31, 51-59.

Maki, Hideki, Megumi Hasebe and Yuka Morita (2012c) "The *All-Round Level B* Version of the Minimal English Test (MET ARB)," *Bulletin of the Faculty of Regional Studies, Gifu University* 30, 55-60.

Maki, Hideki, Megumi Hasebe, Megumi Kato, Shogo Tokugawa, Chise Kasai, Toshiro

Umezawa, Sachie Ono and Jessica Dunton (2012d) "Progress in the junior Minimal English Test: A Study in Gifu Prefecture," *Bulletin of the Faculty of Regional Studies, Gifu University* 31, 43-49.

Maki, Hideki, Takuya Iijima, Megumi Kato, Megumi Hasebe, Chise Kasai, Satoshi Oku and Jessica Dunton (2013a) "The Minimal English Test: Its Correlation with the University Entrance Examination (English Part) 2012," *Bulletin of the Faculty of Regional Studies, Gifu University* 32, 19-24.

Maki, Hideki, Megumi Hasebe, Takuya Iijima, Megumi Kato, Chise Kasai, Satoshi Oku and Jessica Dunton (2013b) "The METs 6, 8 and 10: Their Correlations with the University Entrance Examination (English Part) 2012," *Bulletin of the Faculty of Regional Studies, Gifu University* 33, 45-52.

Maki, Hideki, Kengo Suzuki, Megumi Hasebe, Shogo Tokugawa, Ru-Wen Zhang, Ling-Yun Fan, Jessica Dunton and Chise Kasai (2013c) "The junior Minimal English Test: A New Crown Version," *Proceedings of the Chubu English Language Education Society* 42, 147-152.

Maki, Hideki and Megumi Hasebe (2013) "The Minimal English Test and the Test in Practical English Proficiency by the STEP," *Bulletin of the Faculty of Regional Studies, Gifu University* 32, 25-30.

Maki, Hideki, Ling-Yun Fan, Megumi Hasebe, Satoshi Oku, Yukiko Ueda and Jessica Dunton (2014a) "The Minimal English Test: Its Correlation with the University Entrance Examination (English Part) 2013," *Bulletin of the Faculty of Regional Studies, Gifu University* 34, 31-36.

Maki, Hideki, Ling-Yun Fan, Megumi Hasebe, Toshiro Umezawa, Satoshi Oku, Yukiko Ueda and Jessica Dunton (2014b) "The METs 6, 8 and 10: Their Correlations with the University Entrance Examination (English Part) 2013," *Bulletin of the Faculty of Regional Studies, Gifu University* 35, 43-52.

Maki, Hideki, Megumi Hasebe, Ling-Yun Fan, Jessica Dunton, Toshiro Umezawa and Chise Kasai (2014c) "The junior Minimal English Tests as Prediction Tests for the STEP Tests," *Proceedings of the Chubu English Language Education Society* 43, 1-8.

Maki, Hideki, Yong-Xin Gao, Toshiro Umezawa, Shigeki Taguchi, Megumi Hasebe, Satoshi Oku, Yukiko Ueda, Masao Ochi, Kosuke Nagasue and Jessica Dunton (2015a) "The Minimal English Test: Its Correlation with the University Entrance Examination (English Part) 2014," *Bulletin of the Faculty of Regional Studies, Gifu University* 36, 31-36.

Maki, Hideki, Megumi Hasebe, Yong-Xin Gao, Toshiro Umezawa, Shigeki Taguchi, Satoshi Oku, Yukiko Ueda, Masao Ochi, Kosuke Nagasue and Jessica Dunton (2015b) "The METs 4E3, 4E4 and 6: Their Correlations with the University Entrance Examination (English Part) 2014," *Bulletin of the Faculty of Regional Studies, Gifu University* 37, 45-54.

Maki, Hideki, Wen-Qi Ren, Can Wang, Megumi Hasebe, Shigeki Taguchi, Satoshi Oku, Yukiko Ueda, Masao Ochi, Kosuke Nagasue and Jessica Dunton (2016a) "The Minimal English Test: Its Correlation with the University Entrance Examination (English Part) 2015," *Bulletin of the Faculty of Regional Studies, Gifu University* 38, 59-64.

Maki, Hideki, Megumi Hasebe, Wen-Qi Ren, Can Wang, Shigeki Taguchi, Satoshi Oku, Yukiko Ueda, Masao Ochi, Kosuke Nagasue, Michael Sevier and Jessica Dunton (2016b) "The METs 4E3, 4E4, 4E5 and 6: Their Correlations with the University Entrance Examination (English Part) 2015," *Bulletin of the Faculty of Regional Studies, Gifu University* 39, 1-10.

Maki, Hideki, Shu-Jing Wu, Zi-Wei Xu, Yue-Huan Zhang, Megumi Hasebe, Shigeki Taguchi, Yukiko Ueda, Masao Ochi, Michael Sevier and Jessica Dunton (2017a) "The Minimal English Test: Its Correlation with the University Entrance Examination (English Part) 2016," *Bulletin of the Faculty of Regional Studies, Gifu University* 40, 23-28.

Maki, Hideki, Toshiro Umezawa, Megumi Hasebe, and Michael Sevier (2017b) "The METs 4E3, 4E4, 4E5, and 6: Their Correlations with the TOEIC IP," *Bulletin of the Faculty of Regional Studies, Gifu University* 41, 21-30.

Morii, Nanami (2018) *The Center Test Versions of the Minimal English Test: A Study of Correlations Between their Scores and the Scores on the College TOEIC*, Bachelor's thesis, Gifu University.

Nakagawa, Rieko and Yuriko Yamawaki (2004) *Guri and Gura: The English Version*, Translated by Peter Howlett and Richard McNamara, Tuttle Publishing, Tokyo.

Nation, Paul (1990) *Teaching and Learning Vocabulary*, Newbury House/Harper Row, New York.

日本英語検定協会（英検）(http://www.eiken.or.jp/)

O'Grady, William, Miseon Lee and Miho Choo (2003) "A Subject-Object Asymmetry in the Acquisition of Relative Clauses in Korean as a Second Language," *Studies in Second Language Acquisition* 25, 433-448.

Perlmutter, David (1971) *Deep and Surface Structure Constraints in Syntax*, Holt, Rinehart and Winston, New York.

Pienemann, Manfred, Malcolm Johnston and Geoff Brindley (1988) "Constructing an Acquisition-Based Procedure for Second Language Assessment," *Studies in Second Language Acquisition* 10, 217-243.

Rizzi, Luigi (1990) *Relativized Minimality*, MIT Press, Cambridge, MA.

斉藤栄二・高梨庸雄・森住衛・渡邉時夫・ほか31名（2005a）*New Crown English*

Series New Edition 1, 三省堂, 東京.
斉藤栄二・高梨庸雄・森住衛・渡邉時夫・ほか 31 名（2005b）*New Crown English Series New Edition 2*, 三省堂, 東京.
斉藤栄二・高梨庸雄・森住衛・渡邉時夫・ほか 31 名（2005c）*New Crown English Series New Edition 3*, 三省堂, 東京.
Tohsaku, Yasu-Hiko (1994) *Yookoso!: An Invitation to Contemporary Japanese*, McGraw-Hill, New York.
VassarStats: Website for Statistical Computation (http://vassarstats.net/)
White, Lydia (1988) "Island effects in second language acquisition," *Linguistics Theory in Second Language Acquisition*, ed. by Suzanne Flynn and Wayne O' Neil, 144–172, Kluwer, Dordrecht.
White, Lydia (1989) *Universal Grammar and Second Language Acquisition*, John Benjamins, Amsterdam.
White, Lydia (2003) *Second Language Acquisition and Universal Grammar*, Cambridge University Press, Cambridge.
Wu, Qing-Yu (2011) *The Minimal English Test: A Study in Inner Mongolia*, Master's thesis, Gifu University.
Wu, Shu-Jing (2018) *The Japanese Center Test Versions of the Minimal English Test for High School Students: A Study in Hebei Province of China*, Master's thesis, Gifu University.
Xu, Zi-Wei (2018) *The Minimal English Test and the junior Minimal English Test for High School and Junior High School Students: A Study in Liaoning Province of China*, ms., Gifu University.
柳井久枝（1998）『4 Steps エクセル統計』オーエムエス出版, 埼玉.
Yoshimura, Juri, Megumi Hasebe, Hideki Maki, Chise Kasai, Toshiro Umezawa, Kenichi Goto, Jessica Dunton, Sachie Ono and Takahiko Kishi (2011) "The junior Minimal English Test (jMET) as a Prediction Test for More Comprehensive English Tests: A Study at a Junior High School in Gifu Prefecture," *Proceedings of the Chubu English Language Education Society* 40, 81–88.

索　引

1. 日本語は五十音順に並べた．英語（で始まるもの）はアルファベット順で，最後に一括した．
2. 数字はページ数を表す．

石黒　33, 52
内モンゴル　73, 77
英検　1, 30, 33, 94-97, 143
笠島　80, 83, 86
関係節　97, 107, 108, 111-113
韓国　73, 74, 101, 102, 107
呉姝静　147
小林　1, 2
呉文亮　147
斉藤　90
徐子崴　147
進研模試英語　13, 28, 29
成美堂　1, 6-8, 13, 17, 18, 34, 52, 147, 148, 175
センター試験英語版 MET　115, 128
大学英語考試 4 級　143
多重比較　98, 99, 105, 106, 110, 112
中国　56, 73, 74, 76, 77, 123, 125-129, 140-143, 145
日本英語検定協会　30, 94
日本語能力試験　5, 6
長谷部めぐみ　147
美誠社　33, 52-54
非対称性　101-105, 107-113
フォード丹羽　2
普遍文法　98, 100
翻訳テスト　102, 108, 109, 111
森井那奈美　147

柳井　2
李　129
劉怡　147

CET 4　143-145
Chomsky　98
Cloze Test　16, 22
College English Test Band 4　143
Dawson　129
ECP　98, 100
Educational Testing Service　22
eMET　148
Empty Category Principle　98
Goto　14, 16
GTEC　13, 29, 30
Hasebe　30, 55, 79, 83, 85, 98, 101-103, 105-111
hMET-C　129, 132, 134, 142-145
jMET-C　129-131, 140-145
Kanno　98
Kasai　24, 27
Kawana and Walker　6, 13, 52, 55, 57, 79, 125, 147
Kent　129
Lasnik and Saito　98, 100
Lee　101, 102
Ma　56, 129, 140-144
MET 4 文字以下版　16, 33, 37, 57, 61,

62, 74, 76
MET 5 文字以下版　33, 37, 62
MET 6 単語目ごと版　16, 33, 38, 62, 77
MET ARB 版　52
MET-C　129, 136, 138, 143
MJT　3, 5, 6, 10
Morii　55, 116, 123-125
Nakagawa and Yamawaki　79
Nation　1, 13, 24, 25, 27, 74, 75, 97
New Crown　79, 90
New Horizon　79-83, 85, 88, 92
Niinuma　57, 61, 62, 70
Paul Nation's Vocabulary Size Test (PNT)　1, 13, 24, 25, 27, 74, 75, 97
Perlmutter　98
Peter Howlett and Richard McNamara　79
Pienemann　98
PT　2, 3, 6

SPOT　2, 3, 6, 10
That-Trace 現象　97, 98, 100
The College Scholastic Achievement Test　73
The Global Test of English Communication for Students　29
The junior Minimal English Test (jMET)　80, 83, 86, 87, 90
TOEFL　1, 97
TOEIC　1, 13, 22-24, 33, 97, 123-125
TOEIC ITP　23, 24, 123-125
Tohsaku　3
Visual Analogue Scaling (VAS)　99
White　98
Wh 疑問文　97, 98, 101-111
Wu (2011)　77
Wu (2018)　55, 116, 126-128
Xu　55, 116, 125, 126, 128
Yoshimura　82, 83

著者紹介

牧　秀樹　（まき　ひでき）

岐阜大学地域科学部教授．1995 年にコネチカット大学にて博士号（言語学）を取得．研究対象は，言語学と英語教育．
　主な著書・論文：*Essays on Irish Syntax* (Dónall P. Ó Baoill 氏と共著，2011 年，開拓社)，*Essays on Mongolian Syntax* (Lina Bao, Megumi Hasebe 氏と共著，2015 年，開拓社)，*Essays on Irish Syntax II* (Dónall P. Ó Baoill 氏と共著，2017 年，開拓社)，"The Minimal English Test: A New Method to Measure English as a Second Language Proficiency" (Kenichi Goto, Chise Kasai 氏と共著，*Evaluation & Research in Education* 23, 2010 年)，「The Minimal English Test（最小英語テスト）の有用性」(長谷川信子編『日本の英語教育の今，そして，これから』2013 年，開拓社)，など．

The Minimal English Test
（最小英語テスト）研究

Ⓒ 2018 Hideki Maki
ISBN978-4-7589-2263-0　C3082

著作者	牧　秀樹
発行者	武村哲司
印刷所	日之出印刷株式会社

2018 年 10 月 23 日　第 1 版第 1 刷発行

発行所　株式会社　開拓社

〒113-0023　東京都文京区向丘 1-5-2
電話　(03) 5842-8900（代表）
振替　00160-8-39787
http://www.kaitakusha.co.jp

JCOPY　＜出版者著作権管理機構　委託出版物＞
本書の無断複製は，著作権法上での例外を除き禁じられています．複製される場合は，そのつど事前に，出版者著作権管理機構（電話 03-3513-6969, FAX 03-3513-6979, e-mail: info@jcopy.or.jp）の許諾を得てください．